Complete Security Control

LAN and

Peter T. Davis

Windcrest®/ McGraw-Hill
New York San Francisco Washington, D.C. Auckland Bogotá
Caracas Lisbon London Madrid Mexico City Milan
Montreal New Delhi San Juan Singapore
Sydney Tokyo Toronto

To Janet, for her understanding, patience, and love.

To Kelly, for her inspiration, humor, and love.

To Ruth, for her guidance, nurturing, and love.

FIRST EDITION
SECOND PRINTING

© 1994 by **Windcrest,** an imprint of McGraw-Hill, Inc.
The name "Windcrest" is a registered trademark of McGraw-Hill, Inc.

Printed in the United States of America. All rights reserved. The publisher takes no responsibility for the use of any of the materials or methods described in this book, nor for the products thereof.

Library of Congress Cataloging-in-Publication Data

Davis, Peter T.
    Complete LAN security and control / by Peter T. Davis.
        p.   cm.
    Includes bibliographical references (p.   ) and index.
    ISBN 0-8306-4548-9   ISBN 0-8306-4549-7 (pbk.)
    1. Local area networks (Computer networks)—Management. 2. Local area networks (Computer networks)—Security measures. I. Title.
TK5105.7.D384   1993
005.8--dc20   93-28064
                                                                     CIP

Acquisitions editor: Brad J. Schepp
Editorial team: Joanne M. Slike, Executive Editor
                Lori Flaherty, Supervising Editor
                Theresa Burke, Editor
                Jodi Tyler, Indexer
Production team: Katherine G. Brown, Director
Design team: Jaclyn J. Boone, Designer
              Brian Allison, Associate Designer
Cover design: Holberg Design, York, Pa
Cover photograph: ©W. Cody/Westlight.
Marble photograph: ©H. D. Thoreau/Westlight

WU1
4490

Contents

Notices x
Acknowledgments xi
Introduction xiii

Part one: The problem

1 **LANs: The corporate lifeline** 3
   Information equals power 4
   The changing LANscape 6
   Power to the people 7
   Understanding the problem 8
   Understanding management's need for control 9
   The need for security 10
   Self-assessment quiz 14

2 **What is a LAN?** 15
   LAN components 18
   Communication palindrome: ISO OSI 19
   Getting the data out 20
   Topologies 21
   The network interface 23
   The big three interface standards 24
   Protocols: the rules of the road 27
   How fast is data transmitted? 32
   Which LAN is best? 33

Part two: The framework

3 **What is a threat?** 37
   Threats 38
   Threats to a LAN environment 38
   Threat scenarios 41
   Vulnerabilities 42
   Exposures 42

4 **What is a control?** 43
   Types of control 45
   Areas of control 46
   Potential control issues 46
   Control process 48
   Relationship to management cycle 51
   Relationship to total customer service 53
   Relationship to risk analysis 54
   Controls & people 54

5 Managing risk: cost-benefit analysis 57
Costs, benefits—& risks 58
Risk 59
Risk analysis 60
Management decision 63
Control implementation 66
Effectiveness review 66
Final words on risk management 66

Part three: The solutions

6 Securing the LAN 69
Information systems ethics: an oxymoron? 70
The first step: administrative & organizational security 74
Disaster preparedness 88
Working with people: personnel security 94
Protecting the office: physical & environmental security 94
Riding the waves: communications & electronic security 95
Iron age: hardware security 98
Picking one's brains: software security 99

7 Applying controls to hardware 117
The message is the medium: cabling 118
Making the connection 123
Are you being served? 123
Sharing peripherals 126
Workstations: the local intelligence 130
Fault tolerance 134
Backup strategies 135
Static, noise, surges, brownouts, blackouts & other power problems 138

8 Applying controls to software 143
It takes all types 144
Network operating system 146
Operating system 181
Network management software 183
Application software 185

9 Applying controls to communications 199
Internetworking & connectivity 200
Communication security guidelines 200
Network components 200

Part four: The future

10 Future LAN security issues 211
  Wireless technology 214
  Cooperative computing 217
  Telecommuting 220
  Imaging: the last frontier 222
  Rightsizing 237
  LAN disaster 243

Appendices

A LAN security checklist 247

B Password dictionary 253

C LAN products 259

D Organizations 275

  Bibliography 279
  Glossary 293
  Index 313
  About the author 333

Notices

3Com	3Com Corp.
Apple AppleShare AppleTalk Macintosh	Apple Computer, Inc.
ARCnet	Datapoint Corp.
DEC VMS	Digital Equipment Corp.
Excel MS-DOS	Microsoft Corp.
HP Hewlett-Packard	Hewlett-Packard Co.
IBM IBM PC IBM AT IBM XT EISA PS/2 OS/2 LAN Server NetBIOS SNA Token Ring Structured Query Language	International Business Machines, Inc.
LANtastic LANBIOS AILANBIO Network Eye	Artisoft, Inc.
Lotus 1-2-3 Symphony	Lotus Development Corp.
Novell NetWare (all versions)	Novell, Inc.
Sun	Sun Microsystems, Inc.
VINES StreetTalk	Banyan Systems, Inc.
WordPerfect	WordPerfect Corp.
Xerox Ethernet	Xerox Corp.

Product names are used throughout the book in an editorial manner only. Uses of product names, or the use of any trade name, do not convey endorsement or other affiliation with McGraw-Hill or the author of this book.

The trademark of other products mentioned in the book but not listed here are held by the companies that produced them.

Acknowledgments

A special thanks to Chris Anderson, Art Appelberg, Gerry Grindler, Tony Humble, Jim Kates, John Kearns, Kevin Kobelsky, Craig McGuffin, Gord McKay, Pat Moriarty, Will Ozier, Chuck Perkins, Richard Rueb, Sheryl Teed, and Hal Tipton for helping me grow as an information systems professional. Thanks also to Ryan Fennema, Kenn Hyslop, Darren Jones, Donna McFadden, Brian Nancekivell, and Malcolm Stokes for material used in this book.

Thanks to Mary Ainsworth and Carl Jackson for helping me get this book published, Brad Schepp for going to bat for the book, Lisa Black for administrative help, and everybody who encouraged me to write the book.

During my career in information systems, I have met and talked with many individuals. I also have read many articles, manuscripts, books, and manuals. I would like to acknowledge and thank these sources whose work I have synthesized in this book. I have given direct attribution where I felt it was appropriate (and in some cases known). Please let me know if I should give direct attribution for any part of this book in a future edition.

Introduction

When I originally started writing this book, my intention was to write a generic "how-to" book on information systems security. Although general information systems security would have been a worthy topic, I felt that I could make a greater contribution by limiting the scope to local area networks (LANs). A number of reasons exist for limiting the scope of this book.

First, I found no books that addressed only LAN security and control. Sure, books exist about LANs, with an obligatory chapter on security. I even saw books on telecommunications security. One publisher has a book on NetWare security filled with hundreds of screen shots. McGraw-Hill published a book entitled *The Stephen Cobb Complete Book of PC and LAN Security*. While the McGraw-Hill book is excellent, it focuses more on PC issues rather than LAN issues. (It would make a good companion to this book, if you are really serious about security for your network.) However, through all my searching, I did not find any books focusing on LAN security.

Second, security is a vast and complex subject, and difficult to condense to one volume. Thus, I decided to focus on one area that is rapidly gaining in popularity in almost every organization. Even with the limited scope of this book, it was difficult to include the depth of review required for some controls. My apologies to security experts and purists who may find this book facile in some aspects, but my book was not intended for you.

"Who did you intend to read the book?" you may ask. I intended this book for those individuals struggling with the implementation of a LAN. This book fills the gap for those individuals looking for straightforward security help for their LANs. It does not matter whether you are a user of a LAN, designer of a new network, manager of an old network, security administrator, owner of the network, or a senior manager who wants to understand the risks facing the organization. If you are interested in protecting your organization's most important asset—information—this book is for you.

I aimed this book at a wide audience because I believe in the need to proselytize network administrators and their users on the pressing need for information systems security. One more technical book about encryption, while not without merit, does not help to warn corporations and governments about the risks involved when operating a LAN.

I have included everything you need for a basic understanding of the issues, so you need not be an expert to get the most from this book. Experts will benefit since this book will act as a tickler list or aide-memoire for reviewing their security.

Material in this book has been organized to lead you through a review of your security or potential security if you are just thinking of implementing a LAN. Thus, I encourage you to read the book in sequential order. Chapters tend to build on each other. For instance, I introduce risk concepts early in the book so you will think about them throughout.

In Part one, "The problem," I discuss the background issues. I describe the effect LANs have had on information systems security, and why they have had the effect that they have.

Chapter 1, "LANs: The corporate lifeline," explains the shift to an information economy and how networks have facilitated the shift, and why the shift has caused problems.

Chapter 2, "What is a LAN?" describes the basic components of a LAN, including network standards, topologies, and protocols. This chapter also provides a basic vocabulary for the rest of the book.

In Part two, "The framework," I explore the framework for looking at your LAN security.

Chapter 3, "What is a threat?" defines the concepts of threats, vulnerabilities, and exposures and builds some threat scenarios. This chapter also provides basic vocabulary on information systems security needed throughout the remainder of the book.

Chapter 4, "What is a control?" describes the nature of control and the different types of controls. You learn about the control process and its relationship to management control, total customer service, and risk analysis.

Chapter 5, "Managing risk: cost-benefit analysis," introduces you to risk management terminology. You learn how to develop a risk management program for your organization in this chapter.

In Part three, "The solutions," we turn our attention to solutions for our LAN. You learn tips on how to secure your hardware, software, and network components.

Chapter 6, "Securing the LAN," introduces LAN security concepts. These are the basic building blocks for security: administrative and organizational controls, personnel controls, physical and environmental controls, communications and electronic controls, hardware controls, and software controls.

Chapter 7, "Applying controls to hardware," provides specific solutions for cabling, interfaces and connectors, servers, peripherals, and workstations. You learn about fault tolerance, duplexing, and power supply systems.

Chapter 8, "Applying controls to software," also provides specific solutions, but for software. The chapter covers "shrink-wrapped," operating system, and applications software. Specific applications are discussed, such as electronic mail and client-servers. This chapter also includes descriptions of and tips for AppleShare, LANtastic, NetWare, OS/2 LAN Server, and VINES network operating systems security.

Chapter 9, "Applying controls to communications," provides real solutions to communication exposures. The chapter introduces you to repeaters, bridges, routers, brouters, gateways, and modems and provides you with security tips on their use. Internetworking concepts and pitfalls are also covered.

Because networks and security solutions are not static, Part four, "The future," consists of my insight into what you already should be worrying about.

Chapter 10, "Future LAN security issues," looks at some issues to be faced in the not-so-distant future by organizations with LANs. You learn about several exposures associated with wireless technologies, cooperative computing, telecommuting, imaging, and rightsizing.

I have provided several useful appendices to supplement the information in the books.

Appendix A, "LAN security checklist," provides a useful starting point for your review of LAN security at your organization.

Appendix B, "Password dictionary," lists the words used in a previous dictionary attack. You might want to avoid using these words as passwords.

Appendix C, "LAN products," provides product and contact information for LAN security and control products.

Appendix D, "Organizations," lists those groups who can further help in your understanding of security, audit, and control. These groups can perhaps help take over where this book ends.

I have included some other beneficial information in the back of the book to assist you in your overall understanding of information systems, security, audit, and control.

Select Bibliography is a comprehensive list of books, manuals, publications, periodicals, and articles for information systems. The Glossary contains definitions of the major networking and information processing terms used throughout the book.

Lastly, I hope you learn as much from reading this book as I did writing it. Enjoy.

Part one
The problem

The genius of modern technology lies in making things to last fifty years and making them obsolete in three.
— **Anon**

There's no such thing as "zero risk."
— **William Driver**

LANs: The corporate lifeline

We are living in interesting times and a time of great change! In *Megatrends,* author John Naisbitt identified a restructuring of the North American economy (1982). Alvin Toffler (1980) identified the same trend in his book, *The Third Wave.* This significant trend, or wave, was the shift from an industrial-based society to one based on the creation and distribution of information. With the end of the industrial age and the arrival of the information age, a corresponding shift in the balance of power has occurred.

During the industrial age, power came from capital. Industrialists made more money by reinvesting their capital. Society lived by the Golden Rule: he who had the gold made the rule. An important paradigm shift, however, has taken place. Our economy no longer relies on machine-intensive industries. The sunset industries of the American northeast are in decline, and information-based industries are on the rise. Why are these industries on the rise?

Information equals power

Information, and the knowledge derived from information, equals power. In the information age, power comes from the timely use of information. Prior knowledge of any significant event, such as the date of the start of the Gulf War or a merger of two corporations, can lead to the acquisition of great wealth. People make money because of their knowledge of impending government legislation, such as tax law changes or coming land expropriations. Large corporations have habitually used historic and demographic information to increase profits. American Airlines and American Hospital Supply (now Baxter), two organizations repeatedly glorified for their emphasis on service, quality, innovation, and speed, use information technology to gain a competitive advantage.

Innovative corporations redefine how their industries operate and move the yardstick for measuring excellence within those industries. Corporations entering those industries must meet or exceed the new standards developed by the innovative companies to be competitive. The intelligent use of information leads organizations to a competitive advantage and, ultimately, wealth. Information is the lifeblood of the organization, and it is making its way down a new corporate lifeline. Microcomputers joined in a local area network (LAN) are this lifeline and could very well be the primary information delivery vehicle of the future.

The development of these lifelines is a relatively new phenomenon. Until the widespread availability of microcomputers in the 1980s, most corporations kept their data on computers locked in glass rooms attended by the high priests, priestesses, and their acolytes. Figure 1-1 illustrates a typical mainframe environment of the early 1980s.

These keepers of the data jealously guarded that data because they alone realized the power of it. The introduction of the microcomputer, however—originally scorned by International Business Machines and Digital Equipment Corporation—led to the democratization of information, thus releasing the

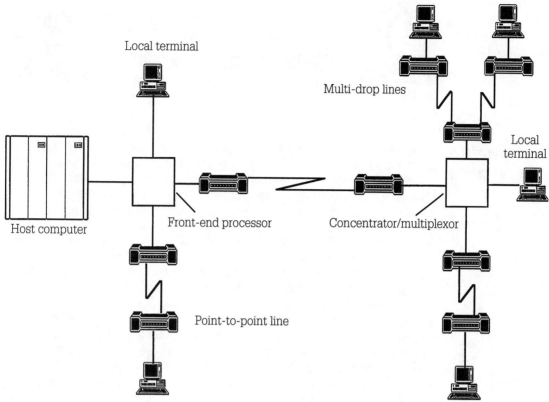

1-1 *Typical early 1980s mainframe environment.*

power gained by wielding that information wisely. The coming of LANs has even more profoundly affected the office environment. No longer do department managers need to negotiate with data processing departments to develop applications. The mainframe's hegemony was over! Managers discovered that microcomputers allowed them to develop their applications more quickly and cheaply. After managers struggled for years with programming staff and vendors promising *vaporware*, these managers managed to develop real-life applications. Soon, they realized even more power could be obtained by combining their data with their neighbor's data.

At first, department managers communicated via modems and telephone lines, as shown in FIG. 1-2, but this mode of communication quickly proved inadequate. As personal computers (PCs) became more powerful, new technologies allowed PCs to be strung together so they could communicate. The linking of these two convergent technologies, computers and communications, has released the full power of the information society and was the genesis of the LAN and the subsequent widespread sharing of programs and data.

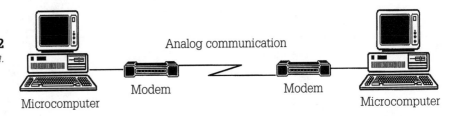

1-2 Pc-to-pc communication.

The changing LANscape

Organizations increasingly share programs and data by using networks in their long-range information technology strategic planning. The term *networking* has meant more than just coupling hardware; it has meant a change in hierarchical structures. Almost 2,000 years ago, the Chinese introduced hierarchies. Western civilizations have embraced them ever since.

Most large corporations ascribed to multilevel hierarchical control structures. These hierarchies are seizing up, however, because of their stifling bureaucracy. In the bureaucratic command and control model, management passes information as orders down the chain of command. The results similarly wind their way back up the chain. These multiple layers then serve as information conduits up and down the chain. Every stop on the chain represented a level of control—a chance for another level of management to exercise its control. Managers could make Go/No-Go decisions at any point in the approval process. Even delaying a decision was a form of control. These organizations soon die, however, just as previous plodding behemoths such as dinosaurs became extinct.

Networks are changing these organizations and their manner of business, as shown in TABLE 1-1. These changes lead to flatter, less hierarchical structures. Flattening of the organization occurs because employees can obtain the information they need easily. They rely less on help from their superiors as the information gap narrows. Team spirit, information sharing, and ultimately power characterize these new organizational structures. The sharing of information throughout an organization is necessary to move decision making to the point where individuals can take action.

Table 1-1
The shifting organization

Superior	Customer
Static hierarchy	Flexible and flat
Superior focus	Customer focus
Control	Vision
Compliance	Initiative

This sharing of information has caused problems, however. Throughout history, human beings have been much better at gathering information than controlling it. Information, however, is a valuable commodity that needs protection, and a great deal is at stake. The power and complexity of our technology is exploding, and our control systems have not kept pace. Power demands control. The installation of LANs presents an almost contradictory situation regarding the use of the facilities and the control of the data on the LANs. Hierarchical levels are controls in themselves. Each expense or issue must pass muster at every level, yet LANs are eliminating these levels. LANs contribute to the decentralization of processing data and the data itself. Decentralizing the processing and the data has increased the security exposures, however, a corresponding increase in control has not occurred. Those organizations that cannot or will not control their networks face confusion or disorder, or "LANarchy."

Power to the people

On the one hand, LANs provide and encourage advanced data transmission and sharing. On the other hand, data-control objectives require that the access to and the use of the data be managed. This dichotomy is the crux of the problem: when an organization maintained information centrally, protection was fairly straightforward because the information administrators built fortresses around the central depositories of data. The introduction of coupled PCs, however, has muddied protection requirements. PC LANs are creating turf battles in many large companies, where systems and telecommunications departments fight over LANs (although user departments are successfully implementing most LANs without the help of either group). The assumption that both telecommunications and systems groups make is that LANs are like mainframe computers and require centralized management and control. These new networks, however, are *not* like the old environments. The old information technocracies must adapt. The Gartner Group (1990) reports:

> [Information Systems] must support and sustain (new organizational styles) by providing access to information and knowledge, the means for facile communications and the basis for new self-sufficiency among users across different functional disciplines. Already, progressive IS organizations have added formal objectives to their charters to optimize user access to heterogeneous data and encourage user self-sufficiency. This represents a radical shift from a financial-control orientation to user-empowerment.

Specialized groups fought the battles over data control because they realized the importance of the data, and that user-empowerment threatened their livelihood. These groups tenaciously defend their role as information handlers and oppose advances creating new organizational forms that make the groups and those who manage them redundant.

In addition to these struggles, business faces another shift that affects the distribution of power. Alvin Toffler (1990) believes a widespread decline has occurred in the prestige of professionals from all walks of life. As an example of this social change, he sees the collapse of the respect for physicians as "the punctured power of the god-in-a-white-coat." He concludes, "The case of the dethroned doctor is, however, only one small example of a general process changing the entire relationship of knowledge to power in high-tech nations." The physician's downfall is akin to the emperor's new clothes. Online access to medical information has de-mystified the profession to patients. Toffler further explains, "In many other fields, too, closely held specialists' knowledge is slipping out of control and reaching ordinary citizens. Similarly, inside major corporations, employees are winning access to knowledge once monopolized by management. And as knowledge is redistributed, so, too, is the power based on it."

To support the flattened structure and the insatiable thirst for information, an organization needs to change its management structure from support of a vertical hierarchy to support of horizontal processes. At the same time, the organization must maintain control over its information. The information flow must shift from a strict vertical orientation to horizontal. The managers must convince management to see beyond old turf wars by taking responsibility for specific processes instead of traditional functions, which means sharing information across various functions and business units. In conjunction, these strategic business units must also share control of the information.

Understanding the problem

A brief look at a LAN will help in understanding how it can help solve the problem while still being the cause. A LAN is a communications system that allows several information processing devices to link with one another over a limited distance. LANs have developed over many years and are now a rapidly growing direction for offices using multiple microcomputers. Generally, a LAN is several microcomputers linked by cables and communications software within a geographically small area such as an office building. LANs also allow multiple users to share data, files, and programs within the system. A LAN is installed for several good reasons. If a data file must be updated concurrently by different departments, it is difficult to develop effective procedures that allow standalone personal computers to do the job, whereas LANs solve the problem well. LANs are also necessary to avoid major problems with redundant data or text, or when program files are being exchanged on diskettes using the sneakernet, making it difficult for users to ensure their versions match the master copies of the programs. A final reason for building a shared PC environment is when PCs are installed in numerous departments within the company.

You should not install a LAN just to share printers or read-only data. The disadvantages of a network simply outweigh the advantages if you only want to share devices and read-only data. Besides, a hardware switch is much more economical. If you have budget or time constraints or system security is a major consideration, you should not install a LAN either. Having said this, however, some of you will still install one. Building a LAN creates unique problems. When personal computers are connected to a network, they are not so personal anymore. With whatever advantages a LAN offers, changes in how an organization looks at microcomputers occur. What few companies remember is that when 30 or 40 machines are connected together, they create a system. Most companies still treat a LAN as separate components and not as the sum of the components. With the leaps in memory chip integration, storage speed, and capacity that have occurred, a company now has a $5,000 system with the same raw processing power that cost $500,000 only 5 years ago. If you have a 30-node LAN and each node has 2 megabytes (MB) of memory, you have more power than an IBM mainframe computer or a DEC minicomputer. That is a lot of power to control!

The power can only be controlled by securing the data. One way to look at this statement is problematically:

SECURE DATA = POWER

Where:
- S = Serviceable, wearing well or durable
- E = Effective, operating, or functioning
- C = Complete, or having all parts and elements
- U = Usable, or fit for use
- R = Reliable or dependable
- E = Efficient, or performing in the least wasteful manner
- D = Defensive or resistant to attack
- A = Available or ready for use
- T = Timely, appropriate, opportune, or occurring at a suitable time
- A = Authentic, factually accurate, or reliable
- P = Pertinent or relevance
- O = Obligation, or moral or legal duty
- W = Way, method, or means for attaining a goal
- E = Economy, or thrifty management of money and materials
- R = Responsible, answerable, or accountable, as for something within one's power or control.

Management needs to secure data to provide adequate control. Why does management need control?

Understanding management's need for control

As organizations change hierarchical control, management's responsibility for control within the organization increases. Legislation, such as the *Foreign Corrupt Practices Act* of the United States, places the onus of due care on management. Case law in North America and elsewhere shows a definite tendency toward the accountability of management for its staff. Frequently, an organization's stakeholders or shareholders hold management responsible for breaches in trust and the lack of due diligence. Security losses are just one example of when management can be liable personally if negligence is proven.

Management's basic responsibility is to effectively utilize resources to meet the organization's goals. Normally, meeting this responsibility means maximizing profitability. If we accept this maxim, it is hard for most managers to rationalize security expenditures.

Environmental pressures, such as, shareholders, mergers, acquisitions, and competition, pressure organizations to focus on short-term profits. Management justifies this approach because it assumes it will not be there for very long anyway. If these individuals in management are moving up the success ladder, they figure they will be in their jobs for only two or three years. Following this assumption, management figures why worry about a hurricane wiping out the network when a disaster only happens once every 20 years. If, however, the continued viability of the company is a concern to management, security expenditures that do not contribute directly to the bottom line are at the bottom of management's priority list. Security can be temporarily sacrificed, resulting in short-term profits, but also damage the organization because of a customer's loss of confidence or trust.

Both approaches described above are a big managerial crapshoot. Most managers believe that losses or disasters will not happen to them. Only the unlucky ones get caught and must face the consequences. Good managers, however, think in terms of long-term success and resist tempting shortcuts that endanger longer-term potentials.

In a weak economy, security administrators, auditors, and trainers are usually the first casualties of layoffs. This fact, coupled with the uncertainties of the economy, the competition, the technology, the politics, and the social environment, make for a volatile mixture. At the very same time management requires good controls, they get rid of their control experts resulting in an unfortunate situation.

People go beyond being a resource. Their knowledge, skills, and experience are invaluable, but their importance is greater than that. Management must carry out actions through and with people. Effective managers are therefore dependent on people to make and carry out management's action plans. In other words, for management to be successful, it must understand people and control systems, and the effect management has on people. Again, this is a difficult task in organizations where management has not inculcated values, and employees feel threatened.

A central truth of life is that conditions are always changing. Some changes are accepted easily, while others are met with great resistance. Another central truth, however, is that your organization does not operate in a benign environment. Some hostility generally exists because the organization, individuals, and society itself do not necessarily share the same goals. Goal incongruity forces the need for security.

The need for security

Just about every unclassified network has been penetrated once. Hackers, crackers, cyberpunks, data diddlers, private investigators, high-school students, university students, and disgruntled staff are all potential threats to your security. They are the curiously bent, the politically motivated, the criminally involved, and the psychologically unbalanced.

The term *hacker* originally was nonpejorative and applied to members of the model railroad club at the Massachusetts Institute of Technology (Levy 1984). Club members spent hours "hacking" pieces of the railroad layout and rearranging them. Hours and hours were spent working and reworking the layout. These engineers then turned their energies to the Institute's minicomputer and applied the same hacking philosophy to it: they spent hours trying to improve routines and save precious bytes of memory. Swapping information was an accepted part of the computer ethos among hackers in the 1970s. Hackers were pioneers in the computer field, and many of them went on to found computer companies. *Crackers* is a term more properly applied to system penetrators and other electronic vandals.

Cyberpunks, the second generation of hackers and crackers, subscribe to an arcane code of honor and look upon hacking as a rite of passage. They are at once explorers, voyeurs, investigators, burglars, vandals, trespassers, and spies. Many cyberpunks ascribe to the notion that big business and the government are the enemy. The Chaos Computer Club of West Germany had a member named Hans Hübner, nicknamed Pengo, who sold military secrets to the East. Other cyberpunks think nothing of ripping off their phone company because they believe the company is making obscene profits. Kevin Mitnick of the U.S. Left Coast repeatedly programmed phone switches to do his bidding. Their stories are told in *Cyberpunk* (Hafner and Markoff 1991). These people find coping with the real world difficult, so they escape into a make-believe world. In this unreal world, their peers respect them only for their technical prowess.

This theme forms the basis for *True Names* (Vinge 1987). Debby Charteris, a senior citizen living a quiet, desperate life, masquerades on the Other Plane as Erythrina, a powerful, attractive person who combats evil. Similar plots are repeatedly found in the science fiction and fantasy genre. Authors such as Cherryh (1988a, 1988b, 1988c), Sterling (1988, 1990, and 1992), Gibson (1984, 1986, and 1989), Vinge (1987), and Brunner (1976) have fed the imaginations of these disenfranchised individuals. The problem will most likely grow as the Nintendo generation hits maturity in the late 1990s.

Hackers start by pushing the security envelope of LANs. Hackers are the first to go in, then the cyberpunks, then the crooks, and finally the cops. The greatest threat to LAN security is from career criminals and their confederates who work in your own organization. Law enforcement officials believe that today's hackers become tomorrow's criminal. Echoing law enforcement's sentiments, William Gibson (1984), author of the now famous cyberpunk cult book *Neuromancer*, wrote "The street finds its own use for technology."

It is not just the criminally bent that those concerned with security need worry about, but also the academically inclined. In May 1990, Robert Tappan

Morris, a 24-year old computer science graduate student at Cornell University in Ithaca, New York was convicted for making a "deliberate and full-scale attack" on the Internet, a computer network that comprises more than 1,200 separate computer installations at corporate, university, and military sites. His intrusion disrupted computer installations across the United States and reportedly cost as much as $100 million to repair. Individuals like Morris remind us of a sorcerer's apprentice—someone who has difficulty controlling one's spells, such as Mickey Mouse in *Fantasia*.

When the intruders are no longer university students proving their wizardry, but technoterrorists hired to create havoc, the situation becomes serious. Possible terrorist operations include bank fraud, embezzlement, and theft of trade secrets. These terrorists could recruit today's data diddlers. *Data diddlers* are a more insidious type of cyberpunk, because they modify data for fun or profit—such as school grades, credit ratings, security clearance information, and salaries, for example.

Professionals will soon replace the amateurs. A number of trained spies are unemployed now as a result of the new political environment. Espionage is one method in which the Soviets believed they could bypass embargoes on high-technology products. The Commonwealth of Independent States, known formerly as the Soviet Union, has long been active in obtaining high technology from the West (Metcalfe 1988), and even had an agency responsible for the coordination of the activity. It is not just the Soviets, however.

American law enforcement officials recently caught the Japanese buying high technology. It is not just an international problem between countries, however. Corporate espionage is a fact of life. Depending on the industry, companies routinely purchase software, competitive sales figures, and strategy reports that are supplied by fired or disgruntled employees seeking revenge or profit. To illustrate, I was laid over in Chicago's O'Hare Airport recently and had a casual conversation with a man seated near me about computer fraud. He related a story about a computer consultant who had worked for his father installing illegal software. He proudly told me this consultant "borrowed" unpurchased software, modified it, and then installed it at his father's manufacturing plant. The consultant, who was in his early 20s, charged $16,000 for the work—$24,000 less than the $40,000 for a legitimate license of the software. Ethics is discussed in a later chapter.

Most technocrats believe their microcomputers are valuable friends, but your microcomputer can betray or even doublecross you. Turning a personal computer against its owner is a technological challenge, but a determined individual can turn a microcomputer into a deadly electronic device whose use results in dire consequences. The individual can be a revengeful, hateful person; a deranged individual; or a resourceful, well-trained programmer led by a terrorist group or foreign government.

Unknown individuals pose a considerable risk to your organization. These external agents, however, are still less likely to cause problems than your own staff. Disgruntled employees can deliberately bring your system down or erase backup files. Most security experts agree that individuals from within an organization commit the majority of computer crimes or abuses, yet the hacker who commits only 2 percent of computer crimes makes the newspapers and magazines. Crime is more likely to be perpetrated by outsiders using company insiders as pawns.

Another less-obvious threat to security is from management itself. Management demands systems that increase user productivity. Buyers of software translate this need and push for ease of use. Being easier to use often makes microcomputer systems and software more vulnerable. Paradoxically, users demand more ease-of-use software yet higher levels of security. The problem is that it is often difficult to have both. The move towards *open systems*, where organizations can buy equipment from different manufacturers and link them together, requires common standards for networking.

Common networking standards and greater ease of access benefits legitimate users. They also speed the spread of viruses. These standards also allow attackers to access even more machines. If these machines allow your users easier access, just imagine what they do for attackers!

Manufacturers of computer technology stress that users need to be more vigilant in their administration of security, because a manufacturer can only do so much to protect an organization's investment. Security must become increasingly important within organizations as more valuable applications run on microcomputers linked together in a LAN. Once LANs are connected through telephone lines to the outside world, they immediately become vulnerable to all the vagaries of that outside world.

A responsible manager can no longer assume that the environment is benign, and to assume so in the face of the evidence presented is naive. To survive in the future, managers must establish a dynamic security strategy. As Sun Tzu wrote in *Art of War* (Clavell 1983), "Security against defeat implies defensive tactics; ability to defeat the enemy means taking the offensive. Standing on the defensive indicates insufficient strength, attacking a superabundance of strength."

Acknowledging a hostile environment is half the battle, but not sufficient to win the war. You also must acknowledge that the organization's information holds value to you and someone else. When I evaluate security at organizations, I invariably hear that nothing of value exists on the network. I quickly find this to be false after a few questions. Perhaps a short self-assessment of your LAN can help you decide if you should be concerned about security.

Self-assessment quiz

- Do you process information about or belonging to your clients?
- Do you process any human resources information about your staff?
- Would any information leaked from your files cause embarrassment to clients, customers, management, fellow workers, or staff?
- Are you in a highly competitive industry?
- Are you required by law or contract to ensure security?
- Do you have military contracts?
- Are you a third-party provider of computing services?
- Do you have militant organized labor?
- Are or did you go through a downsizing of your business this year?
- Are you the target of any fanatical special interest groups?
- Is your business built on trust and the customer's confidence?
- Are you affected by privacy legislation?

If you answered yes to any question, you should read on. If you answered no to all questions, you are a lucky individual and should tell your organization so. Most people must read on to prepare themselves against the threats to their LAN.

The remainder of the book tours LAN components, exposures, and controls. In Chapter 2, the basic components of a LAN are introduced. Threats are explained in Chapter 3 and controls in Chapter 4. From there, risk management is discussed in Chapter 5 and LAN security concepts in Chapter 6. Chapters 7, 8, and 9 provide real solutions to hardware, software, and communication exposures. Finally, Chapter 10 looks at some issues to be faced in the not-so-distant future by organizations with LANs.

2
What is a LAN?

What is a local area network (LAN)? Asking 100 people probably results in 100 different answers. A generally accepted definition of a LAN is not available because of the rapid changes in technology and the frequent misuse of the terminology. For purposes of this book, LANs can be characterized as follows:

- Intracompany, privately owned, user-administered, and not regulated by the government.
- Structured. LANs are integrated into a discrete entity with devices interconnected by a continuous medium.
- Limited in geographic scope, with devices physically separated but not mobile. (The maximum distance, depending on the technology, is about 50 miles.)
- Supportive of full connectivity. Every user device on the network can potentially talk with every other user device.
- High-speed. LANs are not subject to speed limitations imposed by traditional common carrier facilities.

Within this definition, LANs can be used to connect more than personal computers (PCs). They can connect alarm systems, telephones, and videos. LANs can be used to connect anything requiring an exchange of high-speed data. For instance, cable television systems are *broadband* technology-based and can be referred to as LANs. (Broadband technology is explored further in this chapter.)

LANs are becoming more widespread to increase the productivity of PCs as a desktop tool. A strong argument can be made for LANs based on the productivity gains made possible by sharing data across a network. End-user computing and office automation, a category that includes personal computing, information centers, and office automation systems, now accounts for a growing portion of the information technology budget within an organization. Applications include electronic communications such as mail and messaging, office administration functions such as word processing, and the exchange and sharing of corporate and confidential information.

LANs increase any potential security risks by increasing the number of users who have access to a greater range of information. The United States General Accounting Office reported the following in August 1990, entitled *Computers And Privacy: How the Government Obtains, Verifies, Uses, and Protects Personal Data.*

> Federal, state, local, and private organizations have access to personal information maintained in many federal agencies' computerized systems through various types of networks. Some 707 of the federal agencies' 910 largest systems (78 percent) are accessed through one or more communications networks; . . . 379 (42 percent) are accessed through a local area network.

On the corporate side, less than 20 percent of the microcomputers installed are networked, according to International Data Corp., which concluded in a study released in 1992. The study predicted, however, that this figure could grow to 50 percent very rapidly. The *1991 Steelcase Worldwide Office Environment Index* report claims that 88 percent of Canadian, 85 percent of United States, 80 percent of the European Economic Community, and 64 percent of Japanese office workers use computers as part of their job. Further, the Business Research Group reported in their 1991 *PC LAN Integration and Management User Trends* that 51 percent of the 400 sites at Fortune 1000 companies were interconnected. What do all these figures mean? They mean that many microcomputers exist with potentially exposed information on them.

A requirement exists to protect confidential and corporate information by making it inaccessible to those who do not need to see it, as well as a need to protect such data from inadvertent or deliberate destruction. Adequate assurance must also be maintained for the accuracy, completeness, availability, and validity of data. Effective computer security is crucial to safeguard systems that provide essential services. Why are we so concerned with securing networked microcomputers?

Simply put, establishing a connection between two or more computers has two basic implications for security. First, you now have more to lose. This statement is true from the viewpoint of the individual user as well as from a network perspective that the whole is now greater than the sum of its parts. We have created concentrations of data. Willie Sutton reportedly said when asked why he robbed banks, "Because that's where the money is." By implementing a LAN, you have created a magnet for intentional abuse because that's where the data is. Emma Nicholson, a Conservative Member of Parliament in England, has said "Electronically stored information is the New World's gold and needs different measures of protection."

A group of PCs connected to a LAN can do far more sophisticated tasks than a group of unconnected machines, so LANs are now performing mission-critical work, work that is essential to the organization's continued existence. Logically, if we accept the fact that we can realize productivity gains from LANs, then we can conversely realize losses as well. The more one has to gain, the more one has to lose.

Second, you now have more ways to lose your data. You have at least two points of entry, as well as a communications media of some type. You can choose to ignore these implications and wait until the horse has left the barn before you close the door, or you can purchase a padlock for the paddock. This is then the major security decision management faces. Fram, a car parts manufacturer, had a famous commercial, oft quoted by security professionals: "You can pay me now or you can pay me later." This sentiment applies directly to security. Your organization can either predict and prevent threats or it can recover (maybe) from the consequences of those unprevented threats. The remainder of this chapter focuses on the LAN itself, before discussing potential problems and solutions.

LAN components

The growth in the use of microcomputers created the need for PC networks. These networks led to software and hardware that was originally developed for larger computers and networks to be adapted for PC network use. Today's PC networks comprise several major components. The first is hardware, such as microcomputers, printers, disk drives, facsimiles, and modems. The second is the wiring or cabling that connects the hardware. In a cable LAN, twisted wire, coaxial, or fiber optic cable connects network devices. If the cable is long, repeaters are used to boost signals. Most newer buildings now rough in cabling during construction so that electrical, telephone, and data outlets are available for computers. In private branch exchange systems (PBX), standard telephone lines connect the various devices. The PBX is a switchboard that interfaces between an organization's many lines and the public lines of the telephone company.

The third component is the LAN interface. Each hardware device, such as a microcomputer, attached to the network has a network interface card installed to manage the transmission process. The fourth component is the network controller, which is the brain of the network. The controller is either a chip on the interface, a hard disk drive, or a dedicated device. The controller is considered the brain because it controls traffic on the network, detecting and preventing data collisions. The fifth component is the file server, which is usually a hard disk drive that contains the communication and user programs. The sixth component is a communications interconnection device, such as a router, bridge, or gateway. These devices allow the LAN to connect to other LANs, metropolitan area networks (MANs), wide area networks (WANs), minicomputers, and mainframes. Interconnection allows the LAN to talk with computers almost anywhere in the world and draw upon the greater computing power and storage capacity of larger systems.

These six components might or might not exist in every LAN. Some manufacturers offer different types of LANs. The choices that exist are overwhelming to manufacturers. They cannot afford to make all possible combinations of components and protocols, yet they also cannot afford to make products that work with only a few LANs. Because of this dilemma, the industry has worked as a whole to develop standards for manufacturers and consumers alike. *Standards* are agreements that promote connectivity between products of different manufacturers. Theoretically, any device adhering to the published standards can connect to any other device adhering to that same standard. Practically, this is not always the case, because the developers of the standards failed to specify all aspects of interconnection, or some manufacturers offer nonstandard system enhancements.

Communication palindrome: ISO's OSI

The lack of LAN standards is not the central problem; the abundance of LAN standards is. An important milestone in the development of LAN standards was the International Standards Organization's (ISO) publication in 1977. The Open Systems Interconnection (OSI) model specified the functionality of communications in seven layers of hardware and software. The OSI model represents how ISO wants LAN products developed, but LAN vendors do not necessarily follow the model in designing products. Most LAN systems are layered in a hierarchy similar to the OSI model, however. The layers usually divide the network into its physical media, low-level communications protocols, and network/application services.

Low-level protocols specify, for example, exactly how data packets sent across the network should be organized and labeled, what route the data should take, and what to do when the data does or does not arrive. Part of the specification of a protocol is how it communicates with the layers above and below it.

Most managers and network administrators do not need to know the technical details by which each layer does its job, but it is useful when working with LANs to know the names of the various protocols and their various responsibilities.

As mentioned, the OSI model divides LAN responsibilities into seven layers and provides for communication between the layers. The seven layers of the OSI model are as follows, with the top layer (Application) being the most abstract, and the lowest layer being the most basic, or hardware-specific:

- Application
- Presentation
- Session
- Transport
- Network
- Data Link
- Physical

Level 1, the Physical Layer, specifies the physical medium, signal strengths, and distances. The physical medium includes the cabling, which is the physical data path between devices on the network. Level 2, the Data Link Layer, specifies the strategy and mechanisms for accessing the cable and the form of the transmitted data. Level 3, the Network Layer, specifies the route of data from one node to the next. Level 4, the Transport Layer, specifies how to handle errors and the retransmission of data. Level 5, the Session Layer, specifies the maintenance of data links between nodes. Level 6, the Presentation Layer specifies the code and data conversion for application programs. Level 7, the Application Layer, specifies file service protocols used directly by an application.

Layers 1 and 2 of the OSI model are the physical LAN hardware: the cable, the hardware that accesses the cable, and the software that manages the hardware. Usually this hardware is a board installed in a PC, but it can be implemented in other ways, such as on a single chip. Besides housing the physical connection to the cable, this board or interface also can contain software that manages the lowest level of communication between the workstation and the network.

The *network interface* defines the method used to send and receive data between the computer and the cabling system, the rate of data transmission, the size and consistency of the message unit packets, and arbitration of multiple-station access to the cable system. To a large extent, the selected interface constrains the cable layout, called the *topology*, and the type of cable that can be used.

Simply put, Layers 3 and 4 are the communication protocols. *Communication protocols* are precise rules for communication between two devices, two software programs, or a device and a software program. Layers 5, 6, and 7 are usually the operating system (OS) functions that provide services to applications. For example, data compression and encryption could occur at the Presentation Layer. Presently, Apple's AppleTalk architecture is the only major microcomputer LAN that consists of separate protocols that correspond precisely to all seven layers of the OSI model.

Getting the data out

Data moves from one device to another by moving through the seven different layers. For example, when a user selects some data within an application, the PC program sends a request to the OS for access to the correct file. The OS determines whether the request can be met locally. If it is a local request, the OS handles the request by opening the file and transferring the first record into memory. Alternatively, the OS sends nonlocal, or network, requests to the communications program for handling. The communications program packages the request and passes it to the network interface in the PC. When the device is ready to send a request over the LAN, the interface places the request in packets. Each packet usually consists of 1024 characters of data and has an assigned code that identifies the sending and receiving devices. The sending station then listens to the communication line to determine if the line is free. If it is free, the interface passes the packets to the cabling system and places the request on the line. If the line is not free, the sending station waits a few microseconds and listens again. Once the request is on the line, it is carried along to the server. Each device listens for packets addressed to it, and the interface in the server removes the packets as they arrive and passes them to the server's memory. The file server then sends an acknowledgment to the user for each packet it receives.

The file server examines and processes the request just received by issuing a read instruction to the disk. As the system reads the data, it transfers the data to the memory of the file server. At this point, the process reverses. The data passes from memory to the interface in the file server. The interface then repackages the data and passes the packets, one at a time, to the cable. The user's interface receives the packets, one at a time, and transfers the packets to memory. As with the server, the user sends an acknowledgment to the file server for each packet received. The application program then waits for the next request, and the process starts all over. Remember that this all occurs concurrently with other requests of the file server from other users. Note that the speed and manner of these transfers depends somewhat on the network topology.

Topologies

The use of the term *topology* defines the cable layout, which is affected by the type of network interface device. A topogy is a network configuration that describes the cabling layout. LANs are one of three common topologies: bus, ring, and star.

Bus configuration

A bus configuration does not have a central controller, as illustrated in FIG. 2-1. Coded messages travel over a line that connects all workstations. Only designated workstations can recognize the coded messages meant for them. The major drawback of the bus configuration is the collision rate, which is higher than that for the other two configurations.

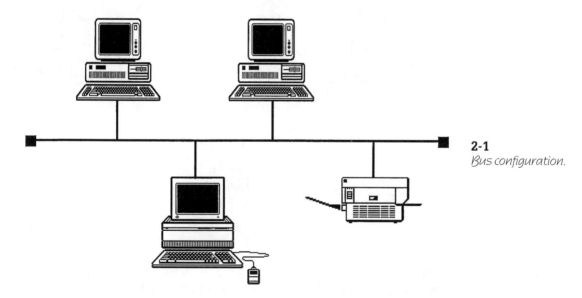

2-1
Bus configuration.

One advantage of this configuration, however, is that cable costs are comparatively low because each workstation is hardwired to one bus. Conversely, in a star configuration, individual cables run from each workstation to the central controller.

Ring configuration

In a ring configuration, each workstation has an equal opportunity to enter the network. There is no controller all workstations physically connect to each other to form a ring. In most networks of this type, workstations are connected to a router or medium attachment unit (MAU), rather than to every other workstation and server. Token-passing or collision detection protocols regulate the ring configuration. This type of configuration is a closed-loop topology in which data passes in one direction from station to station on the LAN. Figure 2-2 shows the ring or loop configuration. Each workstation on the ring is cabled to both the next station and the previous one. Each workstation thus acts as a repeater, passing data to both the next workstation on the ring. The next workstation receives the data from the previous station and transmits to the next station, and the data flows around the ring.

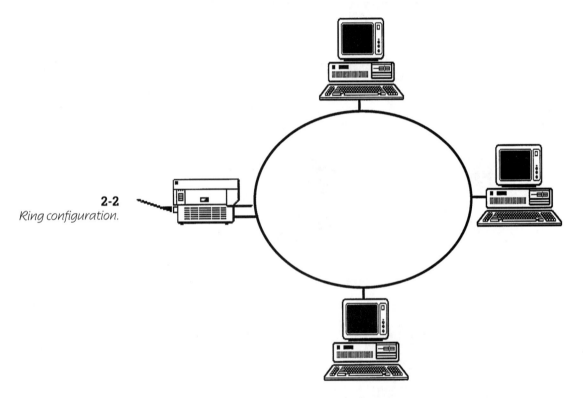

2-2
Ring configuration.

Star configuration The star configuration, as shown in FIG. 2-3, is like the original version of a telephone system, where an operator acted as a central controller and directed calls from different locations. With this type of topology, all communication activities must be directed through a central controller. For example, if a node wants to send a message to the server, it waits for the controller to poll it, and then it sends the message to the controller. The controller, in turn, sends the message to the server during its poll cycle.

To allow stations to be easily connected and disconnected in the network, all cables go through one or more central hubs. At the hub, each workstation connects to the next and previous station. These hubs automatically bypass

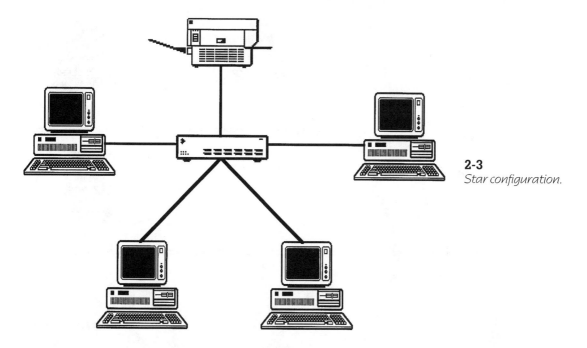

2-3
Star configuration.

disconnected or powered-off stations, maintaining the integrity of the network.

Because all messages pass through the controller, however, delays can be a problem in periods of heavy traffic. A star configuration is traditionally slower than the other network configurations, a major drawback of this configuration.

Tree configuration

Because of the problems with a basic star configuration, the tree topology was developed. The tree topology, or distributed star, consists of several linear buses daisychained together. For example, a linear bus attaches to a hub that splits into three linear buses, with each one splitting into three more linear buses, as shown in FIG. 2-4. At this point, we now have 13 linear buses. As you can see, the successive splitting of buses forms branches as the network grows.

The splitting of buses can continue, creating more linear buses from those split from the original bus, thus keeping the attributes of a star. The advantages of a tree network are that they are easy to expand, and fault isolation is simplified. However, tree networks depend on higher-level buses, and when a primary bus fails, the dependent lower branches also fail.

The network interface

Networks can control data sent and received through the use of an interface. The *network interface* determines the method used to send and receive data, the rate of data transmission, the size and consistency of the data packets, and access method, as well as the network topology and cable types.

What is a LAN?

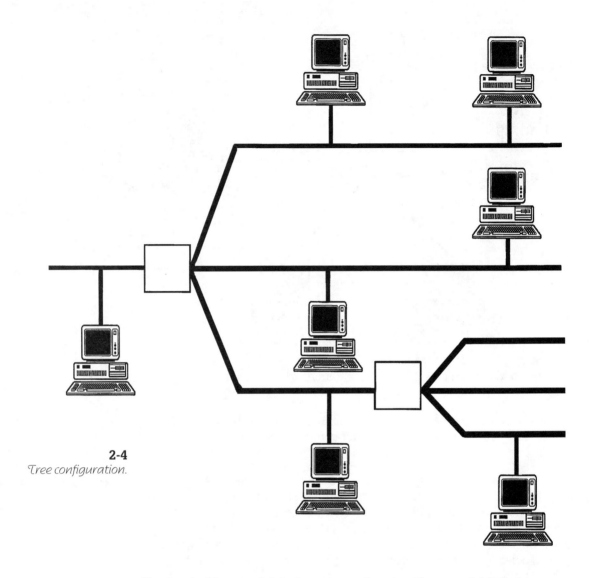

2-4
Tree configuration.

Vendors build network interfaces to conform to either an established standard or proprietary designs. The interface standard generally specifies packet structures, cable access methods, signal strengths, cable types, and cable distance. The standards usually do not specify the hardware and software interfaces to particular microcomputers or operating systems. Therefore, differences can exist between interfaces that subscribe to the same standard. There are three primary network interface standards.

The big three interface standards

The three largest network interfaces, in terms of the number of installed nodes, are Ethernet, ARCnet, and Token Ring. Other LAN interfaces grew out of these three. For instance, Sun, Hewlett-Packard, 3Com, and Digital products grew out of Ethernet, and most Novell NetWare systems use ARCnet or Ethernet hardware. IBM developed Token Ring to tie its networks together. Digital, Sun, and Hewlett-Packard developed Token Ring integration strategies for their machines. Figure 2-5 shows a pie-chart breakdown of the popularity of the different network interfaces of the Fortune 1000 networks, and FIG. 2-6 shows a breakout of the eight most popular interfaces. Although FIG. 2-5 and 2-6 show Ethernet and Token Ring running fairly evenly, an increase in Token Ring usage could occur as large IBM customers implement OS/2. A growing preference for Token Ring is shown in FIG. 2-7.

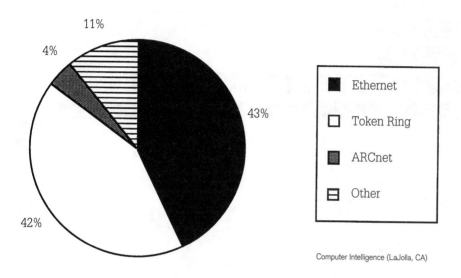

2-5
Popularity of the big three interface.s

Computer Intelligence (LaJolla, CA)

Xerox originally developed Ethernet, and Datapoint developed ARCnet. ARCnet, developed in 1978, is acceptable for small networks but lacks the throughput required for the 1990s. ARCnet also lacks endorsement from the Institute of Electronic and Electrical Engineers (IEEE), one of the standard-setting organizations, and this is a serious drawback to its acceptance in large organizations. ARCnet does, however, have an American National Standard Institute (ANSI) standard, and an IEEE committee is working on a similar one. Most impartial observers agree that both Ethernet and Token Ring offer excellent performance. The choice, therefore, must be made on cost, connectivity, and support.

LocalTalk is a network wiring scheme frequently used to connect Macintosh microcomputers. The hardware required to interface with LocalTalk is included with Macintosh microcomputers, so an extra network card is not needed. LocalTalk is very slow, in fact, ARCnet is 10 times faster, but the wiring for LocalTalk is inexpensive and easy to install. Ethernet and LocalTalk use the collision-detection protocol, and the other two interfaces use the token-passing protocol for their media access control technique. *Protocols* are what define the rules for workstations that have data traveling along the electronic roadway and are discussed in the next subsection.

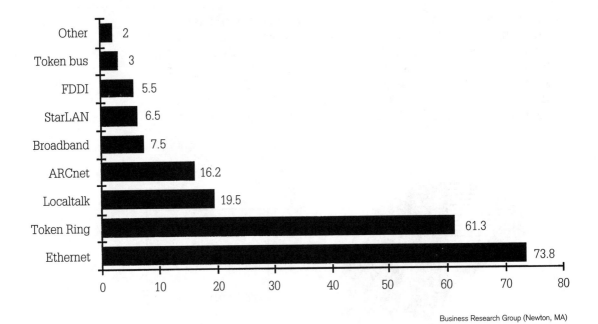

2-6 *Percent of installations from survey of 400 users.*

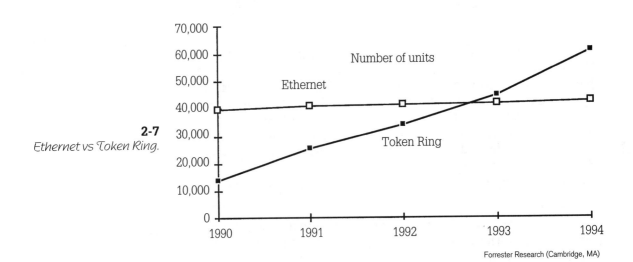

2-7 *Ethernet vs Token Ring.*

Protocols: the rules of the road

The term *protocol* once referred to the proper form for addressing letters to the Papal Nuncio. It also once referred to the letter of introduction carried by a court emissary to another land before a state visit. Some protocols are entrenched, even inviolate. Protocols permeate our existence—Robert's Rules of Order and Emily Post's rules of etiquette are two examples.

The information technology industry also thrives on protocols. Like other terminology used by the information technology world, the new definition is similar in meaning to the older definitions. For data communications, protocols describe any set of rules that allow different machines or software programs to coordinate with each other without ambiguity.

Generally, these rules of communication are how a system talks and expects to be talked to by another system. Systems are considered similar if they use the same protocols. If the systems use different protocols, they can still be made to talk with each other through certain hardware or software that translates from one protocol to another. The Data Link protocol, the second OSI layer, manages data transmission. The two most common media access protocols are carrier sense multiple access with collision detection (CSMA/CD) and token passing.

Collision detection

Collision detection is a *contention*-access method, because network workstations compete for cable access. When a PC broadcasts a message, another PC in the network listens to the cable to see if anyone is transmitting. If the PC does not hear another signal on the line, it transmits its packets of information. If the PC does hear another signal, it waits, checks the line again, and sends its information when the line is free. The data of two workstations ready to use the network will collide occasionally, and one workstation must then back off. During periods of heavy activity, the probability of these collisions is high. On detecting a collision, workstations involved wait a random period (to reduce the possibility of re-collision) and then transmit again. When data collisions increase and performance degrades rapidly, the network approaches its saturation point. Saturation is a rare point in well-designed and managed networks.

Figure 2-8 illustrates the collision detection protocol. Collision detection is analogous to the old party telephone lines still used in some parts of the world. If you want to use the phone on a party line, you pick up the phone and listen. If you don't hear anybody talking, you can make your call, but if someone is on the line, you must hang up and try again in a few minutes. When you hear a dial tone, you know you can complete your call.

Carrier detection is a probabilistic protocol because no node is guaranteed a transmission window on the network, and, consequently, response time for a given transmission cannot be guaranteed. If enough bandwidth exists, the probability of a node transmitting within a reasonable time is very high.

What is a LAN?

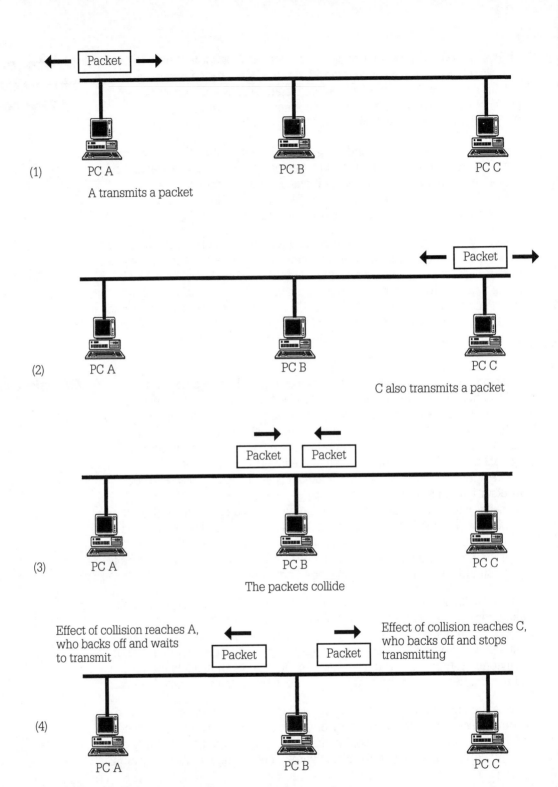

2-8 Collision detection.

Token passing

In token passing, a *token*, which is a predefined bit pattern, circulates in the network in one direction only. When a workstation receives the token, it is permitted to use the network and send a packet of information. If a workstation does not have the token, it must wait until the token is passed to it before transmitting. When the workstation finishes transmitting, the token passes to the next workstation. A token that has information added to it is called a *frame*. If a workstation receives a frame, the workstation takes the appropriate information intended for it before circulating the token in the ring again. The token circulates in the ring until it arrives at the sender node; the sender then acknowledges receipt of the message by the recipient, and the token is freed to be used by the other workstations. If a station receives a free token, that is, a token without data attached, it can attach data to the token and send it on its way.

The packet, which contains source and destination address information as well as data, must be received and retransmitted with the token by each station on the ring in succession until it reaches the destination station. The destination station reads the data from the packet, changes one attribute (called the acknowledgment bit) on the packet and then retransmits the packet and token to the next workstation. The acknowledgment bit signifies to the sending station that the information packet was received by the receiving station. When the sending station receives the packet and token again, it strips off the data and sends the free token on to the next station.

Figure 2-9 illustrates the token passing protocol. Part (a) of the figure shows token passing for a bus configuration, while part (b) shows token passing for a ring configuration. Essentially, token-passing systems are *contention-free*. Instead of contending for network access as in collision detection systems, each station waits its turn until it receives the token. In token-passing systems, network access is guaranteed, while access is random in collision-detection systems. Performance in heavy traffic is usually better than in contention systems.

Future protocols

New microcomputers with an insatiable thirst for information will quickly exhaust the present capabilities of Ethernet and Token Ring. Experience with new technologies, such as multimedia, shows these interfaces are inadequate. Network managers grappling with these technologies are looking at Fiber Distributed Data Interface (FDDI) based networks. FDDI is a 100-megabit-per second protocol that uses a token-passing ring structure for fiber-optic cabling.

The FDDI standard addresses three areas of application:
- Backend LANs
- High-speed office LANs
- Backbone LANs

Backend LANs are used in a computer-room environment to interconnect mainframe computers with mass-storage devices. These LANs provide bulk

A

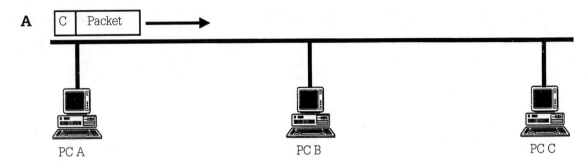

A transmits a packet addressed to C

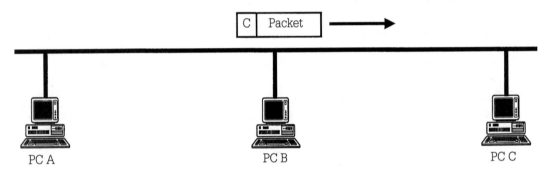

B reads address, packet is not addressed to B, B ignores it

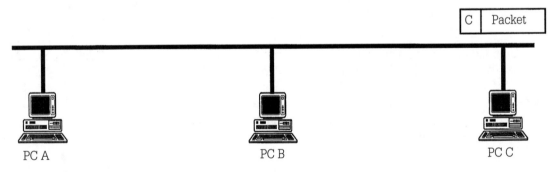

C reads address, packet is addressed to C, C copies it and places token on network

2-9 *Token passing.*

B

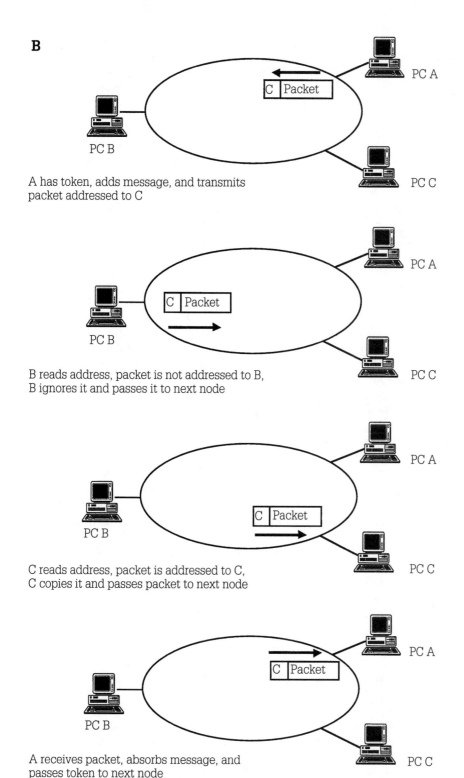

Ring configuration.

A has token, adds message, and transmits packet addressed to C

B reads address, packet is not addressed to B, B ignores it and passes it to next node

C reads address, packet is addressed to C, C copies it and passes packet to next node

A receives packet, absorbs message, and passes token to next node data transfer among a few devices in a small area where reliability is important. High-speed office LANs can meet the high data needs of today's office applications, including distributed data processing, facsimile, and image processing. The backbone LAN interconnects other LANs and standalone equipment on a large site.

Bandwidth to the desktop is an issue that managers need to begin planning for today, especially considering today's media issues. Much attention has been focused on delivering 100 megabits per second (Mbps) of data to the desktop, which is an incredible amount of information!

How fast is data transmitted?

In a network, data can be transmitted in two ways: broadband or baseband. Broadband transmission uses a frequency-division technique similar to that of FM radio, and baseband transmission uses a voltage fluctuation method.

Baseband can be used for voice or data transmissions. Voice and data transmissions typically occur through telephone lines and operate at speeds between 300 and 9,600 bits per second. Broadband channels transmit at rates up to 50 million bits per second. The higher the bandwidth selected, the greater the volume of data that can be transmitted but the higher the cost. Situations exist where broadband networks are more appropriate than baseband networks. Because of the high initial design, engineering, and installation costs of broadband networks, college campuses, large manufacturing facilities, and large, single-company office buildings are types of candidates for these broadband LANs.

When talking about speed, terms such as "kay," "meg," and "gig" are tossed around. What do these terms mean? They are the phonetic pronunciation of scientific notations. These terms are the standard metric prefixes used by the Système Internationale (SI) convention for scientific measurement. If the system describes items based on 10, such as dollars, then they denote the power of 10, such as $1000=10^3$. When used with a binary system, however, items in a system denote the power of 2, such as, $1024=2^{10}$. Table 2-1 lists the scientific prefixes used in computers and communications. The smaller prefixes are rarely used, although a definition does exist for a picosecond, which is a trillionth of a second: it is the time it takes for a New York cab driver to honk after the light turns green. The larger measurements, however, are much more common.

Technicians measure LAN speeds in kilo-, mega-, and gigabits. Storage capacities are measured in kilo-, mega-, and gigabytes. Manufacturers measure disk access time in milli- and microseconds. These measurements are being pushed every year. For instance, the mainframes of the early 1970s had 2 megabytes (MB) of memory. The microcomputer I used to write this book has 4 MB of memory which can be upgraded to 16 MB and 80 MB of hard disk storage. The book itself is approximately 800K, or three-quarters of a "meg." Optical disks today measure capacity in gigabytes. These numbers are staggering when you consider 1 gigabyte (GB) of data is a small library,

**Table 2-1
Scientific prefixes**

Prefix	Decimal	Binary
Atto	1000^{-6}	$1024^{-6} = 2^{-60}$
Femto	1000^{-5}	$1024^{-5} = 2^{-50}$
Pico	1000^{-4}	$1024^{-4} = 2^{-40}$
Nano	1000^{-3}	$1024^{-3} = 2^{-30}$
Micro	1000^{-2}	$1024^{-2} = 2^{-20}$
Milli	1000^{-1}	$1024^{-1} = 2^{-10}$
Kilo (K)	1000^{1}	$1024^{1} = 2^{10} = 1,024$
Mega (M)	1000^{2}	$1024^{2} = 2^{20} = 1,048,576$
Giga (G)	1000^{3}	$1024^{3} = 2^{30} = 1,073,741,824$
Tera	1000^{4}	$1024^{4} = 2^{40} = 1,099,511,627,776$
Peta	1000^{5}	$1024^{5} = 2^{50} = 1,125,899,906,842,624$
Exa	1000^{6}	$1024^{6} = 2^{60} = 1,152,921,504,606,846,976$

and a 1-GB disk can store the equivalence of information recorded in 2,000 binders; 400,000 sheets of paper; 25 40-MB hard disks; or 900 1.2-MB floppy disks!

As you can see, many factors must be considered when purchasing and installing a LAN. Many different combinations of protocols exist for LANs as well, and determining the best one is a difficult process. The answers to the following questions might help with the decision.

Which LAN is best?

- Will processing be distributed?
- Will access be distributed?
- How will microcomputers be connected?
- What sorts of applications will be processed?
- Where will the microcomputer data be stored?
- Who will update the data?
- Who will have access to the data?
- Who will document changes to the data?
- Is user response time important?
- How much does the system cost?
- Is security important?
- Can the organization support the network?

Choosing the right LAN enhances the security, integrity, and availability of data. Despite your choice, your LAN will face threats that put your data at risk. The subject of threats is the focus of Chapter 3.

Part two
The framework

Technological progress has merely provided us with more efficient means for going backwards.
— **Aldous Leonard Huxley**

The characteristic of the exploding technological society is that changes sooner or later must take place in a fraction of the time necessary even to assess the situation.
— **John Wilkinson**

3

What is a threat?

A widely misunderstood concept is the notion of a threat. Many people have difficulty with the concept of a threat and all its components. No discussion of security, however, would be complete without discussing threats and their management.

A few years ago, I was auditing a bank with assets over $60 billion. Our audit led to the conclusion that end-to-end testing was needed because of the complexity of the online banking application. We also concluded that security needed to be moved out of the systems group and given its rightful place in the organization. As exposure possibilities, we listed system unavailability and integrity problems. The chairman's reaction to our findings was in essence, "Quantify and qualify or be quiet." To a consultant, this directive sounded like Nirvana, and we were licking our lips over all the potential work. It turned out, however, that he wanted the quantification done on our time. It was a challenge well worth pursuing, but alas, not one you can do while working for a "Big Few" accounting firm.

Within six months of the audit, however, the bank had a serious outage of its online banking network that lasted more than two days. In the end, the network outage cost millions and tarnished the bank's image. The outage occurred because of an undiscovered flaw in a rate table. The flaw in the rate table went undiscovered because of a flaw in the testing process. These flaws cascaded until the online retail banking computers were shut down across Canada. Coincidence you say? Possibly, but I like to think we had uncovered the symptoms of that problem in our audit. LANs are not much different from any other network and are susceptible to the same class of threats. Let's look at some terms before moving on to a discussion of these classes of threats.

Threats

People or events that exploit system vulnerabilities are aptly called *threats*. Most experts believe that the biggest threat to information security is errors by honest employees, followed by malicious attacks by dishonest or disgruntled employees. These facts probably surprise most people because it is the external threats, such as acts of God or hackers, that get the press.

Threats to a LAN environment

Table 3-1 shows specific threats in one column and the corresponding method of attack to your LAN in the corresponding column. Data can be changed or deleted during transmission or storage. An attacker can modify or delete information while it is stored on the file server. One threat is *message-stream modification*, where the attacker selectively modifies, deletes, delays, reorders, or duplicates real messages.

Disclosure is the threat most people intuitively associate with security. Fundamentally, disclosure occurs when someone gains access to information without authority. Disclosure could result from loose lips, weak access control, or eavesdropping. Eavesdropping occurs when an unauthorized individual passively taps lines to listen secretly or record traffic. Inferences of information can be made from observing the number and duration of

Table 3-1
Threats to a network

Threat	Attack
Denial of service	Acts of God
	Message or session blocking or interruption
	Theft of assets
	Virus/worm
Disclosure	Eavesdropping
	Emanation interception
	Masquerading
	Message forwarding/printing
	Unauthorized access
Masquerading	Forging
	Password determination
	Spoofing
Message modification	Unauthorized changes
	Wiretapping
Repudiation	Reneging
Sequence modification	Masquerading
	Reneging

connections, message format characteristics, origin or destination identities, routing, and traffic patterns. Information about who is communicating or accessing data could be a target of eavesdroppers. These inferences can be made using a technique called *content analysis*. During World War II, intelligence agencies analyzed patterns in thousands of print media to glean information. Valuable information can also be obtained by monitoring the volume or timing of traffic between users and locations. For example, a flurry of messages to a military base could suggest a pending attack, or an increased volume of messages between investors could reveal a financial strategy. This threat is sometimes called *traffic analysis*. Passive taps do not lead to any unauthorized change in the state of the intercommunicating systems. In truth, the contention-access method of interfacing taps the line and listens to traffic itself before jumping in.

Masquerading is the reuse of validated messages by either an authorized or unauthorized individual. One masquerades by assuming the identity of a legitimate user or process after getting proper identification through wiretapping or another means. The identity can be obtained in several ways; frequently, they are obtained by guessing passcodes users create.

Reneging is a method of attack by an entity who is involved in a communication and who falsely denies having participated in all or part of the communication. Thus, the entity disavows any knowledge of the message. This form of attack is also known as *repudiation*. *Forging* is when one party changes or fabricates a message and then claims that such information came from another party.

The wiring between terminals and servers can easily be monitored in many organizations. In some organizations, staff personnel routinely monitor message traffic on the LAN. Inexpensive and readily available diagnostic tools can also intercept data as it crosses the network. Consequently, message contents can be revealed with access codes and corresponding passcodes. Further, individuals can listen to information exchanged on the LAN by intercepting electromagnetic emanations.

Wiretapping is when an individual cuts in on or taps a communication channel to intercept a message. An unauthorized individual actively taps lines to introduce, alter, misroute, delay, reorder, or delete messages. The operative word here is *actively*. If the tap is passive, the threat is either traffic analysis or eavesdropping rather than wiretapping.

Spoofing is when an unauthorized individual deceives the recipient into believing that the individual is another person authorized to perform that function. This threat is similar to masquerading; however, masquerading usually involves the reuse of messages. One method of spoofing involves monitoring an insecure communications line, sending a false logoff message back to the user, then using the line as one's own.

This method of spoofing was similar to the trick making the rounds several years ago. An individual would write a program that masqueraded as a sign-on screen. When the user entered a user identification (userid) and password, the program informed the user that the maximum number of users was logged on and to try later. Meanwhile, the perpetrator captured the userid and password, along with the associated privileges of that user.

Denial of service is the prevention of authorized access to the system or the delaying of critical operations. This type of threat could consist of a variety of natural or manmade events that have the potential to deny operations. Denial of service could be very costly to an organization. For example, assume one of your customers is trying to contact you to place an order, and an individual is monopolizing your lines. That customer could then contact another supplier, thus resulting in loss of business to your organization.

We have primarily looked at intentional threats, but a LAN faces unintentional threats or acts as well. Some of these threats include the following:

- Spikes, surges, and brownouts that cause equipment malfunctions.
- Natural disasters, such as hurricanes, tornadoes, and earthquakes.
- Major accidents, such as chemical spills or train derailments.
- Human error, such as a dropped device or a deleted file.
- Inexperienced users, who do not understand security needs.

- Carelessness, such as inattentiveness when connecting or disconnecting devices on the network.
- Damage from accidents, such as tripping over a cable.
- Water damage from sprinklers, overflowing bathroom facilities, and air conditioners.
- Programming errors.

A *threat agent* is the perpetrator of the threat. The agent can be either human or machine. Simply, it is the vehicle for carrying out the threat. When an unauthorized individual taps your line, the threat agent is that individual.

Now that the terminology has been defined, it can be applied to real-life scenarios. Note that threats can be acted out in many ways. Following are two simple scenarios that have dire consequences.

Threat scenarios

At 8:00 AM, Hy Kent enters the offices of SouthWest Trust Company, just as he has done hundreds of other times. But this is not like other times. No, today is different. Hy is pretty typical in many ways. After graduating from a university with a history degree in the 1970s, he drifted from job to job until he settled down as a programmer at SouthWest. His personal life was not as settled; Hy is in his late thirties and still single. The bachelor lifestyle kept Hy busy and tired. Because of his lifestyle or maybe because of another reason, senior management habitually passed over Hy for promotion. Today, Hy is going to get even with his employer.

SouthWest has a large LAN Hy uses to develop his database applications. Because SouthWest is a security-conscious company, it has taken privileged status away from Hy, but Hy doesn't need privileged status anymore. Last night, he was browsing the Computer Freaks and Geeks Bulletin Board, which is where he found a shareware program called GETIT.COM, which he'll use to change his salary information.

Hy starts his workstation and installs his program on the hard disk. Then he starts the program and calls over the network administrator, Tex Jones, with a request for help. Tex is always willing to help and logs on to Hy's microcomputer. After helping Hy, Tex excuses himself to attend the weekly problem resolution meeting. Tex doesn't realize that he has unwittingly become Hy's accomplice. Hy's program was a password grabber, and he now has Tex's user code and password. These can be used to access the payroll file.

Hypothetical you say? Maybe, but this scenario really happened. Hy, however, was not a disgruntled employee but a computer specialist testing the LAN security.

Any organization could easily control these threats. Four controls exist that could have prevented the password from being compromised—a diskless workstation, a software audit, procedures that prevent software install, and education of staff.

Another risk exists because of the broadcast nature of an Ethernet LAN. Any packet of information can be retrieved by any station on the LAN. The process is, to some extent, simple. An attacker first looks for and finds an accessible workstation directly attached to the network. This person loads monitoring and diagnostic software from a bulletin board onto the workstation. The software monitors network traffic by capturing a sufficient number of packets. Using the diagnostic software, the attacker decodes the contents of the captured packets to identify interesting addresses. The attacker then sets the diagnostic software to capture only packets to the identified interesting addresses. The attacker then looks for and finds logon sequences with passwords for applications. With the information furtively gathered, the attacker logs on and extracts confidential data. Even a moderately knowledgeable individual can execute this type of process. You could control this type of threat using the controls listed for the previous scenario, as well as encryption.

Vulnerabilities

Some organizations are more open or vulnerable to some threats than others. Similarly, some LAN topologies are more vulnerable than others. Organizations without the proper network climate are much more vulnerable to threats than those that implement controls.

The three LAN topologies are vulnerable in different ways. For example, because bus and ring networks do not have a controller, they can be more susceptible to unauthorized use. Potentially, a user could, without detection, tap a node wire and establish an apparently authorized session. The ring network is also sensitive to sabotage because one failure can cause network disruption. Online applications that handle heavy network traffic cannot afford such disruptions.

Exposures

Exposure is the extent of the loss should an individual exploit a system vulnerability. Threats can put your organization at risk to the following exposures:

- Erroneous recordkeeping
- Unacceptable accounting of assets
- Business interruptions
- Erroneous management decisions
- Fraud
- Statutory sanctions
- Excessive costs
- Loss or destruction of assets
- Lost business opportunities
- Competitive disadvantage

The fact that organizations do not suffer these exposures every day proves that they can be controlled. In Chapter 4, an in-depth discussion of controls is presented.

4

What is a control?

All aspects of human activity, inside an organization and within society at large, need control as a process. Would you travel on city streets in a major urban center without speed limits, stoplights, or street signs? Would you fly by plane if there were no air traffic controllers? You get the picture; the results would be chaotic. Controls are therefore necessary to define expected behavior or, as in the examples, to maneuver a car in traffic or a plane in the sky.

Control as an organizational activity—or as a component of any organizational activity—exists at all levels within that organization and is the concern of many different individuals within that organization. Its basic nature can be understood in terms of the major phases of the total management process. The total process begins with planning and the related establishment of objectives. Organizing and the necessary providing of more resources—including people—supports planning. Managers can then act to meet these previously established objectives. These operational actions are typically not enough, however. Things seldom work out exactly as planned. Our underlying knowledge and estimates are never that good. Besides, people are human, and humans make errors.

Environmental conditions also change from when the objectives were initially set. We therefore need supplementary measures and actions to provide appropriate readings on our progress and to provide the basis for further actions that can better assure that our objectives can be achieved. These measures and actions are commonly called *feedback*. We also need procedures that assure desired types of actions and prevent undesired ones. The control function is what provides these supplementary measures, actions, and procedures.

The control function cannot exist unless we have objectives. If we do not know where we want to go, we can hardly know what measures and actions should be taken to get us there. To paraphrase the Cheshire Cat's advice to Alice: If you don't care where you're going, any road will take you there. An oft-quoted phrase, "If you fail to plan, you plan to fail!" summarizes this point best. Taking supplementary actions brings us back into the actual management process to take further managerial actions. Thus, control exists as an independent but essential phase of the management process. Figure 4-1 illustrates the control function.

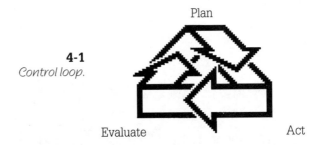

4-1
Control loop.

Victor Z. Brink and Herbert Witt (1982) provide an excellent scenario of the control function. They describe a very simple illustration of a boat setting sail for a given port with an estimated time of arrival. During the trip, the skipper charts the boat's progress. Because of prevailing winds, engine problems, or whatever, the boat veers off course. To compensate where necessary, the skipper must chart a new course, change direction, and possibly alter his speed. The skipper also might need to revise his estimated time of arrival. In this example, the skipper is the control function because his role is to consider and evaluate the impact of developments in actual progress and provide a proper basis for needed supplementary action. He thus contributes to reaching his destination on a timely basis and in the most efficient manner.

Types of control

Control is always tied directly to objectives. While the nature and scope of the objectives can vary widely, how management exercises control can also vary. For the purposes of this book, three different types of controls exist: preventive, detective, and corrective.

Preventive

Preventive controls, or *yes-no* controls, keep undesirable events from occurring. In a LAN environment, setting up automated procedures to prohibit unauthorized system access and to force appropriate and consistent action by users serves as a preventive control. An example of a preventive control is an access control system, which limits user access to a system.

Because preventive controls are unlikely to be 100 percent effective, they should operate in combination with detective controls, which identify errors or events not prevented. It might not be cost-effective to prevent all errors at the source, which is the purpose of preventive controls, so complementary detective controls can protect the system from the error.

Detective

Detective controls, also known as *steering* controls, identify undesirable events after they have occurred. Detective controls have two characteristics. One, the system identifies and records user activity, key transactions, and unusual conditions and keeps exception and summary reports that ensure a thorough and accurate audit trail. Two, a management hierarchy is in place to review the reports, identify any abnormalities, and act appropriately.

Detective controls identify expected error types as well as those not expected to occur. Because preventive controls could fail or be bypassed, detective controls provide redundant review of the error types that need to be prevented. This dual coverage alerts users or management to irregularities in the system or process when they occur. Redundant controls are not always cost-effective, however, and could be employed after the fact or on a sample basis only.

Detective controls are a major focus of audit evaluation, because they can be applied after the fact to information from a specific period or time. The detection of errors in audit testing can point out errors in preventive, detective, or corrective controls. For example, the network operating system can record any attempted access via dial-up, and management can then receive and review the record daily.

Corrective For each detective control there should be one or more corrective controls, depending on the type or extent of the error. Some errors might only be reported, some might be removed from processing and reported for possible further action later, and others might require immediate corrective action before further processing. Corrective controls cause or encourage a desirable event or corrective action to occur after an undesirable event is detected. This type of control, also known as *post-action* control, takes effect after the undesirable event has occurred and then attempts to reverse the mistake.

In dealing with errors of omission, a system is vulnerable when it does not take corrective action to an identified exception. The system should have preventive controls in place to prevent or prohibit no action in response to an action. For example, senior management should be notified when the responsible manager does not clear access attempts.

In dealing with errors of commission, a system is vulnerable when an exception arises and it makes an improper response. In this situation, systems should have controls in place to correct the error. When an improper action occurs, especially in a LAN environment, that action takes place before it can be prevented. In this instance, an audit trail is essential in providing the information needed to correct the error and control the loss.

When designing or evaluating corrective controls, you must relate the control to the event that caused or allowed the error. A corrective control should function close to the source of the error and provide feedback that can improve the prevention of errors. Errors not related back to the source might result in excessive cost, because no incentive exists to reduce error rates. Corrective control processes should be subject to the same scrutiny as other processes to prevent and detect any errors introduced during correction.

Areas of control For LANs, controls can be thought to be in one of four categories: management controls, hardware controls, software controls, or communication controls. Management controls are when infrastructures of policies, procedures, and methods are created in support of management's objectives. Hardware controls are provided by or in conjunction with the physical equipment, and, similarly, software controls are programmable and reside on the system. Finally, communication controls protect the data transmissions. Each of these control categories is discussed in turn. Before looking at specific controls, however, some associated problems need to be considered.

Potential control issues The proliferation of PCs has helped companies perform their duties with greater efficiency. Still, due to the lack of a corporate integration effort, some companies find themselves with different processing platforms (e.g., DEC, IBM, or Macintosh). Is there a central resource pool that has the answers and the knowledge to successfully bridge the gap between the various systems?

Perhaps one should be established. Following are similar questions that need to be answered for an appropriate amount of control to exist.

Do standards or guidelines exist for installing hardware and software? Are these standards regulated through corporate standards and guidelines? How is the data transmitted? Is all data encrypted upon transmission? Encryption is especially important when one organization is housed in the same building as other organizations. Does virus protection and detection exist? Viruses are of particular concern as more users connect to networks, resulting in the networks being more vulnerable to unauthorized activity.

Is application and network software authorized; that is, is it licensed? Is the software as efficient as possible? Efficient software is necessary because much of corporate processing and electronic mail relies on the LAN. Does the LAN administration function continually evaluate new products and recent releases of existing products?

Are business resumption plans and procedures in place? A plan and specific procedures are especially crucial to ensure uninterruptible LAN processing. In some LAN installations, if one PC goes down, the entire network goes down, which is an unacceptable state. Are physical access controls to the file server sufficient to prevent unauthorized actions against the server?

Another potential control issue is how formal the safeguard is. Controls can be subdivided into formal and informal, as shown in TABLE 4-1. Traditionally, informal controls applied to senior management, who rely on their cognitive skills, and formal controls applied to clerical staff, who rely on their technical skills. The flattening of the organization has meant a shift from formal controls to informal controls for everyone.

Having developed these issues or concerns, we can now look at the control process and how it can help us with the issues.

Table 4-1
Formal vs informal controls

Informal controls are . . .	Formal controls are . . .
Trust	Policies
Competence	Standards and procedures
Shared values	Processes
Strong leadership	Laws
Clear accountability	Regulations
Openness	Organizational structure
High ethical standards	Centralized authority/decision-making

Control process

Another way to understand better the nature of control is to understand the nature of the control process. The control process includes the following, each of which are described in the next subsection.

- Developing objectives.
- Measuring results.
- Determining performance gaps.
- Analyzing differences.
- Determining appropriate managerial action.
- Taking action.
- Continuing reappraisal.

Developing objectives

The first step in the control process is determining what we want to do, which we previously defined as developing objectives. The objectives can be defined from a macrocosm or microcosm view. At the microcosm level, these objectives are referred to as standards and procedures. The common characteristic is that a determined objective exists for the standards and procedures.

Generally, management must be responsible for assuring the proper design and adequate control of any LAN. Major control objectives can be derived from this general principle. Management should perform the following:

- Establish policies to address the selection and installation of any LAN.
- Establish procedures ensuring the confidentiality of data.
- Provide adequate controls to ensure protection of the LAN from physical threats.
- Ensure the uninterruptible and reliable operation of the network.
- Establish controls over changes to the configuration of a LAN that will ensure uninterruptible and reliable operations.

These objectives are very high-level and provide no real direction for management. Subobjectives, however, can be developed from the major objectives. Subobjectives are described next that can be used as guidelines for secure operation of a LAN.

Within the control objectives described next, room exists for interpretation of adequacy, which is how managers earn their money. The responsible manager, after proper assessment, is the only one who can decide what constitutes adequate controls. Management can gain adequate information for this assessment by performing a risk analysis, which is covered in Chapter 5.

The business requirements to be satisfied by the network should be defined in writing Management should issue written policy statements prescribing the procedures for selecting, acquiring, and installing networks. These statements should include responsibility and authority for these steps.

A feasibility study should be prepared to identify reasonable alternatives and the costs and benefits of those alternatives
Your organization should have a written policy that outlines requirements for analyzing the costs and benefits of any proposal. For example, the network selected should provide significant operational improvements and benefits to justify the cost of its implementation.

Network architecture standards should be in place Agreement should exist on the types of hardware and software to be supported by your organization, including topologies, transmission media, and network operating system software.

An assessment of the threats and risks to the LAN should be conducted Security safeguards should exist that correspond to the risks and that comply with the organization's policies, standards, procedures, and guidelines. Periodic and formal monitoring of these safeguards should also occur.

Formal contingency plans should be developed and tested At a minimum, mechanisms should exist to ensure the uninterruptible processing of information, including backup.

Appropriate security training for staff should be conducted
A formal and mandatory security program should be designed for managers and all those who use the LAN workstations in their daily work.

Controls should exist to ensure the accuracy, completeness, authorization, confidentiality, and recording of data Access to computer resources, data, and software should be restricted to employees who need it in the performance of their duties. There should be a separate policy and standards for controlling access to the data on the LAN.

Copyrighted software license agreements should be adhered to properly Procedures should be in place to review periodically the network software.

Physical security should be adequate to protect the LAN network
The LAN's components, including transmission media, workstations, and servers should also be protected.

Changes to the network should be adequately controlled
Procedures should exist for covering the authority and responsibility for the physical components of the network. These procedures would include the process for changing the configuration and notifying users of the changes.

Measuring results

Assuming the objectives are measurable, the second step of the control process is to measure actual performance of the controls. We need to know what progress is truly being made toward the objectives. Only by measuring performance can we properly compare and analyze what corrective action must take place.

Determining the performance gap

We can now match the data of actual performance against the previously established objectives. This allows us to identify performance gaps, which are frequently called variances. This comparison can be conducted for current periods or for longer, cumulative periods. Although the comparison is a specific step in the control process, it is often combined with the reporting of actual results in practice. Clearly, these comparisons depend on actual performance and the objectives in the same manner—a need that must be anticipated.

Analyzing the differences

The next step is to decide what caused the differences reported. This step is to identify the various causal factors, plus any efforts necessary to measure the effect of each of the factors. The approach in part consists of pushing backward for more detailed information about the various activities. An effort also exists to discover both immediate and more systemic causes. At the same time, a judgmental evaluation occurs of how important individual factors really are as causes. Evaluating the importance is the essential step in using the results portrayed in the preceding steps. It is the responsibility of every manager, whether the actual evaluation is done personally or by a third party.

Determining appropriate managerial action

Analyzing what caused the differences unavoidably blends to some extent with determining appropriate managerial action. Sometimes, the responsible manager participates in part or all of the analysis. Often, however, this step is done by a separate analyst, so that this analyst also can make recommendations for managerial action. Actual management action in any event rests with the person who has line responsibility for the operational area and LAN. The available alternatives must be evaluated, and the very important judgment reached about what, if any, specific action should be taken.

It is useful to note also that the responsibility for proper analysis and determination of appropriate managerial action is the responsibility of the manager in charge of the activities delegated to subordinates or other staff groups. This is consistent with every manager's responsibility for final acceptance of goals and objectives.

Taking action

The judgment just reached about appropriate managerial action must now be implemented. Management now must issue the needed instructions for control performance in a way that considers the required urgency, the level of personnel to be dealt with, and the complexity of the actions to take. The action to take might be something that can be done quickly—such as rescinding a user's access code—or it might extend over a long period—such as implementing encryption on the network. Always, however, there is a further control problem as to what follow up should be taken to satisfy the responsible manager that appropriate action was, in fact, taken.

In some situations, the proper action that should be taken might be to do nothing at all. Perhaps the cost of correction outweighs the risk. Or, perhaps there is knowledge of future developments that are adequate to cure the existing problem. It needs to be recognized, however, that taking no action is itself a decision, and hence a responsive action.

Continuing reappraisal

A final step in the control process is appraising the results after the actions have been selected and completed. Appraisal is, in effect, a further check on the soundness of the earlier analysis of needed action and the manner in which the actions were actually taken. This final step closes the loop and links one control cycle to the next. This continuing reappraisal thus blends into the next measurement of progress analysis, and determination of further managerial action. Indeed, post appraisal is a continuing action that reflects the input of changing conditions, more experience, and greater knowledge of factors.

Relationship to management cycle

I have already shown that the control process begins with defining objectives and ends with achieving those objectives. The process has mostly to do with the effectiveness of management's actions in meeting the organization's goals. It is helpful to see how the control function interrelates with the major stages of the management cycle—planning, organizing, staffing, directing, and controlling. Figure 4-2 illustrates the management cycle.

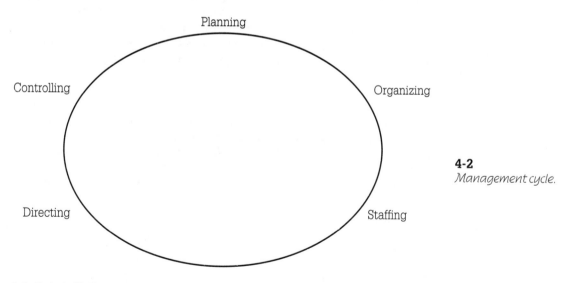

4-2
Management cycle.

R. Alec Mackenzie, "The Management Process in 3-D," Harvard Business Review, November-December 1969.

Planning

Planning involves developing goals, objectives, critical success factors, and forecasts for the organization and its components. These objectives provide the reference point for the supporting control objectives. Complete and comprehensive planning thus is the basis for the control function. I believe, however, that management recognizes the need for complete and comprehensive planning. I also believe, however, that anyone interested in developing and improving effective control must be concerned with the adequacy of the planning. It follows then that good planning is needed throughout the organization to provide good control. For example, management must show commitment to security through its approval and promotion of related policies, standards, and procedures.

Organizing Organizing concerns itself with the structure of an organization and is also important to the control function. It is through organizing that positions and responsibilities are defined and authority determined. In this way, organizing provides the control framework: if you want effective control, you must provide the right organization and the right reporting relationships. You can do this by improving the soundness of the organizational design. Good organizing is therefore an element of effective control.

Again, management must promote security by including basic security responsibilities within individual job descriptions. In addition, management can designate a person or function as having primary responsibility for security of the LAN.

Staffing The selection, orientation, training, and development of staff creates control problems. A discussion of these problems is provided later. Briefly, however, human beings, who have a natural aversion to controls, implement and administer these same controls. Thus, achieving effective control requires proper staff conditioning. Generally, control effectiveness increases with training about the human aspects of control. An important cornerstone of any effective security program is a security awareness program.

Directing Directing is concerned with delegating, motivating, and coordinating staff. It also deals with managing differences and change. Managers must administer the control system and take the necessary corrective actions. How a manager carries out these functions can either support or detract from the control system. This means effective control requires a manager's support, usually achieved through motivation. Security as a performance criterion is a strong motivator. Managers must inculcate positive values in staff to ensure effective security.

Controlling The management cycle usually ends with the controlling function. Controlling includes establishing a reporting system, developing performance standards, measuring results, taking corrective action, and rewarding behavior. Managers' enthusiasm for controls is severely dampened if they perceive implementing effective control is negatively rewarded. For example, it is difficult for managers to focus on effective control when the company focuses on short-term profits. Likewise, it is difficult for managers to carry out effective control when they see other managers not punished for compromising control. Again, upper management must set objectives for security and stand by them.

Relationship to total customer service

Dr. Michael Hammer, a preeminent authority on information systems and their application in business strategy, wrote a now-famous article for *Harvard Business Review*. In "Reengineering Work: Don't Automate, Obliterate," he writes the following:

> It should come as no surprise that our business processes and structures are outmoded and obsolete: our work structures and processes have not kept pace with the changes in technology, demographics, and business objectives. Mostly, we have organized work as a sequence of separate tasks and employed complex mechanisms to track its progress. This arrangement can be traced to the Industrial Revolution, when specialization of labor and economies of scale promised to overcome the inefficiencies of cottage industries. Businesses disaggregated work into narrowly defined tasks, reaggregated the people performing those tasks into departments, and installed managers to administer them.
>
> Our elaborate systems for imposing control and discipline on those who actually do the work stem from the postwar period. In the halcyon period of expansion, the main concern was growing fast without going broke, so businesses focused on cost, growth, and control. And since literate, entry-level people were abundant but well-educated professionals hard to come by, the control systems funneled information up the hierarchy to the few who presumably knew what to do with it.

LANs discourage these information silos and promote decentralization. Formal controls are progressively less effective as decentralization increases. The least helpful in LAN situations is a set of formal controls that implies there is only one correct behavior for all the different situations employees encounter. The more uncertain the task, such as those faced by knowledge workers, the more employees depend on values instead of formal controls to guide their behavior.

That is where the corporate culture kicks in. Culture is the values, beliefs, and norms a group shares. A positive culture is what enables some organizations to be leaders in security. Banks, for instance, have internalized security. Trust and security are necessary and unquestionable values for a bank. A negative culture, and an over-reliance on formal controls, is what leads some companies to ignore security. Real leaders are crucial to security because their words and deeds are the touchstones of a culture. Implementing security in environments where the leaders have not bought in is a difficult, if not impossible, task.

No company can implement security unless its top management is visibly, constantly, and sometimes irrationally committed to security. Setting up security controls is so much work that it only gets accomplished if the people at the top lead the charge. When they don't, the organization naturally turns inward and concentrates on processes that are less demanding. Everyone succumbs to the pressure of just doing their jobs instead of providing security.

Relationship to risk analysis

Evaluating risk for protective objectives focuses on the nature and scope of what impact particular types of potential deficiencies would have on a system, and the feasibility and cost of controlling the risks. Managers perform this type of risk evaluation for every situation. When carried out, risk analysis can be a useful guide to the types of controls, and the extent of their use, that make good business sense. What further complicates the evaluation are the often existing conflicts between reducing potential losses and the broader management needs and operational objectives, such as lower costs and short-term profits. Controls cannot be set up without a thorough cost-benefit analysis, or, in our terms, risk analysis. Risk analysis and the whole notion of risk management is discussed further in Chapter 5.

Controls & people

Controls affect people, and human nature being what it is, this causes problems. The basic source of the problem stems from the fact that most individuals instinctively like independence and freedom of action. The very fact that you require someone to do something makes them tend to view such a control with aversion and even hostility. Individuals can spend tremendous amounts of energy trying to get around the simple precepts of passwords. These individuals will write elaborate programs to change their password and then change it back—they will spend all this effort just to avoid thinking of a new password.

The extent of the tolerance for controls depends to a considerable extent upon the individual—intelligence, experience, cultural background, and emotional stability. It is safe to say, however, a normal tendency exists to resent controls and thus resist them to some extent. Their acceptance does, of course, depend a great deal on how management develops, presents, and administers the control. Therefore, you should anticipate these problems and develop action plans to minimize control animosity among employees.

First, the organization must develop a total reputation for ethical integrity and competence. As discussed in Chapter 6, this reputation should be developed at the top and communicated downward by word and deed. Second, people do not follow blindly like sheep if they do not understand the rationale. You must explain in plain language the rationale for any proposed control. Otherwise, staff will surely resent any control they do not understand and appreciate. The use of a password may be patently obvious to your security administrator and auditors, but completely lost on the rest of your staff.

Third, you must allow for people's feelings. A control has a greater chance of survival if presented with courtesy and reasonable consideration, as well as with an opportunity for adjustment. You cannot legislate encryption controls today and expect them tomorrow. Controls suffer from cultural lag. People do not question the use of key locks and combinations, but they do question the need for encryption. Someday, encryption might be as pervasive as locks, and no one will question its use.

Fourth, people resent controls that they perceive you do not have the authority to impose on them. They will not use password controls if they believe the passwords are a technical solution to a technical problem. The answer is to have controls sponsored by individuals with sufficient authority and a legitimate right. A corporate security policy should be endorsed by the company president and not the vice president of systems.

Fifth, controls derived by consensus have a greater chance of success. The control consultation process should be as broad as it is practical. Finally, the manner of administration affects the success of the control. Administration should not be arbitrary and should show an understanding of the problems involved. People affected by the controls need to know there is an interest in problems and a willingness to listen to solutions from all sources. Although you might follow this advice, you might still face control problems.

Control problems

What are some operational problems relating to the control cycle? What should be controlled? What are the critical resources? What resources are the most valuable in relation to the others? What are the largest expenditures for the network? Which network costs provide the greatest possible savings? What is the impact of controls on the company's continued existence? What combinations of controls are required? And at what cost? Are the controls consistent with the flattening of the organization and the decentralization of authority? How can control objectives be defined? How will the control objectives actually be established? All these control problems are explored throughout the remainder of the book.

Managing risk: cost-benefit analysis

To the casual observer, most security people suffer from an unhealthy paranoia. They are looking for *spooks* in every closet and *bugs* on every line. Some security practitioners I know fit this description, but most do not. Most are dedicated professionals who understand the critical success factors of the business. They believe controls should be implemented when and where compelling business reasons exist.

Still, there are some factions who follow other strategies. For example, one faction espouses a baseline of control. This baseline is a minimum set of controls that can be thought of as one of the costs of doing business. Others follow different strategies. Some security strategies involve developing safeguards in reaction to specific losses. Strategies carried out in this manner are akin to coral reefs, layer built upon layer, with layers not required dying and falling away. Strategies also exist based on bubble-up improvements that have no significant effect on the total security. These strategies normally are not cost-effective.

The majority of security professionals believes an effective control program is one where the cost of setting up protective mechanisms is optimally balanced against the reduction in risk achieved. Implementing security without a control program is like rearranging deck chairs on the *Titanic*—it looks good, but provides little long-term relief. The process of attempting to achieve a tolerable level of risk at the lowest possible cost is *risk management*.

Risk management is an element of managerial science concerned with the identification, measurement, control, and minimization of uncertain events. Managers must address risk management from a multidimensional as well as multidisciplinary perspective. It must be recognized as a continuing, formal planning technique, which includes a whole range of existing management tools, such as budgets. The multidisciplinary perspective stems from the security levels explored in the following chapters; the interrelationship between the different levels creates the multidimensional perspective.

Management's resistance to costs with uncertain payoffs and paybacks difficult to quantify is understandable; however, security has become an important performance parameter. When exposures are not recognized, loss potentials inaccurately quantified, and risk control and financial opportunities overlooked, a company's attainment of its objectives is hindered and its financial rewards reduced. The net cost of risk can be measured, budgeted, and controlled. Where we can reduce this cost, profits can be increased.

Costs, benefits— & risks

The traditional equation of costs and benefits is no longer enough to justify a LAN strategy. In a highly distributed world with microcomputers, complex networks, and database systems, risk has become the third factor in the management equation.

Most management decisions involve the assumption of risk—the chance that the results will be different than we hoped. Decisions made in spite of uncertainties and in recognition of them are generally accepted as essential to dynamic, successful organizations. Usually, the key to success lies not in the willingness to accept uncertainty or assume risk, but in the ability to recognize and quantify risk and to handle it in an objective way. Every manager must face and manage risk in some form. Risk can be reduced considerably, or substantially eliminated, by better information about operational and environmental factors.

As stated, these decisions call for information. The limitations are the costs of obtaining the types of information desired. There is a cost to perfect information. Increasingly, one confronts uncontrollable factors affecting desired results. To some extent, we can reduce this risk by statistical calculations of probabilities. However, here also are increasingly substantive limitations. The overall result is that total certainty is impossible because of both practical and absolute limitations. Seeking a level of no risk is impractical; you must reach a level of risk that is acceptable to your organization.

Management actions must reflect the levels of risk deemed acceptable to the responsible manager. Usually, a correlation exists between the potential available profitability and the extent of risk, but there is also the varying capacity to survive failure and operational losses. There also are varying inclinations to take risk. Psychologically, risk perception differs widely from one person to another. Some people are risk averse while others are risk seekers. Generally, values guiding people's behavior are more negative on the negative than positive on the positive side, which means that people are more sensitive to increases in loss than increases in gains and are therefore risk averse. Risk averters are usually willing to pay less than the expected monetary value of fair gamble. Their utility for monetary amounts increases at a decreasing rate. Simply put, some people are gamblers and take chances, while others suffer distress from taking chances. Managers must therefore make evaluations within the parameters of authority and preferences. Although managers have different risk sensitivities, they need not have different methods for quantifying risk.

The increased awareness of the need for security has resulted in the need for a method to quantify threats to a company. Risk management provides a cost-effective program for reducing risk to an acceptable level. The risk management program provides management with much needed information for basing questions and allocating dollars. Management is provided with information so it can decide whether to accept a loss by controlling the threat or accept the risk. Risk management is to security what requirements definition is to systems development. Figure 5-1 shows the management process of risk.

Risks can only be reduced, retained, or transferred. They can also be managed. You must identify threats, predict exposure to the threats, rank the

Risk

Risk Management Policy
- Overall objective of the organization
- Strategic assessments
- Financial strength
- Willingness to take risks

The above forms the basis for the policy that creates continuous possibilities to analyze and treat the risks of loss within the organization.

Risk Analysis
- Identification of risks and losses
- Evaluation of the severity and probability of losses
- Assessment of priority for action

Involvement in these areas increases risk awareness.

Risk Retention
- Analysis of loss records for trends and basic causes
- Selection of suitable methods for financing residual risks of loss

Risk Reduction
- Measures to reduce or eliminate risks or losses
- Investigation of the possibility of transferring risks

Risk Transference
- Assessing extent of exposure
- Selection of suitable insurance

5-1 Risk management.

exposures by priority, and then implement controls where cost-justified. An effective risk management program encompasses four distinct phases: risk analysis, management decision, control implementation, and effectiveness review.

Risk analysis

A risk analysis of each LAN is necessary to quantify the losses that you would be subjected to if information were disclosed to unauthorized persons, damaged, or destroyed. The two key elements in risk analysis are a statement of impact relative to how badly a specific difficulty would hurt if it happens, and a statement of the probability of encountering that difficulty within a specified period of time. Both parameters are needed to describe risk in terms of cost per unit time, such as dollars per year.

Your risk analysis can be either quantitative or qualitative. Quantitative methods yield data that describe the cost of potential problems in terms of cost per unit time, while qualitative methods help set priorities. Qualitative methods do have scientific merit for the following reasons:

- The method is planned.
- Judgment is based on fact.
- The measures are reliable.

- The calculations are public.
- The conclusions follow from the data.

Risk analysis can be subdivided into nine steps:
- Asset identification.
- Asset valuation.
- Threat identification.
- Vulnerability identification.
- Threat/vulnerability merger.
- Predictive analysis.
- Loss cost analysis.
- Risk assessment.
- Safeguard identification.

Asset identification   The first step in any risk analysis—either qualitative or quantitative—is the identification of assets needing protection. Assets are identified at the lowest level practical.

Asset valuation   In *Guideline for Information Valuation*, the ISSA Corresponding Committee chaired by Will Ozier suggested that the value of information is associated with one of the following conditions:
- Exclusive possession. Information has value to the organization that possesses it, for example, a trade secret.
- Utility. Information is as valuable as the use to which it is put. Information that cannot be used can have a negative value, such as legal sanction.
- Cost of creation/recreation. Information initially costs money to create.
- Liability. The holder of the information may incur a liability for its protection, such as for national secrets.
- Convertibility/negotiability. Information holds at least the value of the information it represents, for example, a funds transfer.
- Operational impact. How valuable the information would be to the enterprise if the information was unavailable.

You can use many methods for valuing assets. In the same guideline, the committee set any of the following methods for valuing assets:
- Policy/fiat/regulation.
- Checklist.
- Questionnaire.
- Consensus.
- Accounting.
- Statistical analysis.

Regardless of the method, valuing data is the hardest part of risk analysis. You should expect to spend a great deal of time and effort on completing the valuation for best results.

Threat identification   Collect and document the threats to your LAN environment. A threat is one or more events that could lead either to intentional or unintentional modification, destruction, or disclosure of the data. Threats include physical threats; natural phenomena, such as storms or earthquakes that could damage or destroy buildings or stop employees from getting to work; as well as manmade threats such as terrorist attacks, union work stoppages, malicious acts by disgruntled workers, fraud, theft, or misuse of equipment. Refer to Chapter 3 for a discussion of the different types of threats. Threat identification also includes the observation and recognition of new threat parameters, new relationships among existing ones, or a perception of a change in the magnitude of existing threats.

By tracing the flow of data through a system, one can pinpoint where in the processing cycle threats could occur. The basic points where threats do occur are as follows:

- Conversion. The physical conversion of source documents to machine-readable form (data).
- Communication (input). The transmission of the input data via the network.
- Receipt. The receipt of data over the network.
- Storage. The storage of data awaiting processing.
- Processing. The execution of application programs to perform intended computations and preparation of the computation results.
- Communication (output). The transmission of the output data via the network.
- Printing. The printing of computer-produced output.
- Usage. The use of data by the recipient, including the storage or location of it while being used.
- Disposition. The disposition of data after the period of use, including the methods and locations of storage, length of time for storage and final disposal, as appropriate.

Vulnerability identification Vulnerability is the cost an organization would incur if an event took place. You must determine how vulnerable your organization is to threats.

Threat/vulnerability merger After collecting the vulnerability data, you must compare it to the identified threats to conclude whether these threats could exploit the known vulnerabilities.

Predictive analysis Data concerning existing safeguards should be analyzed and compared with the threat/vulnerability results to decide if existing safeguards are adequate. This process also includes estimating the likelihood and frequency of occurrence of an event based on statistics, research, and experience.

Loss cost analysis If the risk analysis is quantitative, usually expressed as annualized loss exposures, you must establish and evaluate threat frequencies. These calculations are usually obtained by multiplying the replacement cost of an asset by the annual threat frequency occurrence rate. If the risk analysis is qualitative, you must assign a scale—either alphabetical, numerical, or verbal—to each threat/vulnerability combination for each asset. One such verbal scale assigns threat/vulnerability combinations as *high, medium*, or *low*.

Safeguard identification Selecting a security control mix should include an attempt to assure that all critical functions of the LAN are adequately protected. You must, however, balance the benefits of the various control measures against the costs of their implementation and continued use. When selecting controls, you should consider the following:

- Acceptance. As previously mentioned, control effectiveness relies on acceptance by staff.
- Auditable. Controls must be testable to decide on performance and conformance with specifications.
- Cost-effectiveness. Only cost-justified safeguards should be implemented.
- Degree of automation. Automated controls have a higher probability of success during operation.
- Growth. The safeguard should grow in response to a change within the operation.
- Rigorous. Controls must not rely on secrecy to be effective.

Table 5-1 offers some help on selecting safeguards.

Table 5-1
Threat/control matrix

	Access management	Data integrity	Digital signature	Message encryption	Origin authentication
Denial of service	♦				
Disclosure	♦			♦	♦
Masquerading	♦		♦		♦
Message modification		♦		♦	
Repudiation			♦	♦	♦
Sequence modification		♦			

Management decision

Management's decision involves either a risk avoidance, risk transference, or risk acceptance judgment. Management can acknowledge the risk and its resultant exposure and choose to accept it based on the information provided by a risk analysis, or management can transfer a portion of the cost of the exposure to another agency or organization via a form of insurance, or management can implement selected controls to eliminate or reduce exposure to the risk.

Management's trade-off can be simply stated as

Collective threat − collective security measures = acceptable level of risk

Because adequate security is a relative concept, it is either a managerial policy decision or a technical judgment by a responsible person. To ensure the manager makes the best decision, the best information must be used for decision making.

Managers must review the results of the risk analysis and select a plan of action based on the analysis. They can choose to accept risk as inherent in the business and absorb it. Self-insurance, common in government, is a form of risk acceptance. The manager also has three other possible choices. The manager can change how the organization operates, such as switching from decentralized to centralized processing. The manager can also choose to control or limit the risks using protective measures. Finally, the manager can decide the operation cannot be changed or that controls are prohibitive, and transfer a portion of the risk associated with the operation to others. Table 5-2 lists the decisions faced by management and TABLE 5-3 shows an example of managerial decision.

Table 5-2
Management's decisions

Decision	Action
Avoid the risk . . .	Change the operation
Control the risk . . .	Implement controls
Limit the risk . . .	Buy insurance
Accept the risk . . .	Go ahead as planned

Table 5-3
Risk example

Risk	Disclosure of corporate secrets
Threat	Eavesdropping
Vulnerability	Unencrypted communications
Exposure	Loss of competitive advantage

Risk acceptance Risk acceptance should be initiated when implementing a control causes an unacceptable business impact. Management has acknowledged the identified risk and made a conscious decision to accept that risk based on all available information.

Risk avoidance It is inevitable. Now that your corporation has conducted a risk assessment and feels safe knowing all the risks facing it, somebody comes along advocating "risk avoidance." *Risk avoidance* is those actions taken either to mitigate or eliminate the effect of a potential undesirable act.

Because so many network problems can be anticipated, risk avoidance should be at the heart of an organization's plans. Almost every computer-related disaster can be traced to ignorance of environmental threats or hardware and software design or maintenance deficiencies that allowed minor problems to escalate into major disasters. Even organizations who had disasters occur look at improving their recovery process rather than avoiding the threat. Risk avoidance must be part of security planning.

Uninterruptible power supplies can support file servers and other network resources, thereby ensuring a continuous power supply. Cable scanners can detect wiring faults. LAN analyzers can determine contention problems and malfunctioning devices. Workstations can automatically check diskettes for viruses. Fault-tolerant hardware and software provide fail-safe measures. Duplicate disk drives bypass a single point of failure. Backup of the file server and local hard disk drives can be performed regularly. All of these examples are risk avoidance measures. Thus, there is absolutely no reason why organizations cannot avoid many of the threats facing them.

Risk transference

Residual risk that cannot be reduced or avoided must be financed. Risks can be financed in many ways, with the most important being the following:

- Operating budgets.
- External grants.
- Appropriations of paid-in-capital (reserves).
- Credit.
- Insurance.

Managers must evaluate the advantages and disadvantages of each based on the effect on the cash flow, taxation, earnings, share price, and market standing and position.

Insurance is a method for transferring risk to another organization, in effect, applied risk management. Buying insurance is a form of risk transference. Microcomputers are different from cars, photocopiers, and other appliances, however, and most office policies exclude personal computers. The value of the microcomputer is more than the value of the hardware. When looking for insurance, consider the following coverage:

- Loss of or damage to hardware, including peripherals.
- Loss of or damage to media, including the cost of restoring or recovering files, software and other data.
- Business interruptions.

At least one company offers insurance against computer viruses, software piracy, and toll-call fraud, among other crimes. Commercial banks and other depository institutions can obtain up to $50 million coverage for computer-related crimes.

Control implementation

Once the selected controls are bought or developed, their implementation must be scheduled. Depending on the type of control, some training might be required for users prior to using the safeguard.

Effectiveness review

Periodic review of controls is necessary to identify ineffective, nonfunctioning, or nonessential safeguards. Upgrades in software, hardware, or communications equipment, or the installation of new safeguards, might also result in changes to the risk environment. You should evaluate any changes to decide the impact of these changes on previously accepted risk decisions.

A simple example shows why control reviews are necessary. During the 1950s and 1960s, people judged the threat of nuclear war as highly likely. Because of this perception, they built bomb shelters and stocked them with water, air, clothing, food, and other items of necessity. These same people now have abandoned their bomb shelters—not because the potential devastation is less, but because they perceive the current chance of attack no longer justifies the cost of maintaining the shelters. They reviewed the control and realized that the expense was not justified compared to the possibility of risking nuclear attack. Those people who had previously not abandoned their shelters might have done so when the Berlin wall crumbled, or the USSR divided. Like all good management controls, the effectiveness review brings us back to risk analysis, whereupon the process starts again.

Final words on risk management

Managers should deliberate before assigning individuals to the risk analysis team. The success of risk analysis relies heavily on the team. Individuals should be thoroughly knowledgeable about the area being analyzed before being selected.

Identifying exposures facing a LAN is a task that should only be delegated to staff after great deliberation because of the level of knowledge and experience required in the decision process. It can be an enlightening experience and could lead to system simplification if done correctly.

Qualitative versus quantitative—which is best? That depends. I have implemented both in different organizations. You should base your decision on your organizational culture. For instance, engineering or accounting firms might favor quantitative methods, while an advertising firm might choose a qualitative method. The decision is not important. What is important is that you apply the methodology with consistency.

Finally, many people have criticized risk analysis. They start by saying you cannot value data. Also, they believe you cannot annualize losses. I cannot dispute these claims; however, there is value in applying a cost-benefit methodology to security. If nothing else, risk analysis allows a process for allocating scarce security dollars. Logically, the process makes sense, and as John Maynard Keynes once remarked, "It is better to be vaguely right than to be precisely wrong."

Part three
The solutions

Only science can hope to keep technology in some sort of moral order.
— **Edgar Friedenberg**

It is crucial vision alone which can mitigate the unimpeded operation of the automatic.
— **Marshall Mcluhan**

6

Securing the LAN

A good security program consists of the optimum set of controls. Like a chain, however, your security is only as good as the weakest link. You should not set up your security to be like the Maginot line, which fell so quickly to the Germans in 1940. Hitler ignored the Maginot line and advanced on other fronts, leading to the battles fought in France. People bent on breaking your system will find the holes in your security and will avoid your good controls. Determining the potential security holes, the weakest links in your network, might seem overwhelming, but security comes from the total web of all controls, and everything must be considered. Some controls by their nature, however, are very cost-effective and should be implemented first.

Several control techniques can be easily implemented to secure your LAN. These controls fall broadly into two solutions—technical and managerial. Technical solutions usually involve automated controls. Managerial solutions usually involve written policies, standards, procedures, and guidelines.

Which solutions are the most effective? It is difficult to say. I have never met anyone in the security profession, however, who does not believe security is a management issue first and foremost. This is not to say there are not technical issues that must be solved. The best access control package in the world will not work, however, if you provide many people with powerful privileges. Access control packages work only if you have decided what requires protection and from whom. In this chapter, I discuss management issues before moving on to the more technical issues.

One of the most serious threats to many LANs is the seeming lack of ethics in the business place. Breaches of ethics cause untold daily loss to corporations. These losses occur because of breaches of trust, immoral decisions, focus on short-term profits, and lack of professionalism or pride.

Information systems ethics: an oxymoron?

In the newspaper, we frequently read stories of unethical or unprofessional behavior in our society. It is not unusual to read an article about a stockbroker charged with insider trading—a flagrant breach of trust—or to read about a salesperson who leaves one company, taking the customer list or other confidential information of his previous employer with him or her. Business situations are not the only ones where unethical practices arise. Which one of us, at one time or another, has not copied a record, video, audio cassette, television, or radio transmission? These are all examples of unethical behavior.

The information systems profession is not without its ethical dilemmas. Audits of microcomputers have found games on business microcomputers, even though the company had a policy to the contrary. These same audits revealed unlicensed software on the microcomputers. A microcomputer problem you say. Not so! Companies knowingly use unlicensed versions of LAN software. Companies have sometimes used software without remorse because they were warring with the vendor and felt using unlicensed software was their method of getting even. Or, employees used the software because they needed it, and management would not adequately fund software for the LAN.

Another form of unethical behavior in data processing is the writing and releasing of computer viruses or worms. The present *zeitgeist* regarding computer hackers is that they are clever individuals who should be rewarded. *Zeitgeist* is the term used for the moral and intellectual atmosphere characteristic of an epoch or age, roughly the spirit of the times. Within the current climate, we find it difficult to punish those hackers who destroy networks, software, and data. Many people laud these individuals for their creativity and publicly announce they would hire the hackers. It is this lack of ethics, however, that probably creates the biggest threat to your data! It is difficult to understand how anyone can rationalize this deviant behavior.

Recent court decisions, however, make me believe there has been a reversal of this opinion. I also am heartened by the people at Lawrence Livermore National Laboratory in Northern California. Recognizing that today's children are tomorrow's hackers, Lawrence Livermore developed a 30-minute program on computer privacy, security, and ethics for children from kindergarten to third grade. The video program stars Gooseberry, Dirty Dan, and Chip, a computer terminal with arms and legs. The children seem to understand the concepts better than most adults!

The deterioration, be it real or imagined, of ethical behavior in business can be attributed to several causes. One such cause is what Emile Durkheim has labeled *anomie*, or a state of *normlessness*. The normlessness state arises because societal norms are changing so fast that no one is certain of what is acceptable behavior:

> "It is the same if the source of the crisis is an abrupt growth of power and wealth. Then, truly, as the conditions of life are changed, the standard according to which needs were regulated can no longer remain the same: for it varies with social resources, since it largely determines the share of each class of producers. The scale is upset: but a new scale cannot be immediately improvised. Time is required for the public conscience to reclassify men and things."

Sound familiar? Well, Emile Durkheim wrote this in *Le Suicide* in 1897. This normlessness is characterized by a chaotic business climate in which, as Tom Peters likes to put it, "nobody has a sweet clue what the hell is going on." This is true today because of the *technostress* and information overload that affects the average person. This average person is being constantly bombarded in daily life with information from newspapers, magazines, television, radio, billboards, and other communication media. At work, these people face all kinds of reports, telephone calls, electronic mail, trade journals, and salespeople. The inability of most people to process all this information is highly stressful.

Another cause of unethical behavior in computing is the apparent lack of schooling in ethics. Students of business in general, and computer science specifically, are usually not required to attend ethics classes. Scattered across North America, you can find institutions of higher learning, offering ethics courses to their computing students, but these institutions are rare. Society has abdicated the responsibility for the teaching of ethics to parents, who believe their children are clever if they can penetrate the databases of Sloan-Kettering!

Yet another cause of the morals problem in information systems is the lack of commitment from companies and their management. As previously mentioned, management's commitment is essential to convincing people of the need for controls. Management does not always practice what it preaches, however. One company had a standard of conduct and conflict of interest policy, which are usually good signs.

This company was not in very good shape, though. Lack of ethics and low morale were the main reasons—cheating, lying, and stealing had become widespread. Executive management, instead of punishing problem employees, treated all employees the same, further dampening morale. There was a perceived lack of morality at the top; a "win at all costs" philosophy that permeated its way down the organization. This ruthless attitude was at the root of the unethical behavior and low morale. Management must instead explain the company's purpose to employees and prove its commitment to the purpose through its own words and deeds.

Management blames its own ruthless behavior on increased competition in the business world. Increased competition forced many companies in North America to begin "Work Smarter" programs, which can be loosely translated as cutbacks. As everyone is aware, cutbacks start with discretionary items, such as microcomputer software. Companies that require more and more from their employees yet offer them fewer and fewer resources create an atmosphere that fosters low morale, in turn leading to unprofessional behavior.

All is not doom and gloom, however, and there are steps a company can take to improve morale and promote ethical behavior. For example, companies could develop and adopt a Code of Ethics and Standard of Conduct policy. A code of ethics describes the ideals to which all employees of the company should aspire. The code becomes a summary of the basic principles of conduct all employees should subscribe to when they join the company. The code of ethics should detail how every employee has an obligation to the following:

- Safeguard the company's interests and reputation with integrity, honesty, and objectivity.
- Avoid any conflict of interest issues that may compromise the company's position.

- Uphold the principles of privacy and confidentiality with respect to customers, other employees, and all company business.
- Consult management before publicly expressing personal views on issues affecting the company.
- Maintain a reasonable level of competence, and complete assigned tasks and responsibilities.
- Cooperate with and treat colleagues with honesty and respect and do not misuse any authority entrusted to the employee.
- Conform to all orders, rules, and regulations of the company.

A standard of conduct should outline the various responsibilities for employees. The following are topics that should be included in a standard of conduct.

Employees should be made aware that all resources of the company are for authorized business uses only. One company I know faced a problem when management discovered an employee writing a romance novel on their system, but the company had no policy against it! Along those same lines, all software, system documentation, and other material developed for the company should be for authorized company use only and owned by the company. More than one company has ended in court fighting over the ownership of software written by an employee.

All employees should be accountable for assets entrusted to them and should not intentionally compromise these assets. Accountability is difficult to prove when employees share user identification codes! Employees must not appropriate or disclose confidential information for personal advantage, financial gain, malicious intent, or any other unauthorized purpose. Staff should not be allowed to profit because of a breach of their fiduciary trust with their employer.

Employees must have an obligation to report to management any illegal or unethical practice that comes to their attention because it affects the company. It is usually not in the best or long-term interests of a company for any employee to turn a blind eye to unethical behavior. It is the responsibility of personnel to abide by the company's policies, standards, procedures, and practices. The onus is on employees to conform to the standards of good conduct for the company and society at large.

A service-dominated economy full of knowledgeable workers is substantially different from an industrial-based economy where the required behavior could be explained and dictated precisely. In the information systems environment, a worker must respond thoughtfully and imaginatively to what Jan Carlzon (1987) of Scandinavian Airlines System calls the "50,000 moments of truth." Because it is impossible for management to tell workers what to do in every situation, the company's management must instill the right purpose within every employee, a purpose that is congruous to the purpose of the company itself.

Ken Blanchard and Norman Vincent Peale (1989) coauthored a book entitled *The Power of Ethical Management* in which they suggest you ask yourself three questions when faced with a moral problem. First, is it legal? Legality can be classified as criminal, civil, or company policy. Second, is it balanced? Will you gain an unfair advantage? Will someone else suffer because of your behavior? Third, how will it make you feel about yourself? Can you look yourself in the mirror? If you do not like your answers to any of these questions, you have a tough ethical decision to make. Without a move to a more ethical environment, it will be difficult to figure out who is the enemy in the future business environment!

It cannot be said enough: if you wish to promote ethical behavior, show management's commitment to it and prove to employees the resolve of the company. A demonstration of management's commitment to secure data is an essential cornerstone for LAN security. From this base flows all security requirements.

The first step: administrative & organizational security

Effective external and internal organizational control must exist over processing functions, and management must exercise effective control over the proper use of LAN resources. In Chapter 5, we learned these are basic management objectives—safeguarding assets under their control. Organizations must ensure that structures and senior management support and are committed to an effective network security program. All the various departments and all individuals using network facilities should understand their appropriate role regarding control. They should all understand their responsibility for protecting the confidentiality and maintaining the integrity of any data entrusted to them.

Adoption of a security policy, an example of which is provided in TABLE 6-1, and procedures for the implementation of this policy can demonstrate management's commitment to security. Additionally, these policies provide employees with corporate norms. Once these norms are communicated to all employees, it is reasonable and fair to expect employees to abide by them. Any deviation by employees can be considered insubordination and grounds for punitive action, up to and including dismissal. Management must administer the policy fairly and consistently. Nothing invalidates the policy faster than allowing some valued employees to break the rules with impunity. Once this happens, all employees have the right to break the rules.

To eliminate any question about management's wishes, management should develop security standards, for example, a specified password length. Management must prove its commitment to the standards by consistently and constantly enforcing them. A recent Supreme Court of Nova Scotia decision reinforces this point. Cynthia Conrad worked for 6 years at Household Finance Corp. (HFC) in Halifax, Canada, where she needed a confidential password to access customer accounts. Unbeknownst to Ms. Conrad, somebody used her password to alter account balances. Although

**Table 6-1
Sample security policy**

Introduction	The Organization relies upon the integrity of its data and information systems. To ensure that this integrity is maintained, it is essential that these information systems and data be protected and that the computer-based information systems and the data that they process be maintained in a controlled manner in a secure environment.
Policy	It is the policy of the Organization to protect its information systems and the data they process to ensure: • The confidentiality of information and the security of electronic data processing (EDP) assets; • The continued operation of the Organization's computer-based information systems; and • The exclusive use of EDP assets for purposes authorized by the Organization. EDP assets include computers, computing installations, terminals, supporting facilities, data processing services, and data processing input/output, software and data.
Scope	This policy applies to all EDP assets and personnel within the jurisdiction of the Organization. The scope includes, but is not limited to, central computing facilities, regional processing centers, distributed processing centers, standalone processors, local area networks, wide area networks, metropolitan area networks, data held at service bureaus, Organization employees, and non-Organization personnel under contract to the Organization.
Ownership of EDP assets	For each EDP asset, an owner must be identified who will be responsible for specifying the requisite asset control. The owner is an employee or agent of the Organization asssigned by Senior Management the responsibility for making and communicating certain decisions regarding business control and selective protection of the Organization's assets. The owner is also responsible for monitoring compliance with specified controls.
Custodianship of EDP assets	A custodian and employee, agent or organizational unit of the Organization will be assigned administration or control responsibilities for each EDP asset. The owner is responsible for the assignation of custodianship.

continued

	Any person or function charged with the custodianship of EDP assets is responsible for ensuring the effective safeguarding of those assets and shall be accountable to management.
Classification of EDP assets	All EDP assets despite media or form must be classified and be afforded the protection appropriate to its classification. Owners of EDP assets are responsible for classifying the assets in accordance with classification standards established by the Organization.
Access control	Access to EDP assets must be controlled so that only authorized access is permitted and only those assets necessary to perform the assigned task are provided.
Backup and recovery auditability	Appropriate backup and recovery capabilities must be provided for critical EDP assets. All computer-based information systems must include internal controls capable of establishing an action and accountability for such action.
Security responsibilities	*All Employees* Every employee of the Organization will comply with the information systems security policy, standards, procedures, and directions and owner-established security and control requirements. *Users* All authorized users of EDP assets must use such assets for authorized purposes only and undertake responsibility for their proper use. *Management* Management must ensure that established security and control requirements for EDP assets are met and ensure the controlled use of EDP assets under their respective jurisdiction, and be accountable.
Security awareness	All employees must be aware of those aspects of security required for proper execution of their functions.
Reporting of security violations	All security violations must be reported immediately to responsible management for corrective action.
Risk acceptance	Where owed to business circumstances, either the effective controls cannot be implemented or the risk cannot be transferred to another agency or company, then formal approval to accept this risk must be obtained from the appropriate level of the executive of the Systems Department,

	Information Systems Security, and the division of the owner of the affected EDP asset.
Authority	Chief Executive Officer.
Authority to issue supporting documentation	Chief Information Officer.

HFC acknowledged she had no part in the crime, they terminated her *for cause* on the eve of her promotion and transfer to Ottawa. The cause stated in the proceedings was "a flagrant disregard for the most basic of security measures." She sued for lost wages, wasted relocation costs, and punitive damages and won on all counts.

HFC's policy dictated that employees log off the system when not using their account, and yet Ms. Conrad admitted she might have wandered away from her screen on occasion. The defense pointed out, however, that this was standard office practice. Security had also issued a stamp to Ms. Conrad bearing her confidential password. Policy was silent, however, on the storing of the stamp, and so she kept the stamp in her unlocked desk drawer, as did most employees. Ms. Conrad's lawyer hired a security consultant who testified it was child's play to get passwords—words he backed up with six he had acquired the previous day. HFC's lawyers relied simply on the fact that access was via Ms. Conrad's account and password. HFC was thus found at fault.

The overwhelming conclusion to the case is that should you choose to dismiss someone for violation of security, you better be secure, or at least prudent, in your policy standards. Working against HFC was how the consultant obtained six passwords with absolute ease, along with a lack of a specific policy for handling the storage of the stamp. The lesson is clear, and I repeat that management must prove its commitment to policy and standards by consistently and constantly enforcing them. Table 6-2 is a good example of a password standard that HFC sorely needed.

Management must value information; otherwise, it cannot understand the worth of information and the potential impact through loss or disclosure. Many methods are available for valuing information, some of which were provided in Chapter 5. Security of this information is improved when management assigns accountability for and control over information. A good information protection plan calls for a sponsor responsible for ensuring that

**Table 6-2
Sample password standard**

Introduction	Access control systems involve the issues of authentication and authorization. Typically, an access control system first attempts to authenticate an individual and then, "knowing" who the individual is, attempts to restrict the individual to that which is authorized to the individual. A generally accepted technique for providing authentication is to exchange privileged information or, in general terms, "use a password." The proper use of passwords is an essential first step in establishing effective access control.
Purpose	This standard outlines the basic principles that must be adhered to by all properly implemented password systems. Many definitive statements that could have been made about passwords have been avoided to deal with the general concept of passwords. Particular statements usually deal with the implementation aspects and, hence, are better dealt with at the application level. It is intended that this standard serve as a source of guidance for areas drafting password procedures and designing or implementing password systems.
Scope	This standard applies to all password systems used for automated access control purposes and that protect valuable, sensitive, or confidential assets. Password systems used for physical or logical control and developed either internally or externally to the Organization are covered by this document.
Password application	Documentation or procedures should be generated for each password system within the Organization. This documentation should detail: - Specifics of how the standard is applied; and, - Special considerations or controls unique to the password system.
Deviations	Deviations from this standard for existing, enhanced, and new password systems must be clearly documented and be approved using the Risk Acceptance procedure. Where warranted by the value or the sensitivity of the assets under protection controls that exceed this topic may be required.

When to use password systems	With every controlled access system some form of user authentication is required to ensure that only valid users are permitted by the system. A password system should be considered on a cost-effective basis every time a controlled access system is implemented to protect the Organization's valuable assets. In making this assessment, the aspects of what is being protected and the existing environmental security should be taken into account.
The password system	A password can consist of anything that can be associated with an individual such that this association: - Is a legally binding association (for example, fingerprint, signature); or, - Has an extremely low probability of being guessed or duplicated by an unauthorized individual. Passwords should be associated with a group only in exceptional circumstances. Such usage will be deemed a deviation.
Password generation	A password can be generated by an automated or manual technique. Passwords can be generated in a centralized or distributed fashion. The actual generation of a password should be done so as to prevent any unauthorized individual from determining the password directly, or from collateral information. Passwords should be generated in a random manner to minimize the possibility of a password being determined by an unauthorized individual. Passwords can be derived by transforming a chosen expression.
Password distribution	The distribution of passwords should be in such a form so as to enhance its probability of being retained by the user in a secure fashion.
Creation	Passwords should only be created and received by authorized individuals. Individuals should be authorized on a need-to-know basis. The person who authorizes individuals should be determined at the project level of new systems or otherwise by the level of management designated by policy.
Controlled manner	Distribution of passwords, if required, should be done in a controlled manner through a trusted means to ensure that the passwords are not disclosed to unauthorized persons or physically destroyed.

continued

Acknowledgement	A user acknowledgement of receipt and/or creation of a password should be kept in a central location for audit purposes.
Frequency of change	Passwords should be changed on a regular basis so as to reduce the risk of compromise. This period should be determined so as to accommodate both security and operational requirements. The maximum period for a password's usage must not exceed one year.
Compromise	Passwords that are known to be, or that can reasonably be assumed to be, compromised (that is, known to, or in the possession of, an unauthorized individual), should be removed from the system immediately. For centralized systems, a report should be prepared by the individual experiencing the loss or compromise and sent to the Password System Auditor (PSA) and the Password System Manager (PSM).
Password control	The password system should be capable of securely controlling passwords in the system. In particular, the authentication list must be stored and maintained in such a manner so as to prevent unauthorized access. Authorized access must be controlled by an auditable procedure so that accountability of access and activities performed can be established at all times.
Need-to-know	Such access should be limited to the fewest number of people possible and controlled so that no one individual alone can read the passwords. No hardcopy listing of the authentication list should exist.
Multiple accounts	If a user is to be issued with more than one account-password pair per password system, the access control system should be capable of properly controlling the activities and privileges associated with each of the accounts of this user.
Authentication	The password should be obtained and checked by the authentication system before the access is granted.
Suppression of password	If the password system "echoes" the password to the user, this echo should be destroyed before or immediately after it is turned into humanly readable form.
Logon attempts	The number of consecutive failed password submission trials permitted and the action taken by the system should be such that the user is effectively prevented from guessing any password through trial and error.

Automatic logoff	Where the password system implicitly attaches the authentication to a facility and the facility is liable to be left unattended by the authorized user, provision should be made for automatic denial of access or reauthentication after an appropriate quiescent period.
Expiration of passwords	The password system should disable any password which has expired.
One owner/one account	A single password should not be "split" and given to two or more parties so that joint control may be established. Such control must be by way of two separate passwords.
Reports	The report generator within the password system should be flexible enough to effectively chronicle activity without placing undue burden on the audit function.
Reporting requirements	The password system should be capable of reporting, for audit purposes, on all authentications it makes.
	The password system should be capable of reporting, for audit purposes, on all invalid attempts to authenticate (that is, exception reports). This reporting should occur in a timely fashion. The password system should be capable of reporting, for audit purposes, on all logical maintenance activities performed on the password system. Other forms of maintenance performed on the password system should be logged by a related control system (for example, physical maintenance).
Contingency procedures	The password generation process should be capable of providing new passwords in sufficient quantity and within the appropriate time frame, as required by the user.
Backup password control	If a duplicate password is to be kept for backup purposes, this password should be properly protected and controlled by an auditable procedure that can be used to establish accountability at all times.
	Where warranted by the value and sensitivity of the assets under protection, duplicate passwords must be kept in joint custody. Custodians should not have knowledge of the passwords.
Backup password change	If the duplicate password is used during a contingency period, this password should be changed in an authorized fashion as soon as practicable.

continued

	When an existing password should be investigated or overridden, this will be done by the PSM. The PSM will ensure that the request has been properly authorized before action is taken.
The password system user	Every effort should be taken by the user to prevent any other individual from learning what an individual's password is. The protection to be afforded should be tailored to the medium on which the password resides.
Control of passwords responsibility	A password should never be loaned to another individual. A password should not be passed on when a user no longer requires it.
	A password should be changed or removed from the system immediately whenever the owner resigns, is transferred, or changes functional responsibilities; if such are controlled by passwords. The appropriate maintenance request form should be filed with the PSM by the user's manager.
Password compromise	When the user determines that the password has been lost or compromised, the user is obligated to inform the PSM as soon as possible. The appropriate reports can be filed later.
Password expiry	When a password has expired, all copies of the password should continue to be treated as sensitive information until destroyed in a controlled fashion.

custodians and stewards obey security requirements. Most organizations fail to designate sensitive LAN assets. It is difficult to provide protection when you do not know what you are protecting. Physically marking assets shows a desire to protect the asset. Without marking or identifying your assets, it might be difficult to prove in a court of law that the asset was important to you.

One universal symptom of poor security is the misunderstanding of the value of a company's information. Many companies have little knowledge of this value because they have never assessed or classified their data. Valuation enables the LAN administrator to define access privileges for the various security levels. A check can also be made to ensure that your company meets minimum legal requirements. Table 6-3 provides a sample data classification standard.

The effectiveness of an organization's information security can be impacted by support functions. No matter how much is spent on sophisticated security technology, it can often be circumvented by knowledgeable employees.

Table 6-3
Data classification standard

Introduction	It is important that an organization analyze the sensitivity of its information assets and become aware of the methods for protecting these assets from potential harm. Information is such an asset and is worth protecting.
	Data classification is a security technique that stratifies data into different security levels. By using a classification system, the organization can categorize data and hence be in a better position to protect its data and information from loss or misuse.
	The two primary data classification goals are to assist in:
	- Protecting data that the organization owns or has custodial responsibility for; and,
	- Preserving the continuity of the computing service to the organization.
	Effective classification of data is accomplished through the application of the protection and preservation classification schemes in this standard.
Purpose	This standard outlines the basic data classifications and the method used to assign the classifications to data.
	Classification of the organization's data is essential because it assists management in properly controlling and protecting data. This standard will permit the owner to explicitly state both protection and preservation classifications for data.
Scope	This standard applies to all computerized data, either resident on or directly produced by an information system, where the organization is either the owner or the custodian of the data.
Application	Classifications for protection and preservation are associated with all data so that managers can assign appropriate control measures. Such classifications and associated controls need to be provided for the entire life of the data or information or until the data is appropriately reclassified using the classification process. Managers should review periodically the classification of data under their control.
	Initially, an individual, typically the owner, determines the classification based on an analysis similar to that described in this standard. The resultant classification is then used to configure the data environment to ensure the proper protection of the data.

continued

Protection classification	Protection classifications are used to invoke control measures so as to prevent the misuse, theft, or improper disclosure of information. This part of the standard states those protection classifications used by the organization.
	Sensitive: Loss, misuse, or unauthorized disclosure of *sensitive* data could have a serious negative impact. Such an impact would be very harmful to the organization.
	Confidential: Loss, misuse, or unauthorized disclosure of *confidential* data could have at most a major negative impact. Such an incident would be harmful to the organization.
	Internal Use Only: Loss, misuse, or unauthorized disclosure of *internal use only* data could have at most a minimal negative impact. Such an incident would cause some harm to the organization.
	Public: Loss, misuse or unauthorized disclosure of *public* data would have no adverse effect on the organization. Data in this category has been reviewed for classification but does not necessarily carry a classification designation.
Additional control statements for protection	In certain circumstances, additional controls over and above those associated with a classification are necessary for proper protection. Where necessary, the individual classifying data can apply control statements in addition to applying a classification.
	The list of accepted control statements is:
	DO NOT COPY—Unauthorized reproduction is prohibited.
	ENCRYPT FOR STORAGE—Encryption required for online or offline storage.
	ENCRYPT FOR TRANSMISSION—Encryption required for transmission outside of secured areas.
	FOR XXX USE ONLY—Only individuals with a legitimate need within a specific department or group allowed access.
Protection criteria	To determine the appropriate classification, it is necessary to determine the worth of the data to the organization. This can be done by assessing the exposure represented by the loss of the data with respect to several criteria.

The key criteria for evaluation are:

Customer-related: Does the data identify or relate specifically to any customer of the organization?
Employee-related: Does the data identify or relate specifically to any employee of the organization?
Security-related: Is the data used to effect control or secrecy for security purposes?
Financial: Would loss of the data affect the organization's financial well being?
Competitive: Would loss of the data affect the organization's competitive position?
Integrity: Would loss of the data result in any recovery costs?
Reputation: Would loss of the data affect the organization's image and hence ability to do business?

These criteria serve as an effective basis for most evaluations. If it is felt that these criteria do not adequately describe the import of a particular data set, additional criteria may be added at the evaluator's discretion.

Deriving a protection classification

A classification can be determined for data by assessing the worth of the data with respect to all of the foregoing criteria and then interpreting these assessments. Such an analysis is both generic and subjective in nature.

Generic

Customer-related: If data is customer-related, it is classified as confidential, at a minimum.
Employee-related: If data is employee-related, it is classified as confidential, at a minimum.
Security-related: If data is security-related, it is classified as confidential, at a minimum.

Subjective

Subjective

Impacts for the next four criteria can be found as high, medium, or low according to Table 1. Each criterion is assessed independently. The subjective criterion assessments may be converted to a classification on the following basis.

Sensitive: If one or more of the criteria is rated as high.
Confidential: If one or more of the criteria is rated medium and none are rated as high.

continued

Internal Use Only: If one or more of the criteria is rated as low, and none are rated as medium or high.

Public: If there is no impact to any subjective criterion or other reasonable criterion devised by the assessor.

Aggregate
The classification applied to the data now can be determined by taking the higher of the determined generic or subjective values.

Preservation classifications

Preservation classifications are used to invoke data control measures so as to recover from loss of data or data integrity and hence avoid interruptions in computing service.

This part states those preservation classifications that will be used by the organization.

Critical: Critical data is essential to the organization's continued existence. The loss of such data would cause a serious disruption of the organization's operation.

Valuable: Valuable data is very important to the organization's operation. The loss of such data would cause a major disruption of the organization's operation.

Useful: Useful data is important to the organization's operation. The loss of such data would cause minimal disruption of the organization's operation.

Protection criteria

To determine the appropriate classification, it is necessary to understand the effect on the ongoing business of the organization caused by the loss of the data. This can be done by assessing the exposure represented by the loss of the operation for the following key criterion.

Service Related: Would the interruption in service have any effect on the organization's business?

This criterion should serve as an effective basis for most evaluations. If it is felt that this criterion does not adequately describe the impact of a particular data set, additional criteria can be added at the evaluator's discretion.

Deriving a protection classification

A classification can be determined for a particular data set by assessing the worth of the data with respect to the foregoing criteria. Impact may be adjudged as high, medium, or low according to Table 2. Once the criteria have been assessed, a classification can be derived on the following basis.

Critical: If one or more of the criteria is rated as high.
Valuable: If one or more of the criteria is rated medium and none are rated as high.
Useful: If one or more of the criteria is rated as low, and none are rated as medium or high.

If corruption or loss of the data results in no appreciable disruption of the organization's operation, then no preservation classification need be applied.

Table 1 Impact assessment for subjective protection criteria

Criterion	Impact		
	High	Medium	Low
Financial	Compromise of data impacts the organization's financial situation seriously.	Compromise of data impacts the organization's financial situation to a major degree.	Compromise of data causes minimal financial harm to the organization.
Competitive	Compromise of data results in a serious loss to the organization's competitive position.	Compromise of data causes a major impact to the organization's competitive position.	Compromise of data has minimal effect on the organization's competitive position.
Integrity	Compromise of data results in a serious recovery cost to the organization.	Compromise of data results in a major recovery cost to the organization.	Compromise of data results in minimal recovery cost to the organization.
Reputation	Compromise of data results in a serious impact to the organization's reputation.	Compromise of data results in a major impact to the organization's reputation.	Compromise of data results in a minimal impact to the organization's reputation.

Table 2 Impact assessment for preservation criterion

Criterion	Impact		
	High	Medium	Low
Financial	Loss of the data seriously disrupts the organization's operation or results in serious sanctions.	Loss of the data causes a major disruption to the organization's operation or results in major sanctions.	Loss of the data results in some disruption to the organization's operation or results in minor sanctions.

Therefore, hiring good staff is crucial to good security. As previously mentioned, you should define roles and responsibilities for all staff for two reasons. One, it shows management's commitment to security because rewards are tied to performance. Two, employees are provided direction on acceptable behavior, and therefore have a better idea of how to behave when confronted with a security or ethical dilemma. For those workers who are not full-time employees, you must specify roles and responsibilities into their contracts to further spread the ethos.

Individuals should be charged with the security of specified LAN resources. These individuals should maintain current documentary evidence about the security of these assets and attest to their acquisition, deployment, movement, modification, utilization, disposal, and destruction. Violations or attempted violations of security must be traceable to individuals who can then be held accountable. Tracing violations to determine reasons also helps meet the goals of security.

A security audit program must be established to prove all security measures are necessary and sufficient. The major thrust of the program should be an effectiveness review of controls implemented as a result of the risk management program. Development of contingency plans, including disaster preparedness, is the next essential administrative safeguard.

Disaster preparedness

What is all this fuss about disaster preparedness? Why prepare for disasters when we have never had any problems? These are good questions. A natural or manmade disaster, however, can greatly affect your network, as demonstrated by the following examples.

In September 1989, Hurricane Hugo ravaged Charleston, South Carolina, leaving devastation in its wake. This storm was particularly nasty because it was thought it would stay at sea and miss land. Hugo caused network downtime because of the loss of power in the area, as well as physical damage to companies and their computers.

Likewise in October 1989, the San Francisco Bay Area earthquake resulted in network downtime through the loss of power. Chemical spills in Canada and the United States have prevented people from getting to work. On August 13, 1990, a fire in a Consolidated Edison substation caused a power blackout in Manhattan's financial district, and the 1993 bombing of New York's World Trade Center shut down all those networks as well.

In April 1992, the Chicago River dumped more than 250 million gallons of polluted water through a car-size hole into century-old tunnels. The resulting flood caused power failures and water damage that forced 200,000 people to evacuate the business district. Estimated losses exceeded $1 billion. Also during 1992, a benzine tanker derailment in Wisconsin ended with the evacuation of 25,000 people from the twin cities of Duluth and Superior.

About 4,000 miles away, London was hit with a disaster of its own. Just after Britain's national election, an Irish Republican Army car bomb tore up the city's financial district. Approximately 200 buildings were damaged and losses were estimated at £1 billion. More than 35 firms sought alternate office space. Some businesses were hit so bad that they could not cope with the scale of the crisis even with their contingency plans. One merchant bank was forced to move its LAN to a new location, and business did not return to normal for 10 days. Problems also arose when attempting to reconnect a microcomputer-based departmental banking application to the mainframe. Every year similar disasters result in network downtime, with serious consequences to the organizations.

Picture a Monday morning with staff arriving to discover the network is unavailable. If the network is not available immediately after employee arrival, hundreds of hours of productivity are lost. Luckily, you developed a disaster recovery plan and everyone knows what to do. If you are like most organizations, however, you do not have a *tested* plan. The lack of a plan could have a serious impact on the economic viability of your organization. Estimates have been made regarding how long a company could last without its information systems and data processing, yet these numbers are not particularly relevant to your situation. What is important is how you, as a data processing professional, feel. Security dollars are hard to justify and must provide a warm feeling. To paraphrase one manager, "Do you want to sleep tonight?"

Management must evaluate its information processing position and assess whether it can effectively conduct the day-to-day business of the enterprise. Management must adopt a proactive position for potential disasters instead of reactive. Most firms, however, have been nonactive. Disasters do not happen randomly; they are caused by predictable, preexisting conditions. Even hurricanes, tornadoes, earthquakes, floods, and other acts of God follow predictable patterns. Data centers have hidden vulnerabilities that can be handled or controlled, but management must act to avoid loss. Most companies declaring disasters could have avoided them. Your disaster plans should now have prediction, prevention, and avoidance components. Before you backup, buck up: your environment, policies, procedures, and practices.

A disaster in a network computing environment is any interruption of service significantly affecting user operations. Disaster recovery planning is the process of identifying critical computing resources, determining potential events that could affect these resources significantly and developing a plan for responding to such events.

Disaster recovery planning has two primary goals: to safeguard human life because an organization is responsible for ensuring the safety of its employees, and to minimize the impact on the business.

Why plan?

The planning process

As discussed earlier, an important step in any project is planning. Successful planning leads to a successful plan. The planning steps for disaster preparedness are identification of critical business functions, assessment of related exposures, and determination of disaster impact. Each of these is discussed in the next subsections.

Identifying crucial business functions Through interviews and discussions, you must identify the business functions critical to the continuation of operations. Critical business functions contribute to the bottom line and the success of the company. You must review the critical business functions served by the LAN and select the most appropriate processing alternative necessary to support those business functions.

Assessing related exposures In Chapter 5, a method for identifying threats relating to system unavailability was offered. Threats affecting availability could be intentional or unintentional. Obviously, power failures affect availability. Maybe not so obvious are the deliberate attacks against your LAN. A disgruntled employee could destroy your file server easily and quickly. Accordingly, for planning purposes, threat types are not as important as the impact of those threats.

Determining disaster impact You must assess the costs (both tangible and intangible) of a disaster and its effect on the critical business functions if a business resumption plan is not in place. The shorter the period specified to recover the critical application, the higher the cost to maintain a plan. Conversely, the longer the recovery period, the lower the cost. To develop an effective plan, address the following areas of concern:

- Potential threats.
- Probability of the threat occurring.
- Estimated impact, exposure, or cost of occurrence.
- Solutions for recovery.
- Estimated cost of recovery.
- Priorities for recovery.

The development of detailed plans enables your organization to recover in a controlled and timely manner the LAN, along with the manual activities that support the critical business functions. Your plans should include the following:

- A listing of all critical business applications and their network resource needs.
- A network schematic of all network components.
- An inventory, by location, of all hardware and communication lines.
- An assessment of security given to and the risk of loss of each network component.
- The level of backup required.
- An outline of the levels of risk inherent in the network.

- A projection of disaster scenarios and an assessment of their impact on the organization.
- A set of action plans for each scenario.

A documented plan of the actions that must be taken immediately after the disaster happens would include, for example, names and phone numbers of key individuals to be notified, building evacuation procedures, and those activities generally needed to minimize danger to human life and physical damage to the facility.

Testing the plan

Once you have completed your plan, you must test the plans to decide their completeness and practicality and develop procedures to ensure that the plans stay current. The test plan consists of two tests:

1. Ensuring that hardware and software relied upon in the event of a disaster are compatible.
2. Conducting a simulated disaster test to ensure the plan is workable under adverse conditions. Simulation can involve anything from a limited paper test to a full simulated disaster.

Positive reasons exist for testing plans. These tests allow organizations to determine the feasibility and compatibility of backup equipment and procedures. In addition, testing identifies and corrects weaknesses in the plan. Many organizations find serious problems during testing. For instance, one company who had faithfully sent tapes offsite found during testing that they had incorrectly created the tapes, and the tapes were of little use. You can provide regular training to staff on backup and recovery. People could panic if improperly prepared to deal with a disaster. Practice and training provide confidence.

Another good reason for testing is to prove the ability of the organization to recover and thus increase confidence in the ability of the organization. Some industries, such as banking, are required by law to develop business resumption plans. In the future, plans might be necessary for all public corporations. Auditors might qualify statements *ongoing concern* if management cannot assure the availability of critical business functions. Tests also provide strong motivation to continually maintain the plan, including all those activities necessary to restore and continue operations in either a normal or degraded mode.

Revising the plan

Changes in your software, hardware, and building can create different exposures that make a plan inoperable. You must analyze these changes and make any necessary modifications or refinements to the original plans. You must then retest the plan and go through the process again. The process must be cyclical without an end. Testing of the plan feeds back into threat determination.

Maintaining the plan

Most organizations fail to maintain their plan because it is too much work, their priorities shift, or they lack the will. One organization that successfully recovered from a major fire felt it had achieved success because it had just finished the plan; it was current. This scenario demonstrates the need to assure any plan's currency. You must develop procedures to ensure revision of the contingency plans to meet changing technology, systems, and business requirements.

Ten commandments of business resumption planning

- Protect human life first.
- Write simple, understandable procedures.
- Involve the right people in the development of the plan.
- Train staff on emergency procedures.
- Perform periodic tests.
- Minimize loss and risk to the organization.
- Maximize recovery and the return to normalcy.
- Maintain competitive position.
- Protect the organization from legal suits.
- Assure your insurance coverage ties in with and covers all (or most) expenses of the disaster.

Sample plan

This section provides a sample plan outline to be used for disaster preparedness.

Introduction The introduction includes the objectives, scope, authorization, and premises upon which the plan has been developed.

Disaster recovery plan The disaster recovery plan includes a definition of the organization, objectives, actions, and responsibilities of management and recovery teams.

Recovery strategy The recovery strategy includes a complete overview of the entire plan to reflect all the synchronized actions and events that must happen to effect recovery. This strategy also addresses command posts, extraordinary expense, insurance claims, personnel administration, etc.

Recovery time frames Recovery time frames includes documentation and charts that depict base recovery and operations recovery time frames and critical time lines that show time-related events that must be accomplished to achieve recovery processing at the alternate site.

Qualifying a disaster To qualify a disaster, you need to explain escalation plans, how you chose the escalation plan, and then formulate a plan announcement.

Emergency notification plan The emergency notification plan includes a plan to notify the disaster recovery organization and other key offices, as well as the sequence of notification.

Hardware/software subplan This subplan includes how to recover the hardware and operating system software elements of the LAN after a disaster.

Communications subplan This subplan includes how to recover the communications element of services and specifies maintenance responsibilities.

Applications systems subplan The applications systems subplan includes the plans for recovering applications systems and maintenance responsibilities.

Workstation subplan This subplan lists the plans for recovering key workstations and specifies maintenance responsibilities.

Offsite inventory subplan The offsite plan includes how to cycle and store items offsite, and any actions required during recovery mode.

Plan administration Plan administration includes ongoing procedures necessary to maintain the plan and to schedule and conduct tests of the plan.

Disaster recovery sequence

You come in one morning, and your LAN is gone—what do you do? You know the steps in preparing for the disaster, but there are also steps to take when the fateful event occurs. Following is a useful disaster recovery sequence:

1. Experience disaster.
2. Initiate emergency procedures.
3. Notify site and enterprise management.
4. Assemble recovery team.
5. Assess impact.
6. Make recovery decision.
7. Initiate selected recovery procedures.
8. Transition to selected redundant/backup procedures.
9. Restore emergency service to users.
10. Restore damaged resources.
11. Transition back to restored resources.
12. Restore normal service to users.

Avoiding problems

As discussed in Chapter 5, the best plan in risk management is to avoid the problem altogether. You would not expect a company to have a key position and not have at least one person cross-trained in the job, yet computer systems often do not have adequate backup. Corporations dutifully rotate tapes offsite for several years. During backup tests, however, they discover that the tapes cannot be found or that they are unintelligible because of media errors. Ensure that any tapes sent offsite are retrievable and reusable.

Disaster preparedness self-assessment quiz

After developing a plan, take this self-assessment quiz to gauge your readiness.

- Do you have a procedure to recover applications and data?
- Does the procedure consider what to do if the backup data is corrupted?
- Do you periodically test your disaster preparedness?

- Does your plan include evacuation plans, procedures for declaring an emergency, emergency procedures, and recovery plans?
- Are you a third-party provider of computing services?
- Do you have adequate insurance?

Working with people: personnel security

Have you ever heard this one: "We don't need security, we trust our people." Or this one: "We are just one big happy family." Or maybe even "My staff wouldn't do that, they're too honest." As Michael J. Comer, Patrick M. Ardis, and David H. Price (1988) point out, "He who lives on trust, dies of flatulence." More than one organization has lived to regret misguided trust.

Smart organizations know people are their most important resource. Security measures for these people are critical to a successful security program. The aim of personnel security measures is to ensure the specification of security requirements in job descriptions, that incumbents meet the security requirements, and that adequate security motivation and training are provided. Personnel security can be accomplished by implementing the following personnel policies:

- Job descriptions.
- Security orientation.
- Hiring and firing procedures.
- Candidate screening and checkout.
- Nondisclosure agreements.

Supplying enough employee training is an effective method of avoiding disasters. More than one case has occurred where a computer system has been disrupted because of the actions of poorly trained staff. This situation has probably even happened to you.

Another way of avoiding a disaster is to conduct adequate personnel reference checks. A personnel survey found that an average of one out of every seven candidates for a job lies significantly on their resumes or during an interview. Dishonest job applicants lie to conceal a derogatory background or to enhance their qualifications. Another study reported that most custodial contractors had criminal records. Both instances could be a disaster waiting to happen.

Protecting the office: physical & environmental security

The prime objectives of physical security measures are to deter, delay, defend, and detect. These objectives are the same the police offer when discussing protection of your house or vehicle. First, you try to deter someone by locking your doors and installing a burglar alarm. This step is enough to discourage some amateurs. In fact, simply sticking a decal on your windows informing would-be thieves of an alarm can sometimes act as a deterrent. Second, you install a chain lock on your door, which delays entry a few crucial seconds, enough perhaps that a professional thief may feel it is not worth the trouble. In the burglar trade, however, there's a saying that "there isn't a lock that cannot be picked."

So, for the third step, you install a deadbolt lock to try to defend against a serious attempt to enter. The deadbolt offers some resistance but most likely falls to a determined attack. Failing all attempts to prevent entry, a broken door or an alarm will prove unlawful entry, thus providing detection. Any hardware solution for LANs should be evaluated with these objectives in mind. If you perceive your biggest problem is employee theft, detection is about all you can do, and spending money on the other objectives is probably not justified.

The implementation of effective controls helps to ensure only authorized access to the LAN, that physical protection exists, and that facility-wide protective measures are adequate. Physical protection must be provided from natural and manmade hazards to ensure security commensurate with the sensitivity of the data processed and the service supplied. Physical protection can be accomplished in the following manner:

- Control access to network components.
- Protect against physical damage.
- Protect against power and environmental failures.
- Protect media and supplies.

It is possible that today's office environments are not secure enough for the processing of some transactions. The typical office does not have adequate physical security to prevent unauthorized entry. Banks have been processing fund transfers since the days of the telegraph. These same banks also always put wireroom functions in an area called a cage. These areas were originally bounded by wire-mesh cages. Now, the wireroom is a separate secure environment with strict access requirements. Organizations planning to implement LANs that process confidential information must reassess physical security. Server rooms should be physically secured during regular business hours and access to equipment and information should be controlled outside those hours.

Companies have become relatively blasé about computers and look at them as simply another piece of equipment. Because computers are commonplace, their value is underestimated, often leading to disaster. Walk around your office at quitting time. You see staff locking up their radios and clocks, but very few locking their microcomputers—until, of course they lose one. Securing computers is a management issue, and management needs occasionally to remind staff of the value of the equipment and the resident information.

Communication and electronic controls ensure LANs are not subject to external electromagnetic radiation that can adversely affect performance in ways difficult to detect. These controls also protect transmitted data. The communication network must be analyzed to determine what protection is necessary and to protect the system from access by unauthorized persons. These objectives can be achieved by the following:

Riding the waves: communications & electronic security

- Encrypting data.
- Authenticating messages.
- Shielding workstations.
- Reducing/eliminating radar/radio transmitter interference.

People believe that intercepting transmissions is the stuff of James Bond movies. That is not the case. Intercepting transmissions is relatively easy and even commonplace.

Code wars The Commonwealth of Independent States (the former Soviet Union) does it. The Mossad does it. The Central Intelligence Agency does it. Gangsters and industrial spies do it. There are so many people doing it that it is amazing they are not interfering with each other. What is *it*? Eavesdropping.

National security is not the only area targeted for monitoring, either. Medical and financial records are targeted for their confidential information. Other corporate information is of interest and open to compromise. Protecting information has existed for a long time. Evidence shows Julius Caesar, Chaucer, and Thomas Jefferson all encoded their data.

With the advent of personal computer and telecommunications technologies such as LANs, society is generating and storing more information than at any other time. The need for message encoding or cryptography has never been greater. Cryptography is a major communication security measure. *Encryption* is the transformation of plain text into coded form (encryption) or from coded form into plain text (decryption). It consists of a step-by-step procedure, usually mathematical, for completing a specific function, such as a personal identification number (PIN) verification algorithm. Simply, it is a process where data in its readable form is scrambled into an unreadable form. The transformation is performed using an algorithm: clear text is passed through an algorithm along with a variable piece of data, or key. The process is reversed by passing the cypher text through the algorithm with the same key to decrypt or recover the clear text.

Transmitted information is susceptible to an unauthorized reader if it is unencrypted. Communication channels should be encrypted if shielding is inadequate and data is sensitive. Database information should also be encrypted to prevent one user of a LAN from reading the data of another. Encryption is the only practical means for protecting information stored on devices attached to the network, network servers, or transmitted across the network.

Recent interest in encryption has increased as technological advances have lowered costs associated with encryption while increasing the amount of information exchanged electronically. Most commercially available encryption equipment uses conventional encryption, where two parties share a single key for encryption and decryption. Figure 6-1 illustrates conventional

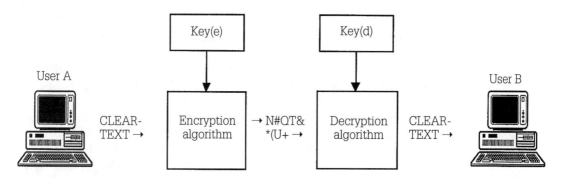

6-1 *Conventional symmetrical encryption.*

encryption. The two principal challenges with conventional encryption is the distribution and protection of the keys.

The alternative is a public-key encryption scheme, where the process involves two keys; one for encryption and another for decryption. Figure 6-2 shows public-key encryption. One key is kept private by the party that generated the keys, and the other is made public. The most rigorously tested cryptographic algorithm available commercially is the Data Encryption Algorithm, commonly called DES. IBM employees originally developed the algorithm, but it is now publicly available. Anyone can obtain the code for the algorithm.

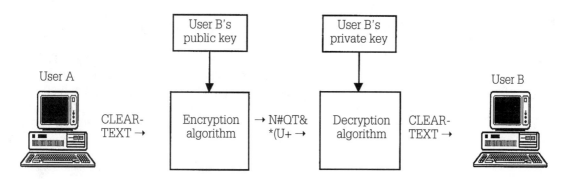

6-2 *Public-key, or asymmetrical encryption.*

Sometimes, integrity of the information is more important than confidentiality. To ensure the identity of the originator and the integrity of the data, message authentication codes are used. Message authentication ensures the veracity and source of messages by processing the messages so additional information is generated and transmitted with the message, which is used for validation at the receiving node. Message authentication should be used for those messages that need write protection as opposed to read protection.

Securing the LAN 97

In the paperless electronic office of the future, message authentication techniques can provide an *electronic signature*. These signatures will be used to sign purchase orders, applications, contracts, and other messages. The desirable features of electronic signatures are that they must be difficult to counterfeit, yet easy to verify. If a signature is always the same, for example, a string of symbols, then it can be easily counterfeited by copying the string of symbols. Thus, the signature must be different every time it is used. To be unique, the signature must be a function of the signed message; hence, the use of message authentication techniques. In the past, it has not been unusual for trading partners to act without signed, sealed agreements that specify what constitutes a signature.

Electrical avoidance tactics must also be taken to protect data. You can install an uninterruptible power supply to guard against power outages and surge protectors to protect against power fluctuations. These devices are discussed in detail in Chapter 7.

Another method of protecting data is *electronic vaulting*. Electronic vaulting allows instantaneous backups to be continually sent to offsite mass-storage devices. Offsite vendors offer *televaulting* services, where the vendor installs a connector at every workstation, terminal, and personal computer at the client's site. Once the system is in place, every keystroke at the device is recorded and transmitted offsite. You can access this information, whenever and however you want.

Iron age: hardware security

On December 17, 1990, Wing Commander David Farquhar left his car in downtown London while he browsed an automobile showroom. He was trying to escape the pressures of the day, including the impending Gulf War. Unfortunately, he left his laptop in his car—a laptop that stored, among other things, General Schwarzkpof's plan for the Allied strike against Iraq—and it was stolen. The computer was returned intact a week later, but not in time to save Commander Farquhar from court-martial. Similarly, a roving band of "computer hit men" from New York, Los Angeles, and San Francisco were reportedly paid as much as $10,000 to steal personal computers with strategic information belonging to senior executives at Fortune 1000 companies.

Hardware is an integral part of every LAN, and physical security exists for all components of the LAN. These securities are covered in later chapters. It is enough to say here that redundant components and diskless workstations can contribute to system availability. Not every company can afford redundant systems to provide service when the primary system has failed; still, other options are available that provide similar benefits. Fault-tolerant systems allow processing to continue when a component fails, equipment is under repair or needs replacement, or new processors or peripherals are added to the system. Recent announcements have proclaimed the genesis of fault-tolerant personal computers.

For some applications, you can buy personal computers without disk drives called *diskless workstations*. Their initialization programs reside in memory on a chip in the workstation, and they connect to the network when powered on. A diskless workstation lacks data storage of its own but is distinguishable from terminals by the fact that it can perform local processing.

Software contributes significantly to system security. Safeguards such as access control facilities, fault-tolerance software, software testing, vaccine software, and audit trails help maintain the confidentiality, integrity, and availability of data. Access controls are the ones most familiar to most people. Many of us have cards for automated banking machines activated by an access code–PIN.

Picking one's brains: software security

It is interesting to note the derivation of the word *access*. Access comes from the French *accedere*, which means to accede. This word derived from the Latin *ad*, meaning to and *cedere* meaning to yield. Synonyms for access are consent, concur, comply, yield, conform, attain, and enter. Thus, a system yields itself to anyone with a proper access code. Because the system yields, it is important that only legitimate users are given access. The following objectives for access control should be met:

- Ensure unauthorized access to either the system or the application is protected by an identification and verification scheme;
- Ensure users are restricted in privilege by using access lists, authorization tables, and resource/user association;
- Ensure user violations (such as illegal operator or user accesses) are recorded on the system log and periodically evaluated;
- Ensure a violation of a security protection measure causes a job or transaction to be terminated or a message written that is in line with the severity of the violation;
- Ensure proper segregation of duties between application programmers and network operators exist; and
- Ensure security procedures are subject to audit and review.

Access control systems involve the issues of authentication and authorization. Typically, an access control system first attempts to identify and authenticate an individual and then, knowing who the individual is, attempts to restrict the individual to only authorized information. Identification of an individual normally involves an access code. User authentication supplied by a password or passnumber can be anything the user has, knows, or is, such as a key, an access code, or biometrics.

A generally accepted technique for providing authentication is to exchange privileged information, or, in general terms, use a *password* or *passnumber*. The proper use of passwords and passnumbers is an essential first step in establishing effective access control. A password or passnumber can consist of anything associated with an individual that is a legally binding association,

User authentication

including fingerprints or signature, or that has an extremely low probability of discovery or duplication by an unauthorized individual.

Passcodes For years, security practitioners have stressed the need for good password systems. The use of the term *password* was unfortunate because it focused on the use of ordinary words. Ordinary words are limited by the space from which the code can come. These authentication keys should be labeled as passcodes. The National Bureau of Standards' *Password Usage Standard* defines the basic elements of a good passcode system as follows.

Authentication period The time for which the authentication of a user-identity is valid is the authentication period. Password system managers must determine the hours users need access to the LAN and restrict their use to those windows. You should set the usage window for hours and days of work. Access must be prohibited outside these windows. The system must log any attempted access outside of approved hours.

Composition A passcode is a sequence of characters selected or generated from a possible password *space*. The password space can have some passwords that are not acceptable. A good password system has a very large space of acceptable passwords. The space should be large enough to make a brute force attack unprofitable, which occurs when the attacker breaks the system by trying all possible passwords. Discovering the password through a search of all passwords should cost more than the value of the information being protected.

Composition is the set of acceptable characters that can be used in a valid passcode. The password composition is affected by the entry device, storage, and verification methods. Passcodes should be generated randomly to minimize the possibility of their determination by an unauthorized individual. Passcodes can be derived by transforming a chosen expression, as shown in TABLE 6-4. Hackers of course have a copy of these transformations, and you can bet they will try them, so be careful how you use this list! Some passcodes to avoid are the following:

- Words in the dictionary.
- First names and last names.
- Street names and city names.
- Valid license plate numbers.
- Room numbers, social security numbers, social insurance numbers, and telephone numbers.
- Beer and liquor brands.
- Athletic teams.
- Days of the week and months of the year.
- Repetitive characters.
- Software default passwords.

Table 6-4
Passcode transformations

Transformation Techniques	Illustrative expression	Resultant passcode
Transliteration	photograph, schizophrenic	FOTOGRAF, SKITSOFRENIK
Interweaving of characters in successive words (or numbers)	database, Peter Davis	DBAATSAE, PDEATVEIRS
Interweaving vowels and consonants	Peter Davis, password	PETERADAVIS, PASESIWORUD
Translation	strangers	ETRANGES, ETRANIERI
Replacement of letter by decimal digit (modulus-10 index of letter in natural order)	babbage	2122175
Replacement of decimal number by letter (with corresponding position, in natural order)	10/12/1492, 10/13/1989	JABADIB, JACAIHI
Insertion of a special character	Peter Davis, database	PETER$DAVIS, DATA&BASE
Shift from "home" position on the keyboard	zucchini, rutabaga	XIVVJOMO, EYRZVZFZ
Actuation of keyboard "shift"	6/6/1944, 1/1/2000	^?^?!($$, !?!?@)))
Substitution of synonyms	coffee break, office party	JAVAREST, BRANCHBASH
Substitution of antonyms	stoplight	GODARK
Substitution of abbreviations	relative humidity	RELHUM
Use of acronyms	computer-aided software engineering, security audit & control	CASESAC
Repetition	tom	TOMTOM
Imagistic manipulation (180° rotation of letters)	swimshow	SMIWSHOM

Length Length is closely associated with composition. The U.S. Department of Defense's *Password Management Guideline* uses the passcode space as a major parameter for figuring out the acceptable length. The length of a passcode determines the potential security of your system. A passcode length of 1 character reduces the potential passcode space to the

Securing the LAN

number of characters in the composition set, for example, 0 to 9 for numeric and A to Z for alphabetic. Increasing the length of a random passcode can make it increasingly more difficult to discover. With each additional character, both the number of possible combinations and the average time required to find the password increases exponentially. A length of 2 characters squares the number, a length of 3 cubes this number, and so on.

Passcodes made up of truly random combinations, however, are harder to remember the longer they get. Table 6-5 demonstrates the effect of passcode length on randomness. Using combinations of seven letters and seven numbers provides for more than 314 passcodes for every man, woman, and child in the United States (78,364,164,096 passcodes to be exact).

Table 6-5
Passcode combinations

Number of characters	Possible combinations (rounded up)	Average time to discover (rounded)
1	36	6 minutes
2	1,300	4 hours
3	47,000	5 days
4	1,700,000	6 months
5	60,000,000	19 years
6	2,000,000,000	630 years
7	78,000,000,000	25,000 years
8	2,800,000,000,000	890,000 years
9	100,000,000,000,000	32,000,000 years
10	3,700,000,000,000,000	1,200,000,000 years

Even a computer that would allow an attacker to test one million passcodes per second would require, on average, close to 60 years to figure out a random 10-character passcode. If, however, the passcode is not random but a 10-letter word from a 60,000-word spell checker, the attacker could figure out the passcode in an average of only 7 days. A significant difference from 1.2 billion years!

Lifetime Passcode security can be improved by frequent change to minimize compromise. A lifetime defines the time a passcode is valid. The useful lifetime of a passcode depends on the following:

- Cost of passcode changes.
- Risk associated with information disclosure.
- Probability of guessing the passcode.
- Number of times a passcode is used.
- Susceptibility of passcode to a brute force attack.

Passcodes should be changed regularly to reduce the risk of compromise. This period should fit both security and operational requirements, and the maximum period for passcode usage should never exceed one year.

Lance Hoffman, in *Modern Methods for Computer Security and Privacy*, offered the following formula for determining the lifetime of a passcode:

$$T = \frac{A^S * R * E}{2}$$

Where:
- T = the safe lifetime of a passcode
- A = the passcode space, i.e., all letters and numbers would be 36
- S = the length of the passcode
- R = the transmission rate of a communications line
- E = the number of characters exchanged in a logon attempt

Distribution Distribution is the transport or transfer of a passcode from source to owner. Distribution of passcodes, if needed, should be controlled through a trusted means to ensure the nondisclosure of passcodes to unauthorized persons. A user acknowledgment of receipt or creation of a passcode should be kept in a central location for audit purposes.

Entry Secure entry of a passcode is often a difficult task. Observers can easily detect passcodes when entered in to an automated authentication system. Unauthorized individuals can "shoulder surf," or steal access codes by reading the numbers or letters over the shoulders of authorized users. Passcodes should only be entered into an automated authentication system if the user can prevent their compromise. If the passcode system echoes the passcode, this echo should be destroyed before or immediately after turning the passcode into human-readable form.

The number of consecutive failed passcode submission trials that are permitted, and the action taken by the system, should be such that the system effectively prevents a person from guessing any passcode through trial and error.

Ownership Ownership is the authorized possession of a passcode. Individual accountability is essential to any secure passcode system and is tied to ownership. Passcodes should be associated with a group only in exceptional circumstances. This rule is desirable even if the group has common access privileges and shares data. Normally, passcodes should not be shared between individuals; sharing of passcodes makes accountability difficult to prove.

Source Passcodes should be selected at random from the acceptable passcode space by the owner, the system, or a security officer. When the passcode originates from a security officer or security system, the user should immediately change the passcode. Only the owner should have knowledge of the passcode to ensure accountability.

Storage Passcodes must be maintained within the computer system so they are protected from disclosure or change. The passcode system should securely control passwords in the system. Specifically, the authentication list must be stored and maintained in such a manner to prevent unauthorized access. Authorized access must be controlled by an auditable procedure, so that accountability of access and activities performed can be established. This step might involve the encryption of the passcodes while they reside on the system or during transmission.

Transmission Transmission is the communication of a passcode from its point of origin for comparison with a valid stored passcode. Passcodes typically authenticate the identity of a user accessing the network. To be authenticated, the passcode must be sent to the file server over the network. Unless the line is physically protected or the passcode is encrypted, the passcode is vulnerable to discovery during transmission.

Passcode guidelines Table 6-6 offers some passcode guidelines that should be adhered to by all users despite the access control system. As you have already seen, words from a dictionary are easily guessed and should be avoided. A comparison of your password file to a standard dictionary probably would result in the guessing of at least 1 in 4 passwords. This comparison is how most hackers and sneakers obtain passwords. Fortunately, software exists that can help users derive strong passcodes. This software helps users select strong passcodes while learning what makes a good code.

**Table 6-6
Passcode guidelines**

Don't . . .	Do . . .
- Select easily guessed passcodes - Write your passcode down - Share your passcode - Include your passcode in any file - Use your passcode forever - Trust anyone else with your passcode - Use the same passcode on multiple systems	- Use nonpronounceable words or phrases - Use an easy-to-remember passcode - Keep your passcode secret - Hide your passcode - Change your passcode frequently - Change your passcode if compromised - Use different passcodes for different systems

It is amazing how many offices you can walk into and find passwords taped to the side of the microcomputer. You can write policies until you are blue in the face and you cannot stop this practice. Bank campaigns have stressed to customers the need to avoid writing their PIN on their card, yet bank investigators will tell you this practice is what accounts for most automated banking machine fraud. This is just human nature, so you must periodically look for passwords.

Jim Kates of Janus Associates tells a story of users who could not wait to share their passwords. Jim was on assignment to test the effectiveness of passwords at a company and he sent a blind letter supposedly from marketing on company letterhead—a relative easy commodity to obtain or recreate—to the employees. The letter explained a new service to be offered to customers and solicited their help in a trial. To participate in the trial, employees need only complete a simple fact sheet. The fact sheet asked for name, position, branch, address, phone number, access code, and password. Employees dutifully supplied this information to Jim. One employee who ran the company electronic bulletin board suggested putting the letter on the board so everybody could participate! Obviously, employees needed education on keeping their passwords secret.

Most communications software packages for microcomputers allow scripts to be developed to help access remote systems. These scripts automate repetitive commands for users. They can and frequently do include access codes and their corresponding passcodes. A periodic review of files on microcomputers can pinpoint these security lapses.

In many companies where I have reviewed security, I have found privileged users with passwords older than 6 months. These privileged users could read or change all data on the network. The longer a passcode exists, the greater the probability of its exposure. Users, especially privileged ones, should be forced to change their passcodes at least bimonthly.

Most users can be convinced to surrender their password if they think they are protecting someone from trouble with the boss. Sneakers often sit down beside a legitimate user and feign exasperation over an attempted logon. They explain how they cannot log on to look at a report that the boss needs urgently. After explaining what the boss will do to them if they do not get the information, they wheedle a userid and passcode from a sympathetic employee. Users must be told not to share their passwords with anyone.

Because users think access control systems are, at best, a necessary evil, they try to short-circuit the controls wherever possible. A good example of this is using the same password on different systems. This might seem like a good idea at first; you can create one good passcode that you can readily remember. I can tell you of instances, however, where a password obtained from a microcomputer also provided access to a dial-in network, a minicomputer, and a mainframe. The passcode might have been adequate to protect the data on a microcomputer, but not the critical information maintained in the corporate systems. So, as the television show Romper Room taught me as a child—"Do be a do bee, don't be a don't bee!" In other words, you must encourage your employees to practice the do's of passcodes.

One last comment on passcodes. Some security practitioners feel passcodes should not be pronounceable. The advantage to this approach is a dictionary attack would not work. An unpronounceable passcode, however, is likely to be written, and I personally do not agree with enforcing unpronounceable passcodes. Passcodes created by a transformation as shown in TABLE 6-4 could be pronounceable but extremely difficult to guess.

Biometrics

As you can see, passcodes are not entirely effective—either because of user carelessness or the static nature of the codes themselves. Because of this, organizations with high security needs have looked for other solutions.

User authentication can be anything the user has, knows, or is. Authentication based on what a person is known as biometrics. Biometrics measure a physical characteristic or personal trait to recognize the identity, or verify the claimed identity, of a person through automated means. Because of their nature, biometric identifiers cannot be transferred, lost, or altered. A properly implemented biometric identifier is positive identification of an individual. Biometrics include behavioral traits, such as handwriting or speech characteristics, recognizable by automated means.

Today, many different types of biometric electronic access control equipment exist, including devices that scan retinas, signatures, teeth prints, thumbprints, fingerprints, voice prints, hand shapes, or the patterns of veins (usually at the wrist or the back of the hand). Other characteristics such as weight and height can be recorded, analyzed, and compared.

Most biometric systems work essentially the same. All systems require a reader—a physical device that reads or scans the characteristic being measured. The scanner is first used to enroll users by recording and cataloging the measured trait. The reader then becomes the logon or locking device. The user offers the trait for measurement to the reader to obtain access. The trait is measured and compared to the catalog maintained by the system. A match allows access; a mismatch allows another attempt or denies access.

The most widely used and accepted characteristic is fingerprints. Fingerprint readers are the most prevalent because they build on the science of fingerprinting. A fingerprint is unique to an individual and, thus, an excellent identifier. A stigma is attached to fingerprinting, however, that could be hard to overcome with your users.

Measuring hand geometry is another popular biometric. The shape and length of fingers and profile of knuckles vary considerably. Using ordinary light, the reader constructs a three-dimensional image of a user's hand and compares it to the catalog. Keystroke dynamics measure the consistency of timing in striking letter groups when a person uses a keyboard. This method is effective for identifying operators who frequently use the keyboard.

Every person has a unique blood vessel pattern in the retina. These patterns on the back of the eyeball are read by retinal scanners. Retinal scanning is one of the most reliable biometric identification methods. It mistakes one person for another only one in a million times with a single eye system, and one in a trillion times with a system that examines both eyes.

Signatures-analysis devices are used effectively by financial institutions to check signatures on instruments. A user signs on a pad that digitizes the signature, which is compared to the signature stored on the system. The system then measures signature dynamics, such as pen pressure, character shape, and pen acceleration.

Voice verifiers work by analyzing the unique characteristics of a person's voice. The voice can be digitized and compared to the catalog for verification. Voice analyzers are popular since they can use existing telephone technology.

Biometrics provide the key to the access control lock, on a LAN workstation, the server, or the room where the device or server is located. While some might consider these devices Orwellian, turnkey biometric systems are available today that provide cost-effective, high security where needed. Until this market takes hold, however, the more mundane high-technology security devices—the magnetic stripe and infrared identification cards—will continue to dominate the market. The migration to the more exotic equipment will occur when biometric technologies become less expensive, less invasive, and more user-friendly.

Whatever identifier is selected, problems are associated with the devices. First, users are reluctant to use these devices. They will likely see biometric systems as intrusive and intimidating. Any organization interested in biometrics should consider user's concerns before implementation because users could be intimidated. Putting your face up to a retinal scanner can be scary. Of the biometrics available today, signature verification is probably the least upsetting.

Second, there are questions of reliability and practicality. First-generation biometric devices were unreliable, which gave the technology a poor reputation. Though persons with cuts and laryngitis might not have passed thumb scans and voice analyzers, biometrics today have much-improved accuracy levels.

Unfortunately, inventive users can subvert biometric systems. If authorized users log on and then share their accounts, you have accomplished very little. Again, ethical users provided with adequate security training are the best security defense.

There are other software safeguards as well. One very effective software control is fault-tolerant operating systems. These systems allow a copy of the operating system to run concurrently on each processor module. Each

Fault-tolerant software

operating system is ready to respond to a failure in the total system. This enables nonstop processing and allows each processor to act as an individual computer that functions independently from all others in the system. Note that quality software also helps to ensure systems are available.

Software integrity

One time-proven technique for avoiding system downtime is to do adequate software testing, including the simulation of expected processing volumes and the execution of programming logic. The information systems group spends a large portion of its budget on errors and omissions; these factors can possibly be reduced with the implementation of access control software to prevent unauthorized access and accidental deletions.

Poor development practices can have several consequences. First, they could lead to a system with vulnerabilities that result directly from undetected errors in software. Second, such a system can be harder to evaluate, because it is very difficult for an independent evaluator to understand or review the implementation. Third, the system can be harder to maintain or evolve, which means that with time, the security of the system might get worse, not better. The answer is to develop and maintain quality systems.

What is quality? Ford Motor Company employees call it "Job One." W. Edwards Deming, revered by the Japanese for his work on productivity, believes low quality means high cost and a loss of competitive position. Executives think quality control circles will help them emulate the success of the Japanese. General Motors' solution to the productivity problem was to establish a "quality of work life" program. Quality is like class. Everybody understands it and likes it, but still finds it difficult to describe. Quality is also a lot like the weather. Everybody talks about it, but no one does much about it. Let's look at information systems quality and what it means to business.

Information systems quality is the degree that an information system meets the goals of its users, managers, and developers. These goals include reliability, efficiency, responsiveness, and flexibility. Information also has time and space requirements. Quality of information is a function of its pertinence and its coherence:

- *Spatial pertinence* refers to the degree to which an item of information is relevant to its intended organizational function. Thus, information must be selected and processed according to a local organization's needs.
- *Temporal pertinence* refers to the timeliness of information.
- *Spatial coherence* refers to the consistency and completeness of information and is concerned with the validity of the interpretation model used for selection and processing.
- *Temporal coherence* refers to the degree to which diverse data elements, such as closing dates and sales figures, reflect the same time period.

Quality defines the value realized from an investment in a data processing activity, measures the effectiveness of that activity, and ensures the trustworthiness of what results from that activity. This last task involves not only detecting defects in both process and product, but preventing them as well. It is the successful marriage of the disciplines of quality assurance and software engineering. The information systems quality, audit, and security disciplines are the main components of information integrity.

Information systems quality includes, but is not limited to, software engineering and software testing. The goals of information systems quality—and the methods used to achieve them—conform to those followed in measuring and maintaining quality in the manufacturing and service sectors. One new method is known as Computer-Aided Software Engineering, or CASE.

Everybody has jumped on the CASE bandwagon. CASE tools automate and integrate the software development steps. They're used for analysis and design, code generation, testing, and maintenance. Present CASE software is weak, however, in integrating these processes. Hence, CISE (or I-CASE) is gaining in popularity. CISE, Computer-Integrated Software Engineering, tries to provide the outputs and inputs from one step to all tasks in the development life cycle. Most programmers have trouble keeping abreast of all the acronyms, let alone using them. Despite what zealots attribute as benefits, it is estimated that less than 10 percent of the programmers in the United States use structured methods for programming! Other studies show, however, that defects decrease with an increase in method.

Quality control to some corporations means periodic review of reports on productivity. The function of quality assurance in many companies is to provide hindsight, to keep management informed about defects weekly. Banks are encouraged by their industry groups to establish a productivity department to measure productivity. Unfortunately, measuring productivity does not improve it.

We can perhaps borrow some techniques from William G. Ouchi (1982) to develop quality systems. For instance, quality control circles use simple statistical techniques, such as scatter diagrams, Pareto diagrams, and control charts, to discover the most important possible sources of trouble that they can govern and eliminate. These concepts form the curriculum of managerial accounting courses. Trying to understand the problem is the first step along the path to solving it.

Engineers have tools for tracking the reliability of components. Some of these measures are Mean-Time-To-Repair and Mean-Time-Before-Failure. The Unisys Corporation has developed a Reliability, Availability, and Serviceability (RAS) model and tracks reliability measurements, such as Mean-Time-Between-Stop, Mean-Time-Between-Incidents, and Mean-Time-Between-Attention. By tracking and controlling these metrics during development and operations, improvements in quality can be made. You cannot control what you do not track.

An organization's commitment to information systems quality will create a working environment in which defect-free and reliable computing happens. Information systems should be designed to function in conformity with the user's requirements and performance specifications. It might not be immediately evident why this conformity is important. It might not be important if your system is a microbased spreadsheet used for comparative or What If analyses. You might, however, be developing a Star Wars system. Is it acceptable if this system is accurate 90 percent of the time? What if your system is used for oil exploration? Or an expert system used for medical diagnosis?

Hospitals, pharmacies, insurance companies, government agencies, and drug companies are applying different computer technologies to facilitate access to medical databases vital to lives and company reputations. Can we allow these systems to contain defects? Roughly 7 percent of hospitalizations relate directly to drug-induced illness, according to Health Information Design Inc. of Arlington, Virginia. How would this number change if medical diagnosis relied on suspect data? System malfunctions are blamed for accidental downings of public aircraft and other life-threatening situations. No doubt you have experienced frustration over a problem at a bank or utility company, only to be told it was the computer's fault.

Today's programmers and scientists concern themselves with the development of artificial intelligence and its offshoots. It is only logical that an inverse relationship exists between expert systems and quality systems. As systems call for less human intervention, the need for quality information systems increases. The good news is that automated systems can stop the randomness of human error.

Many companies report that more than half their programming effort goes into maintenance. For every dollar companies spend to develop software, they spend two dollars to test and maintain that same software. These are estimates because most companies do not know how much of their budget they spend on uncovering and correcting defects. They usually allocate these costs to operations instead of isolating and classifying them as waste. If companies allocated these costs to waste, the variances would call for explanation. Testing costs are usually hidden; therefore, they are difficult to control.

Often, developers install software systems with inadequate testing and debug them in production. The correction of coding and logic mistakes in production is expensive when compared to complete and thorough testing at the various stages of system development. Several people have estimated it costs $40 to correct an error in unit testing, $170 in environment or string testing, and $1000 in systems testing! User relations deteriorate when information systems do not deliver as promised or take too long to implement. These intangible costs could potentially cost the organization as well.

One goal of testing is to identify differences between existing and expected conditions. This is a *white box* test for an error of commission. This type of testing is a negative, destructive process, yet this is the type of testing with which most of us are most familiar. In reality, however, this process is often more defective than the development process itself! Another goal, usually ignored by system testing, is to enable management to estimate the risk of software failure after testing. Tests of this type, *black box* testing, try to uncover errors of omission. This testing is the confidence factor that external auditors refer to when signing-off financial statements and is a business decision. Testing costs increase with a corresponding increase in the confidence level.

To illustrate, the techniques used in quality management are evaluation, verification, validation, and confirmation. The corresponding procedures are review, inspection, test, and audit. Estimates show that a review costs 2 to 5 percent of development costs, an inspection costs 15 percent, and testing costs 50 percent.

Companies argue that they do not do any development and that they are in a maintenance mode. Most corporations undergo a period of renewal, that is if they intend to vie for the future. You are probably familiar with how Coca-Cola tried to change its formula after 90 years. The planning was good; the implementation was not!

Entropy is a physics term that we can borrow for our discussion. This principle of physics measures the disorder or randomness in a closed system. According to the principle, everything that is organized will break or run down unless maintained. For example, an airplane sitting on the tarmac will deteriorate much faster than one flying and receiving regular maintenance. Systems inexorably deteriorate; they need constant maintenance. Therefore, every organization should be involved in changing and ensuring the quality of information systems constantly. Higher-quality code means less downtime, greater system reliability, and satisfied users. These are the basic premises of information systems quality.

Japan has established software factories. These factories have proven, defect-free software routines. They create programs from specifications by stringing these routines together. Because the programs are proven defect-free, they can be assembled at a lower cost with higher quality. Some American corporations will not promote programs into production unless they contain at least 15 percent reused code.

The scarcity of capital, raw materials, energy sources, managerial skill, and market opportunities and the increase in competition demand the improvement of quality in business. System stability is seldom a natural state, especially in today's everchanging world. It is an achievement, the result of eliminating identified causes, leaving only the random variation of a stable process. The solution is not to become Luddites and prevent the buildup of machines, but instead to build quality machines that can be trusted.

Four changes must therefore happen. First, the development process itself must be improved; which might include the implementation of structured methods, such as walk-throughs, CASE, or CISE. It definitely means corporations must change to stay competitive. Second, testing methods must be improved. Defects per thousand lines of code must be decreased. This decrease can improve through the increased use of automated testing tools. An increased emphasis on test planning will also likely help.

Third, management must identify and track various types of errors. It is unlikely that one could eliminate a type of error without first identifying it. Before the recognition of AIDS and Legionnaire's as diseases, no one was developing a cure. Once error types are identified, they can be tracked and eventually eliminated. Management accounting techniques as exemplified in quality control circles should be developed and adopted.

Last, management accounting techniques within the organization must be improved. It is necessary to prove what testing versus maintenance really costs. All errors should be identified as wastage and explained. Techniques within manufacturing are relevant in software development and should be adopted. If the user found that unapproved code changes had caused errors or realized what value for the money they received for testing, then questions would most probably arise.

Most likely, you have heard of "Management by Objectives" and "Management by Walking Around." Well, Bill Perry of the Quality Management Institute has coined the phrase "Management by Embarrassment." It is time someone asked systems development what they are spending the testing money on!

Computer pestilence

After hackers, viruses have received the most press. The popular press has whipped up horror stories on viruses and hacking that are out of proportion to the number of incidents. Reporters like to sensationalize the havoc caused by viruses because they can understand the idea, leading to a perception that viruses and hacking are rife—contrary to the evidence. Not only have reporters grabbed onto viruses and run with them, but so have many authors of security books, and a plethora of books do exist on the subject. I would be remiss if I did not contribute to the lore. So far, the publicity has not shaken the public's faith in information technology. My contribution is short, and I refer you to the bibliography for more material.

Just like the Egyptians who were plagued by pestilence in the Bible, organizations are suffering as well. They are faced with many strains of computer pestilence—bombs, bugs, viruses, and worms. A new threat to LANs is the computer virus. The first recorded computer virus was the *Core*

War game invented by M. Douglas McIlroy at Bell labs in the 1960s. The point of the game was to write a program that would erase the opponent or block its movement.

Although the military has known about computer viruses for dozens of years, viruses only really came into their own in late 1987 when the popular press drew attention to them. A *computer virus* is defined as a program that can "infect" other programs by modifying them to include, say, an evolved copy of itself. A virus is designed to change its form or its target over time. Furthermore, it is self-replicating and attaches itself to either a program or data so it can hide and travel from one computer to another. These viruses are Trojan horses embedded in microcomputer software. They are programmed to erase hard disks, delete critical files, prevent logon by authorized individuals, and distinguish themselves by replicating and attaching to other parts of your system. A destructive virus can spread rapidly through communication networks, infecting unprotected programs and libraries. Software could contain code that could disrupt processing.

The threat increases as microcomputer use grows, users become more sophisticated, and publicity about viruses inspires people to create new viruses. Any computer-literate person with malice aforethought who knows a few techniques, network addresses, user codes, and has a virus-writing kit (such as those for sale in West Germany) could wreak havoc on LANs. By far the greatest risk in the personal computer environment is from the ability of any user to load a new program into the system from a diskette. New programs are bought and installed by anyone who finds them useful. Viruses are either benign—causing disruption but no serious damage—or malignant, destroying data or the integrity of the system. A *logic bomb* is a type of virus triggered on a specified date and time or an occurrence of a specific event or events.

Worms are similar to viruses except that their aim is simply to replicate themselves repeatedly, eventually using all the memory in a computer or the network and preventing anything from being retrieved or entered. The first use of the term described a program that copied itself benignly around the network, using otherwise unused resources. Reading science fiction provides insight into worms. In *Shockwave Rider*, John Brunner (1975) described a tapeworm program running loose in the network. He wrote, "It's definitely self-perpetuating so long as the net exists. Even if one segment of it is inactivated, a counterpart of the missing portion will remain in store at some other station and the worm will automatically subdivide and send a duplicate head to collect the spare groups and restore them to their proper place." Other authors have talked of the same theme. Thomas J. Ryan's *The Adolescence of P-1* (1977) chronicled a fictional account of the development of a worm. In the book, P-1, a software program, wanders from machine to machine storing parts of itself and eventually taking control of 7,000 computers.

IBM systems analysts coined the term *bacteria*—electronic mail that spreads itself to all users when read or otherwise executed. The most famous bacteria was the Christmas Tree, which spread itself until IBM was forced to shut down its worldwide mail system. Others prefer to call this pestilence a *tribble* (from Star Trek), *rabbit*, or *chain letter*. Regardless of their name, these pestilence can cause untold damage if not handled correctly.

Viral symptoms An infected system exhibits a number of noticeable symptoms the network administrator should be aware of. In a favorable environment, a virus can spread rapidly and do great damage. Because of the benefits they bring, modern system environments will likely be more, rather than less, favorable to the rapid spread of viruses. They will be more open and have larger user populations and more contact among the users. For instance, you will likely face more viruses if connected to Internet then if you have a standalone LAN. The first noticeable symptom of a computer virus may be decreased system performance; one reported virus had so filled the network with copies of itself that it was not possible to get warnings to potential victims. Segments of the network showing symptoms or positive test results can then be isolated from other computers.

Practical solutions First, management must set the right tone by implementing and enforcing good security practices. For everyday operation, however, TABLE 6-7 provides guidelines that should be adhered to by all users to limit viruses on the LAN. Remember that education, not eradication, is the number one method for controlling the threat of computer pestilence. Forewarn your employees about viruses—an ounce of prevention is worth a pound of cure.

Network security managers must be aware that viruses represent a real and potentially catastrophic threat, but that users can safeguard their networks to

**Table 6-7
Virus guidelines**

Don't . . .	Do . . .
- Download executable programs from bulletin boards.	- Use only reputable bulletin boards and networks.
- Accept or use unlicensed software.	- Use "shrink-wrapped" software.
- Share program software diskettes with other users.	- Test all foreign diskettes for extended periods on an isolated machine.
- Use precompiled programs.	- Promote programs properly with library management techniques.
- Allow access to microcomputers by unauthorized persons.	- Use access control to prevent unauthorized access to hard disks.
- Leave diskettes unattended.	- Use write-protect tabs on diskettes.
- Ignore virus symptoms	- Install prophylactic and vaccine software.

deter viral infection. Corporations must review their vulnerability to viruses both in physical terms—who has access—and in administrative terms—what policies are necessary.

Fortunately, industrious entrepreneurs developed *flu shot* programs to combat computer viruses. These programs scan all other programs and look for any potentially harmful instructions. These corrective programs only work on known viruses, unfortunately. A prophylactic program, however, might take control when any attempt is made to put data on media and raise an alarm. These programs are loaded into memory and intercept any suspicious activity.

Computerworld and *InfoWorld* have reported "shrink-wrapped" viruses—despite extraordinary precautions taken to screen new software before shipping. In December 1991, Novell warned users of the Stoned II virus in the Network Support Encyclopedia Standard Volume. In the same month, Konami, Inc., warned users about the Stoned III virus in Spacewrecked. The Michaelangelo virus was shipped in da Vinci eMail 2.0 demo disks in January 1992 and in 500 Leading Edge PCs shipped in December 1991. These occurrences were unintentional. Other unscrupulous vendors are now even writing time bombs into their software to enforce software licensing.

Recovering from a virus

Most people know what to do if they have a cold. Drink plenty of fluids and get plenty of rest. Many people, however, do not know how to recover from a computer virus. Following are some steps to take when you discover you are infected:

- Do not panic. Because many of these pestilence are malicious, one false move could wipe out your hard disk. Thoughtful analysis at this point could save months of work.
- Terminate any connections to the outside world. You do not want to risk reinfection while trying to eradicate the virus.
- Try to recall your activities and previous symptoms. These recollections could help recover your system.
- Determine the nature and extent of the infection. You should be aware of what happened. For example, was the fixed disk affected and has the damage stopped?
- Power down the infected system.
- Power up using the write-protected, uninfected, original system diskette.
- Back up all nonexecutable files and screened files to tape or diskette.
- Do a low-level reformat of the infected hard disk.
- Restore the operating system software to the hard disk.
- Reload all uninfected files that were backed up.
- Scan all floppy diskettes you use for infections and reformat those that are infected.

Software licensing

As mentioned, some software vendors are stooping to include time bombs in their software. Also known as keys, traps, or access codes, these devices are set to bring down the software at a predetermined time, usually the expiration of the contract. Because vendors often hide the existence of these devices, users should ask for a warranty against time bombs. LANs are the cause of some of these software licensing problems. Users who once launched one program from a local hard drive now launch a much wider selection of programs stored on a network server, effectively dumping the licensing problem in the lap of the network administrator. These administrators have a difficult time tracking down software use. Most network operating systems do not provide adequate metering and auditing features.

The Software Protection Association (SPA) in the United States and the Canadian Alliance Against Software Theft (CAAST) are working against software theft. They identify companies they suspect have unlicensed software and inform the authorities and encourage prosecution. Authorities already have prosecuted several corporations in the United States and Canada.

Audit trails So integral to control is the comparison of inputs to stored programs that the word control derives from the Latin *contrarotulare*, to compare something "against the rolls," the cylinders of paper that served as official records. Review of audit trails is an old and honored tradition.

The network should provide a comprehensive audit trail that tracks user logon attempts, file access attempts, and many other workstation and network events. Events to be audited are selected by the system administrator. Where warranted, it may be prudent to do dual logging or journaling. Software should write every transaction to the log not once but twice for instantaneous backup and control purposes. Obviously, these logs need not be in the same location. One log could be produced in Toronto and the other in New York, for example.

Applying controls to hardware

If software is the brains of the network, then hardware is the brawn. Hardware consists of the network cabling and devices. Giving thought to hardware security when designing and installing the network will help ensure the network's effectiveness and economy.

The message is the medium: cabling

The transmission media used to build a LAN run the gamut from simple telephone wire to coaxial cable to fiber-optic cables. The price of cable does not in itself tempt thieves, but the value of the data transmitted over the cable does. If information is the lifeblood of a corporation as I mentioned, then cabling represents the vascular system—the arteries and veins. The most common threats to cables are the following:

- Cutting. Cables can easily be cut either inadvertently or deliberately to deny service. Once the cable is cut, the data will not flow on the network until the cut is repaired.
- Damage. Because cable is a physical medium, it is susceptible to all the normal wear and tear of an office. Worn or damaged cables lead to unreliable transmissions.
- Interference. Cables carrying electrical currents are susceptible to interference from other electrical equipment. Even fiber-optic cables using phase conductors or shield wire as fiber carriers are susceptible to electrical storms.
- Radiating. Most wire cables radiate data when transmitting. These emissions can be picked up by unauthorized people who have the right equipment.
- Wiretapping. Cables are susceptible to passive and active wiretaps. The simpler the technology, the easier the tap. Intercepting a transmission on twisted-pair wire is straightforward and inexpensive.

We discuss each of these threats in turn. First, however, a little cable background is necessary. Cables are usually installed in one of three ways: through a wall, over a ceiling, or under a carpet. For example, installers usually put cables for a star network in walls, making telephone jack connectors potential points for tapping. Those connectors, therefore, should be restricted to physically secured rooms, and unused connectors should be restricted to prevent unauthorized access. Cables installed beneath carpets are also susceptible to physical tapping, but cables installed over the ceiling using a metal conduit are the least susceptible to potential wiretapping attacks.

Unshielded twisted-pair

Figure 7-1 illustrates unshielded twisted-pairs (UTP). UTP cable is probably the least expensive cable alternative and has several advantages. First, UTP is already installed in most office buildings and can be used for both voice and data. Most telephone lines consist of two insulated copper wires, called twisted-pair wires, arranged in a spiral pattern. Although primarily used for voice transmissions, twisted pairs can be used to transmit both analog and digital signals. Ethernet, ARCnet, Token Ring, Apple LocalTalk, and other LANs currently support UTP. Because of the standard star-wiring scheme of

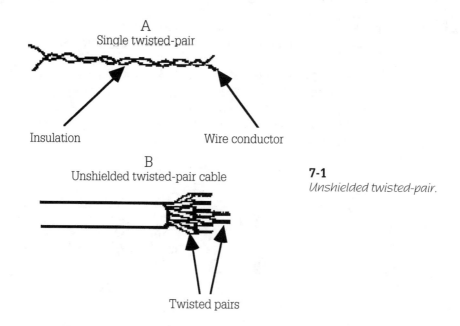

7-1
Unshielded twisted-pair.

UTP (all lines usually connect to a central wiring closet), fault isolation is also relatively easy compared to linear topologies of cable. Star configurations also allow great flexibility.

There are disadvantages though. UTP is relatively susceptible to interference from fluorescent lights and small motors. It also does not support the higher data transmission rates of the latest technologies. UTP is probably the easiest cabling to tap, too, requiring only alligator clips and a tape recorder. Obviously, these requirements are not a real barrier to someone who wants to acquire your data.

Shielded twisted-pair wiring has one or more wire pairs surrounded by a foil or mesh shield, then surrounded by a vinyl or Teflon jacket, as shown in FIG. 7-2. Usually this jacket is plenum-rated, which means that it does not emit noxious fumes into the building ductwork if it burns. A shielded, dual twisted-pair cable, which is the cable usually used with Token-Ring networks, supports higher transmission rates than UTP, and generally runs longer distances. Shielded twisted-pair cabling is less susceptible to interference, but is still easier to tap than coaxial cable.

Shielded twisted-pair

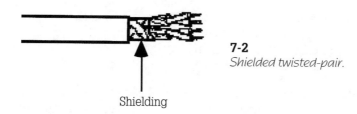

7-2
Shielded twisted-pair.

Applying controls to hardware 119

Coaxial cable A coaxial cable, commonly called a *coax*, is a group of copper and aluminum wires wrapped and insulated to minimize interference and signal distortion. Installers usually bury these cables underground. Figure 7-3 illustrates a coaxial cable. Note that your cable TV system uses coax, which can be used to transmit both analog and digital signals. Coax can be used at higher frequencies and speeds than twisted pairs and is less susceptible to interference and crosstalk. Generally, broadband networks require coax to support the higher transmission rates.

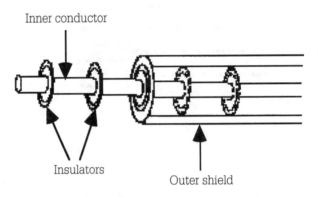

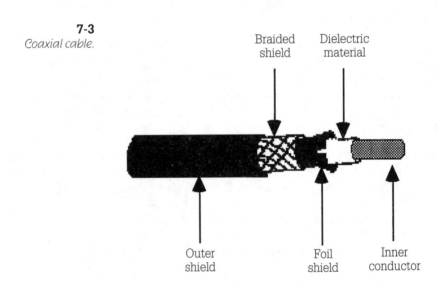

7-3
Coaxial cable.

Fiber optics In their study entitled *Fiber Optics Technology: Markets and Applications for Cables & Components*, Business Communications Co., Inc., of Norwalk, Connecticut, estimates 11 million kilometers of fiber-optic cable to be installed worldwide by 1995. So what is fiber-optic cable?

A fiber-optic cable, or FOCS, consists of thousands of glass or plastic strands that transmit data using light waves. Figure 7-4 shows a fiber-optic cable.

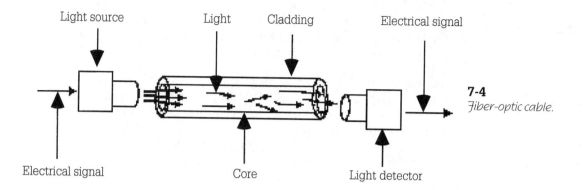

7-4
Fiber-optic cable.

The laser-generated light waves are very concentrated and are of a very high frequency. Fiber-optic cables are much faster than twisted pairs or coax. transmission requiring an hour on copper can be made in less than a second on fiber. Fiber optics also are practically immune to interference and tapping.

Physical tapping of fiber-optic cable is almost impossible because of the speed and the nonradiating method of transmission. Because wires are in general radiating media, they are more susceptible to electronic eavesdropping than fiber-optic cables. Radiated electromagnetic signals can be easily picked up from other types of wire.

The highway to the future

The future of technology will be measured in gigabits—1 billion bits of data or roughly a 20-volume encyclopedia—that can move across the land in barely a second. With that speed and accompanying power, scientists and schools and homes and hospitals could all be connected in one massive computer network that runs on a data highway, or a fiber-optic backbone network. Many people believe that such a backbone will do for the economy and lifestyle what the railroad in the 1890s and the interstate highway in the 1950s did for North America. During the 1992 presidential campaign, then-Arkansas Governor Bill Clinton said, "Just as the interstate highway system in the 1950s spurred two decades of economic growth, we need a door-to-door fiber-optic system by the year 2015 to link every home, every lab, every classroom, and every business in America." President Clinton and Vice President Albert Gore of the United States visited Silicon Valley in February 1993 and restated their belief in the development of an electronic highway.

The U.S. Government has committed money for the development and installation of a fiber-optic network to help share data among the nation's leading research centers. The data highway will run primarily along the fiber-optic cable already laid by the research centers, telephone companies, and government agencies. The new network will supplant the present computer web known as the Internet.

Internet grew out of computer-linking experiments of the 1960s. It now connects thousands of computer networks spread over 35 countries; more than 2 million users go online each day. They use it to pass messages, browse through bulletin boards reporting the latest news in their fields, and even to run experiments on computers that are oceans away.

What will the new network offer that the old cannot? In a word, speed. Today's Internet does a good job of passing text around, but such data-heavy items as books and full-motion video take prohibitively long to transmit. Traffic on the new highway will zoom along at a hundred times today's common Internet speed. With a bigger, faster pipeline, students could search through the Library of Congress, and farmers could read detailed geographical maps from satellite photos for crop data.

Internet and other highways can also provide unknown entry points into your network. If you are a member of the Internet, then Internet intruders equipped with a microcomputer can log onto your network by dialing up access and guessing passcodes. These intruders could then send electronic mail that contains viruses or worms as described in the previous chapter. They could also simply delete or read the data for which they have access. Once these hackers are on your system with the right authority, they can alter audit records to hide their presence, set up accounts, and use the system to crack other passcodes.

Private telephone exchanges

Many LAN systems are attached to a company's private telephone exchange. These telephone exchanges allow employees or customers to dial in and route calls, taking advantage of wide area telephone system lines or placing long-distance direct calls. Hackers have broken into and made unauthorized long-distance calls around the world from these computerized telephone systems. Again, the hackers only had to figure out a three-digit passcode.

LAN configurations

Now that we have looked at various topologies and media, we can put them together. Following are the most common LAN configurations:

- Coaxial baseband bus
- Twisted-pair baseband star
- Twisted-pair ring
- Broadband bus and star
- Optical-fiber ring

Standard LANs

The Institute of Electronic and Electrical Engineers (IEEE) 802.3 Ethernet is a 10-Mbps network using CSMA/CD to control station access to the network. Ethernet is designed to work over a variety of physical media. The IEEE 802.3 standard allows for the following:

- 10Base-T. 10-Mbps voice-grade unshielded twisted-pair wire
- 10Base-2. 10-Mbps baseband thin coaxial cable
- 10Base-5. 10-Mbps baseband thick coaxial cable
- 10Base-36. 10-Mbps broadband coaxial cable
- 10Base-F. 10-Mbps fiber-optic cable

In 1993, vendors proposed an industry standard, 100Base-VG, to enable computer users on 10Base-T Ethernet networks to transmit data at speeds up to 100 Mbps. The proposed Ethernet standard uses voice-grade unshielded twisted-pair wire and a star topology. Normally, Ethernet is a bus topology because network nodes are electrically daisychained on a single cable. Even 10Base-T, which uses a central hub and a physical star configuration, preserves the illusion of a daisychained bus.

Token Ring IEEE standard 802.5 uses a token passing protocol to control access to the network. Typically, Token Ring uses a central hub, that is, multistation access unit, and physical star configuration. Although the IEEE standard specifies 150 ohm shielded twisted-pair wire between the hub and the workstation, IBM specifies several physical media as follows:

- Type 1. Solid wire 22 American Wire Gauge (AWG) shielded twisted-pair
- Type 2. Solid wire 22 AWG shielded twisted-pair plus 4 pairs of solid wire 26 AWG shielded twisted-pair
- Type 3. 4-Mbps 22 or 24 AWG unshielded twisted-pair
- Type 5. 100/140 micron fiber optic for connecting multistation access units (MSAUs)
- Type 6. 26 AWG shielded twisted-pair
- Type 9. 26 AWG plenum-rated shielded twisted-pair

The only standard ARCnet is an American National Standard Institute (ANSI) version that also uses a token-passing protocol. Standard ARCnet is 2.5 Mbps. Characteristically, ARCnet uses either a bus or star configuration.

Making the connection

Most personal computers sold these days will be networked in some form. Although this statement is a fact, most personal computers, except the Apple Macintosh, are not sold with a network interface already built in. In most machines, the network interface is a board that must be installed in the machine. These boards are expensive and have been the target of sophisticated thieves. Locking devices exist, however, that protect the contents of a personal computer. These devices are discussed more fully under workstation security.

The use of network interfaces sometimes provides an additional level of security. Some suppliers have developed locking network connections that ensure their physical connection to the cable. The interface is attached to the thick Ethernet cable by a transceiver. The transceiver functions as the connection device as well as the portion of the network interface that performs collision detection. Locking devices exist that protect these Ethernet transceivers.

Are you being served?

The network interfaces allow workstations to talk to servers. Servers are the heart of the LAN. They provide controlled access to files, shared printers, and other resources. Disks or file servers can be specialized, proprietary computers designed to work with a specific manufacturer's hardware and software or a general-purpose computer. A minicomputer itself can be used as a disk or file server in many situations. General-purpose PCs are most commonly used as file servers in PC LANs. A general-purpose computer usually costs significantly less than a proprietary system.

Disk servers & file servers

Early microcomputer LAN operating system software allowed multiple computers to share a common hard disk to offset the high cost of disk storage. These early systems allowed you to partition a disk into read-only shareable volumes and read or write nonshareable volumes.

Called *disk service*, this approach was the most common method of resource sharing on microcomputer LANs for several years. Problems occurred when two or more users tried to write to the same volume. Each microcomputer using the disk attempted to control it as if it were a local drive. This attempt on the part of the computer was the primary reason most early LANs were error-prone. Because administrators had to grant access to the whole disk, users sometimes received more data than they actually needed.

Because of the problems associated with disk service, *file service* was created. The primary difference was that file servers provided control at the file level rather than the disk level. This finer level of granularity prevented much of the file corruption that existed previously and improved security. Today, most PC LANs use file service. Besides protecting the files, file servers also provide file and record-locking schemes, some measure of security, and print-spooling functions.

Today's file servers rival minicomputer and mainframe systems. Unlike these bigger systems, file servers do not process the data they retrieve, but instead transfer it to some device on the LAN for processing. Data is requested and delivered to devices on the LAN where processing occurs independently, on the individual workstations. Modified data is returned to the file server and the disk is updated. Because of the pivotal role of the file server, extra attention must be paid to its security.

Central-server & distributed systems

Most high-end LAN systems use a central file server approach. One or more computers on the LAN are specifically designated for file-server tasks and generally run software specifically designed for the file-service tasks. Distributed LAN systems provide for the sharing of most resources on the network, which means that each user can offer his or her disks and printers for use by others. Most current distributed LANs like the central servers, use file-server technology. Generally, distributed LANs are potentially more cost-effective, but central-server LANs provide for easier manageability and greater security. The most-effective PC LANs today employ a central-server approach.

Apple's AppleShare software uses a distributed approach. Every microcomputer on the LAN can make files available to every other microcomputer. This arrangement does not require the expense of a central server. It does, however, make security more difficult to administer.

File servers

What makes a computer function as a file server is software. The particular machine used for a file server might be a standard PC, a minicomputer, or a specialized proprietary computer designed specifically as a file server. Regardless of its hardware, it is the software running in the machine that defines it as a file server.

The primary purpose of file-server software is to synchronize access to shared resources. This means that the server software, in cooperation with application programs, ensures that users have simultaneous file access where appropriate while preventing simultaneous access where inappropriate.

File servers also can provide various levels of security and access control, allowing a system manager to designate who has access to resources. In this area, vast differences in capabilities exist between different file server systems. The system manager can set up access by application users, task groups, class of application, or management level. A detailed discussion of access rights is provided in Chapter 8.

The efficiency and sophistication of a file server's data management and retrieval capabilities can also vary widely from one network to another. High-speed disk access techniques, the use of disk caching, and the use of proprietary disk file structures are among the methods used to increase data-retrieval speed.

Two other types of servers are worth mentioning: dedicated and nondedicated servers. Dedicated servers function strictly as servers, and not as a user workstation. These servers generally provide better performance and system integrity than nondedicated servers. Nondedicated servers function as user workstations as well as file servers. Although most manufacturers provide for nondedicated servers, performance and system integrity issues can make this a risky approach. Users and applications can easily lock up a nondedicated server. Nondedicated servers can sometimes provide cost savings, but not if they constantly crash or freeze.

Servers are desirable items. They can and will be carried away by people. You should consider tethering hardware for your server, which is explored further under the discussion of workstations. Because of the physical threats to the server, servers rooms should be access-controlled. Only those individuals tasked with maintaining the LAN should be allowed in to the room at all. With most network operating systems, anyone with access to the server can access all the resources on the system, including print queues and data files. Unauthorized access to the server could lead to a serious compromise of your data.

Hubs Every workstation on a network needs access to the file server. In large star and ring networks, it is highly impractical to connect every workstation by cable to the file server; therefore, a device called a *hub* or concentrator is used instead. A hub is similar to an electrical breaker or fuse box in your house. The main power comes into your house to the fuse box where it splits into circuits to serve your bedroom, living room, and other rooms.

On a star, ring, and star-wired ring network, the hub is the central area where workstations and file servers can communicate. Hubs can be either active or passive. An active hub regenerates the signal as well as provides the physical connection. Most active hubs provide security features, for instance, intelligent hubs prevent eavesdropping and unauthorized access by restricting data delivery and stopping unauthorized users from adding devices to the network. The passive hub serves only as a cable termination and connection device. In truth, a passive hub is an exposure, because it represents a single point of failure.

Sharing peripherals Sharing expensive peripherals was a driving force in the development of LANs. These peripherals included printers, batch processors, facsimiles, modems, gateways, and other network devices. Some of these devices present opportunities for system exploiters and improvement. Access to devices on the network and beyond on other networks needs to be controlled. Connections to gateways for mainframes and other networks, fax machines, and modems must be controlled to ensure that only authorized users have access from the start. Figure 7-5 shows a typical LAN workgroup that must be controlled, including bridges, gateways, and servers.

Print servers Most file server software includes shared print service functions for printers attached to the file server machine. Other machines on a network also can provide shared print service. Some LAN operating systems provide this capability directly; others provide support through third-party utilities.

Print servers often distribute physically shared printers, support specialized printers that require specific control hardware and software, and add printers when a file server's printer attachment capability is reached. These specialized servers were developed because a single user was unlikely to keep a printer busy all the time, but placing the printer on the LAN then allowed it to be shared by all users. Depending on the print-server software, a print-server machine can be dedicated, functioning only as a print server, or nondedicated, functioning concurrently as a user workstation or other server.

The disadvantages of using print servers as workstations are similar to the disadvantages of using file servers as workstations: the workstation may run a little slower when used as a print server, and a user or application could lock it up. The consequences of a lockup on a print server, however, are ordinarily less severe than on a file server. Security problems exist for printer sharing also. For instance, when several users share a laser printer, the printer is usually in a location where at least one user cannot see the printer.

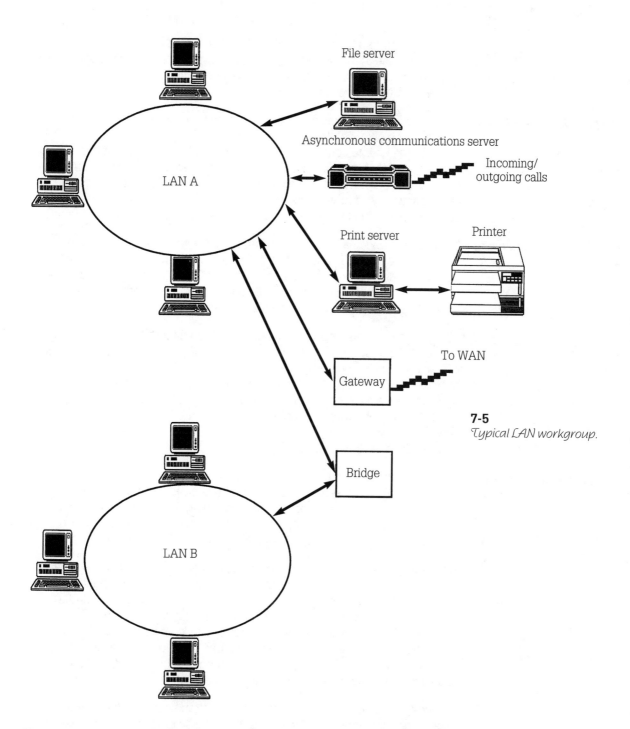

7-5 *Typical LAN workgroup.*

If sensitive reports are printed on these printers, the reports could be exposed to unauthorized people. All the passcode controls in the world cannot help if your sensitive reports sit in the paper trays of shared printers. Fortunately,

Applying controls to hardware

most laser printers have a manual feed option, which allows the user to feed the paper while at the printers. If you have users who, because of the nature of their jobs or the level of training they received, should not use a shared printer, require them to use a monitored printer.

Batch processing servers

Batch-processing servers allow time-consuming tasks, such as lengthy reports, to be offloaded from a user's machine, database, or file server, allowing the user to continue working while the batch processor handles the offloaded tasks. Access to these servers must be well-controlled to protect the information provided in the batch jobs. You should treat batch servers like file servers and provide stringent access control. Unauthorized access to batch reports could lead to the disclosure of confidential company information.

Fax servers

Fax servers provide all workstations on the LAN with access to a single fax service. Network fax services save time and paper, provide higher-quality transmissions, and promise more management and control than traditional facsimile machines. The server can be a workstation PC with an installed fax board, or a special device designed for fax service.

Like the use of shared printers, the use of fax machines poses security concerns. Sensitive reports sitting in the trays of shared facsimiles are exposed to anyone with physical access to the device. Again, it is important to protect the reports through physical access controls. In most cases, you must provide access control to servers processing, transmitting, or printing confidential information. Access control is accomplished by placing the server in a room with key or card access, or in some other way preventing unauthorized walkup access.

Communications servers

Communications servers allow LAN users to share devices such as modems across the LAN. The server is usually a dedicated PC with one or more multiport communications boards and several attached modems. These servers provide either dial-out, dial-in, or both types of service. Dial-out provides modem pooling and dial-in allows remote LAN access.

Dial-out service Dial-out services allow users on a LAN to access remote devices, such as bulletin boards and other networks, by using available modems attached to the communications server, rather than attached to their PCs. Similar to the print servers, these specialized servers were developed because a single user was unlikely to keep a modem busy placing the device on the LAN allowed it to be shared by all users. This sharing results in a reduction of modems and telephone lines; many users can use a small number of modems on an as-needed basis.

The costs of the hardware and software can often be more expensive than locally attached modems, however. Usually, these modems require their own software, limiting the selection of communications software. If dial-out lines are accessible universally, there is also a serious risk of abuse. If users can easily dial out, there will be tendency to connect to bulletin board services and other sources of external data and files. These sources might contain infected programs that could disrupt the network. Developing a policy on dial-out use could save your organization money and time in the future.

Dial-in service   LAN software vendors often provide for remote access through a serial port on a file server. Given the few serial ports that exist on a file server, this is not an ideal solution. Because of the nature of dial-in communications, the serial ports used continually interrupt the computer processes, severely affecting file server performance. Processing speeds for the file server also can become unacceptable because they will drop to modem speeds, for instance, 9600 bits per second.

Some communications servers can be used to dial into the LAN. Users not in the office can dial in and use network services, such as printers, files, and electronic mail. Any dial-in access should be access-code protected. The simplest solution is a modem requiring a user code and passcode. More complex solutions include network-access control devices. These devices should be considered for LANs where security is a concern.

A network-access control device is a programmable network security device that sits on either the analog or digital side of the line. These devices are hardware-independent and can protect many ports and an almost infinite number of users. They also can capture and log user profile and network usage data. Devices operating on the digital side of the line provide a higher level of security and network management. These devices can monitor and filter the datastream during the entire session, allowing the device to control the user's activities even after authentication is complete. Network-access control devices usually operate in the following modes:

- Callback
- Passthrough
- Random password generation
- Encryption

Callback options are fixed or variable. With all options of callback, the system verifies the user's access code and time and date restrictions in the user database. For fixed callback, the user is prompted for an access code and passcode. After caller verification, the system tells the user to hang up and calls the number in the user database to establish a connection to the LAN. When the callback is made, the caller must repeat the passcode to ensure the device reached the correct party. After acceptance of the passcode, the caller is granted access. For variable callback, the system prompts the user for an access code and passcode. Once verification occurs, the caller provides the number to be called back when prompted, and the process is then the same as the fixed callback process.

The passthrough process is similar to the callback. The device prompts the caller for an access code and passcode. Upon verification, the caller is granted access to the LAN without a return call. This mode can be used when the caller is calling through a switchboard and cannot be called directly.

The system creates a unique session passcode for each access attempt using a random passcode generator. Similar to a handheld calculator, the administrator issues a generator unit to authorized users to generate a session passcode in response to a random challenge. Each unit given has a unique DES encryption key, a user-specific access code, and a personal identification number (PIN). In this mode, the network-access controller intercepts each call, verifies the caller's access code—similar to the callback modes—and issues a challenge value. The caller enters the PIN into the generator unit, followed by the challenge value, and keys the displayed generator response. If the response is correct for the user's generator device, the system grants access.

The encryption mode usually combines the DES algorithm in the network-access controller with a remote encryption device attached to the caller's device. The devices acknowledge each other through the exchange of keys. Once the system verifies the caller, it automatically generates and destroys a new session key without knowledge of the user for each connection. A caller accessing the LAN with a recognized encryptor is automatically authenticated and logged, and all communications is encrypted using the DES algorithm.

Serious consideration should be given to security for dial-in ports provided by LANs. Dial-in ports are open windows into your network that must be defended by measures identifying individuals who desire access from remote locations. Hackers can easily identify your dial-in ports. They program their demon dialers to look for modem tones on phone lines. When a modem tone is found, the software records the phone number for later use.

Workstations: the local intelligence

The security of the network must start with one of its most basic components—the workstation. In a LAN environment, the workstation is the most vulnerable. A LAN basically takes several local unsecure computers and attaches them together. Applying controls from the top down can be, at best, unproductive. Therefore, good network security originates from good workstation security. Issues for local workstations include site protection, device protection, electromagnetic radiation, backup, and adequate power supply. Each of these topics must be addressed to provide adequate workstation security.

Because application processing occurs at a user's workstation, performance must be considered when selecting workstations. For most applications, workstation performance is more important than file-server performance.

The workstation is typically unprotected, providing a prime opportunity for intruders. The workstation also can be the first line of defense. Suitably equipped, workstations can control access to the network and the information contained within, and they can be robust, and available when needed.

Environmental control measures for workstations range from simple plastic covers for keyboards to uninterruptible power supplies. Microcomputers are susceptible to environmental contaminants. They are smothered by fingerprint oil, dust, hair, carpet fibers, and oxide particles from floppy disks. These destructive elements cause downtime, errors, and loss of data. The simplest protective measure is to place a plastic skin over the keyboard. Skins are thin, precision-molded, polymer covers that hug the exact contour of the keyboard. The skin will provide protection against disasters such as coffee spills. Cleaners do exist, however, if you forget to use a skin. In addition to protecting your microcomputer, the cleaners function as preventive maintenance. When used regularly, cleaners can prolong the life of microcomputers by safely removing dirt and oxide particles from drive heads. Dust covers made of antistatic material also provide protection against dust and dirt. Other physical protection measures are classified as restraints and act as deterrents.

Key locks & microcomputers

In 1984, IBM stunned the PC marketplace by selling the first PC AT with a locking keyboard. A security-minded individual might think this was a patently obvious idea, but it took a while. Most vendors now sell locking microcomputers of some specificity. My experience with locking devices, however, has not been positive. Usually, the key is left in the device at all times, or it is not used at all. Again, the keys will not be used properly if users do not see either the benefit or management's commitment to their use. Another common method of physically protecting a microcomputer from unauthorized use is a *dongle*. A dongle is a device attached to the parallel port of the microcomputer and acts as an electronic key.

If you decide to use keys or dongles as control mechanisms, you need to monitor their use periodically and establish controls for them. The controls should include issue, use, and return of keys or dongles. Users should be issued keys or dongles, and their supervisors should retain a copy. All keys and dongles should be surrendered when the employee retires, quits, or otherwise leaves.

Device restraints

Computer theft is a serious threat. Most large organizations have lost microcomputers or their components. Yes, even components; thieves will open a microcomputer and liberate network interface and video cards. You can do something about it, however. Tethering kits can secure almost any PC. These kits provide safeguards to chips, boards, and hard drives. Other kits batten down components to desks and other heavy, immovable fixtures.

Disk drive data

Many value-added resellers of microcomputer equipment initialize disks as a service to their customers. Normally, disk initialization is a welcome service, but in one instance of which I know, this service helped spread a Macintosh virus. The reseller installed the system software and, unknowingly, a virus as well. If the owners did not reformat their drive and reinstall the system software, they would have been infected. You must reformat and reinstall software whenever you receive any new equipment. You do not know where that drive has been!

Disk drives are a major source of data that are easily obtained and converted. Most large corporations have experienced the loss of workstations. They just grow legs and walk away. Microcomputers are easily carried, quickly converted, and highly desired. What happens when you realize you have lost a microcomputer? I know, because it happened in my office! First, you try to remember what was on the microcomputer. Eighty megabytes of data is a lot, approximately 36,000 pages of written text. You hope you have some word processing and spreadsheet programs on the disk so the data portion is smaller. You cannot remember everything, and you know you did not use the password option on your files. Oh well, at least you did not keep that confidential report, your credit card numbers, any mainframe passcodes, performance appraisals, and your personal information on the microcomputer. You did? Well, maybe they won't have microcomputers at your next job. Thank goodness you do backup every day and you can get on with your job. What? You cannot find your backup because it was in a disk caddy beside your PC?

Suppose your microcomputer is returned. Do you know if anyone read your files? Did they destroy your hard disk? By now, the item you classified in your inventory as less than your photocopier has caused you a lot of grief. Let's look at another twist on this story.

The U.S. Department of Justice disposed of a computer as it is wont to do periodically. Nobody took the time to reformat the drive, and the computer included information the department preferred stay confidential. The buyer noticed the information and was willing to return it if the Government admitted its mistake. Well, the Government would not, and it subsequently prosecuted the individual. The last I heard, the Justice Department got its information back. This is scary stuff, considering that the release of the information might have been life-threatening.

One last example needs to be presented. A colleague of mine once took a laptop computer with him on a business trip. On the return trip, the individual checked his luggage with the laptop inside. Needless to say, he made it home but his luggage did not. The luggage and laptop showed up three days later, but we could not tell if anyone had turned the computer on or not.

Computer theft is a serious threat. So serious that the industry has taken an important step to solve the problem—the Stolen Computer Registry. Its purpose is to intercept the sale of stolen computers. The Registry publishes a list of stolen equipment to legitimate secondary sales channels. Stolen equipment on the list is confiscated and returned to the rightful owner. Obviously, the registry will not prevent theft, but it could help reduce it.

Removable disks

Some disk drives come with removable media, usually a cartridge. Pros and cons exist with the use of this type of media. Removable media makes it easy to store your data because it can be written to a cartridge and placed in a desk. Because the data is easy to store, it is also easy to steal. Vital corporate information can fit easily on a cartridge. The FBI, however, recommends the use of these cartridges for critical applications. It believes the pros outweigh the cons. You should assess your own situation and decide if this is true for you.

Diskettes & storage

Diskettes, or *floppies*, are a security risk if left unattended. Disk caddies can end the chaos of loose disks. These caddies usually store dozens, if not hundreds, of disks and can be stacked vertically or horizontally in a system. Many people make the mistake of leaving these caddies out on their desks and susceptible to theft. One way of eliminating floppies and their security risk is to use diskless workstations.

Diskless workstations

Diskless workstations are in vogue for two reasons. Clearly, a need exists to prevent the copying of some information off the network onto floppy disks and to reduce the likelihood of a virus being copied from a floppy onto the network. A diskless workstation offers a cost-effective solution to both these problems. The workstations are called diskless because they come without a floppy or hard disk installed. As previously mentioned, they do have local processing capabilities and are distinguishable from dumb terminals. By eliminating the floppy drive, however, it is difficult for users to unintentionally introduce viruses, copy licensed software, or steal corporate information. Another reason for diskless workstations is their higher reliability in nonoffice environments. Floppy drives can be easily damaged by airborne debris in companies or manufacturing plants.

Stopping signals

You are in a highly competitive industry, and someone is stealing your secrets. It is so serious you bring a private investigator in to track the source of the information leaks. A few weeks later, the investigator phones. He has discovered the source of the leak. His evidence points to an inside job—it is one of your personal computers. It might surprise you, but your personal computers are leaking information to electromagnetic eavesdroppers all the time. Most personal computers, monitors, keyboards, and even printers emanate electromagnetic signals that contain all the information they process. An eavesdropper can pick up this data using a television set, a videocassette recorder, and an external oscillator—the electronic equivalent of a Saturday Night Special handgun. This equipment is legal and can be bought as a complete system or assembled from components. The eavesdropper can even listen from two miles away. Your equipment acts as a radio transmitter so it is just a matter of the thief finding a good antenna. Eavesdroppers can receive signals through antennas or by attaching alligator clips to power lines, sprinkler systems, or sewer or bathroom pipes.

Fortunately, there are two security solutions. One works at the source and the other works at one of the leakage points. Microcomputers are available that shield against the leakage of electromagnetic signals. Also, a glass manufacturer has developed a specially coated glazing construction designed to reduce materially the passage of signals into and out of a room.

Fault-tolerance

LANs with mission-critical applications must be available. Industry experts, however, estimate that these LANs suffer a 6-percent downtime. To complete their 1989 study *The Cost of Downtime*, Infonetics interviewed 100 Fortune 1000 information and network managers, whose companies average $1.7 billion in revenue. Major findings of the study were the following:

- The average network is down approximately two times per month for almost five hours each time.
- Companies lose almost $3.5 million a year in employee productivity from downtime.
- Lost revenue averages over $600,000 per annum.
- Companies are only spending $60,000 per annum for LAN maintenance.
- Networks are growing at a rate of 48 percent, and a positive correlation exists between network size and the number of network problems.

A facile example shows these figures are disastrous. Our simple network has 10 workstations used by accounts receivable clerks. For the sake of argument, assume these clerks make $20 per hour (benefits included), work 40 hours per week and 50 weeks per year. Our estimated 6 percent of downtime now is worth $24,000 per annum! These figures go up substantially when we begin to look at the effect on knowledge workers commanding higher pay. We must find ways to reduce these figures. One method is to build in preventive measures instead of developing more and more corrective measures. One highly effective countermeasure is the use of fault-tolerant technologies.

If your calculations justify it, you might want to consider fault-tolerance. What is fault-tolerance? Basically, it involves deciding where the key points of failure are and then building in redundancy for those components. This could mean duplicating, and even triplicating, some components of your system. Nonstop performance can be achieved because, when a component fails, another can take up the task immediately. Two key points of failure include the file server's hard disk and the network operating system. The server's hard disk is particularly prone to failure because it has moving parts. Most other server components have a high infant mortality rate, meaning that if they make it through the first three months, they probably will last a long time.

Anyone who maintains computer hardware knows most devices are serviced for disk problems, that is, bad sectors or ruined read/write heads. Duplexing and mirroring provide relief when a server suffers disk failure.

Duplexing & mirroring

A reasonable method for providing availability at the hard disk is to mirror, or duplex, the disk. Any data written to the primary disk is also written to a secondary disk, which is waiting to take over if it detects that the primary disk is unavailable. Both mirroring and duplexing are now available in hardware, software, or a combination of both. Some products even provide a level of granularity, for example, some allow duplication of data while others mirror only critical data.

While most people see disk duplexing and mirroring as synonymous, differences do exist. Duplexing provides more protection than disk mirroring because it uses two controllers and two drives. The duplicate controllers mitigate a failure of a controller card in the server. If your applications are very critical, this subtlety might be important. Duplexing also improves network performance because you have two controllers accessing two drives, thus cutting the user's access time. Dual controllers also allow reading from one disk, writing to the other, and mirroring of both. Obviously, this duplexity gets complicated, but the advantages of duplexing over mirroring should be kept in mind if performance and availability are critical success factors for your LAN and its applications.

Disk arrays

Users with applications requiring fault-tolerance also might want to consider disk arrays. Disk array systems help prevent data loss as well as improve disk performance. The most widely used disk array system is the redundant array of independent disks (RAID) technology. RAID technology provides error correction, data striping, disk mirroring, and duplexing. Data striping, a new concept, allows you to spread blocks of data across drives.

For error correction, you can dedicate a disk as the parity drive to act as a checksum by summing all bytes of the data and keeping the least-significant two bytes of the results. For example, in a disk array system, the data you write is sent to the array's controller, and each block of information is spread across each drive in the array. The disk array's controller then calculates the parity byte by summing data bits on each drive. When a drive fails, the system uses the parity byte to recover the data stored on the failed drive.

Disk arrays are an excellent solution for operating systems such as UNIX. Other operating systems, such as Novell NetWare, provide similar features at a much lower cost. Chapter 8 discusses NetWare's fault-tolerance features, which provide better performance because its fault-tolerance is hardware-independent, and NetWare does not have to maintain a parity drive.

Backup strategies

When fault-tolerance is too expensive, or you still are not satisfied with relying totally on it, an effective strategy is redundancy. The growth of the microcomputer has brought about the requirement for more and more people to back up their data. Microcomputer users do not usually heed warnings about potential problems if they do not prepare for a disaster. Users adopt a "it won't happen to me" attitude. These facts are borne out in a study done by IntelliQuest commissioned by 3M, which is summarized in FIG 7-6. According to the study, American companies must put out $4 billion a year due to data loss. Most people realize the value of their data only when they have lost it. The value of the data is usually far greater than that of the server

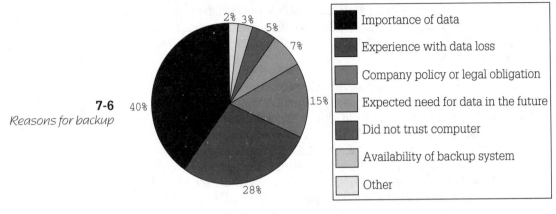

7-6
Reasons for backup

hardware, and often greater than the value of the LAN components combined. Reasons for backup are provided in the figure.

After their first bad experience from failing to back up their data, these same users go through a spiritual enlightenment and begin proselytizing the benefits of backup. These same attitudes have carried over to the LAN environment as well. Backup is a loathsome task that most network administrators take for granted or put off.

Networks, however, are quickly moving away from small workgroups run on single servers to enterprise-wide systems. These larger, more complex systems carry more data, making backup all the more important. Some network administrators have difficulty, however, finding enough downtime to copy a disk-image for each server to tape.

Previously, network administrators took weekly backups of the whole server and performed incremental backups daily. Administrators did not pay much attention to the types of files backed-up or the frequency of file changes. This method, typically using one tape drive for one or two servers, was reliable and worked well for most small networks. Information could be retrieved and restored, provided that the administrator knew on which tape to look.

The bigger the network, however, the less likely these traditional methods for backup will succeed. Clearly, administrators need new approaches. Luckily, backup techniques and strategies are available that allow more flexibility in backups; they can be handled more incrementally, along with better management of backup and restore files and without user intervention.

Backups should be done more incrementally and scheduled on patterns of file change rather than time frames. If the server contains files that are only updated monthly, daily or weekly backups are not necessary. This brings us back to a point previously made: we need to classify and understand the nature of the data on the network. Human involvement in the backup process should be shifted from the traditional role of monitoring progress to the evaluation and planning of the process itself. The ultimate goal is to perform unattended backups, because human involvement always brings random risk into the process.

The success of a backup depends on the completion of the task with little interruption. The greater the capacity of tape drives and other media, the less likely the process will stop because the tape ran out. Most backup products allow for spanning tapes during backup but, without an automated process for change, human intervention is still needed. The need for human assistance was not a problem on mainframes because night shift operators existed to handle these housekeeping chores. There is, therefore, a tradeoff between increased automation of the process and human intervention. Some managers have difficulty with traditional backup or are uncomfortable with the idea of centralized control of backups.

Backup on enterprise-wide systems does need some degree of centralization. It is a control that can be easily routinized once established. As long as the ultimate goal of backup—reliable and easy recovery—is met, managers and users need not be concerned with where or by whom the file was backed-up. Consolidating backup hardware and software should also result in savings in large networks. Obviously, the managers, users, and network administrators need to feel secure and be assured that the centralized method is as good as the decentralized. They need to know eavesdropping on the network is prevented, and the physical backup media is protected.

The primary requirement for a backup system is to get information back. Speed of the backup and restoration is also important, but meaningless if you cannot restore the data. The range of backup hardware is wide. Tape is probably the most commonly used medium. Systems do exist that are based on magnetic disk, optical disk, or even mainframe magnetic disk. There are also robotic media-handling systems such as tape and optical disk jukeboxes. Large networks require high-capacity backup media. Tape is generally the answer because of its low cost, ease of storage, reliability, and widespread acceptance, including in other market segments, such as consumer electronics. These very reasons also make it a target. Thieves can easily steal 5 gigabytes of data without your knowledge!

Recovery requires a fast search-and-restore capability. Disk media have faster search speeds than tape. Compare this to queuing up a song at home on your compact disk and cassette players and you understand the reason. Usually, search and restore speeds are affected by the backup software. Most software cannot use the fast speeds of tape and disk drives. Even with high-speed search-and-read capabilities, most software does not allow for very fast recovery. Backup software for large networks must selectively back up files, and especially be able to consistently bypass unchanging files.

Finally, do not store your backup tapes onsite. Many network administrators store their backup onsite where the backup is open to the same threats as the original copy. You can either electronically or manually send your backup offsite.

Developing a practical, manageable strategy for backup is an arduous task. All the tools do exist to simplify the process; a network manager need only pull the pieces together and integrate them to provide reliable backup and recovery. Planning is essential to the manager. The manager must know what needs backup, how often, and how long it will take. Finally, the manager must know and understand the various software and hardware options available. Successful completion of planning will help to ensure data availability in the face of a disaster.

You will be glad you backed up your data when you experience a power problem.

Static, noise, surges, brownouts, blackouts, & other power problems

Bell Laboratories estimates that your equipment faces 128 power disturbances each month, from indiscernible surges to total blackouts. Like other electrical equipment, LAN file servers and workstations can suffer damage from power problems. Data error, data loss, head crashes, shutdowns, and physical equipment damage are just a few of the results of electrical supply problems.

A file server should be plugged into a dedicated circuit. If one is not available, noise producing equipment, such as photocopiers, air conditioners, fans, and refrigerators, should not be on the same line. File servers should be protected by surge protectors to ward against both surges and spikes, along with power backup systems to protect against blackouts, brownouts, dips, and sags. If possible, the power backup system should include a monitoring function to provide for graceful degradation of the file service.

As a minimum, workstations should be protected by surge protectors. If line noise is a problem, line filters or isolation transformers should be considered. If your environment is dry or static electricity is a problem, static mats or other static control equipment should be used.

Static

Static discharges measure in the thousands of volts, and can easily destroy electronic equipment. Static discharges can be controlled by any of the following:

- Antistatic chair mats
- Antistatic equipment mats
- Antistatic carpet
- Antistatic spray
- Grounding straps
- Touch pads

Antistatic chair mats ground the user, eliminating static discharge, but floor mats cannot drain static electricity when the user wears rubber-soled shoes. Similarly, antistatic equipment mats ground the equipment, and operators touch the mat before touching the equipment. The layers of carbon and a grounding cord zap static on the spot. Specially treated carpet eliminates or minimizes static charge buildup, which is probably the best solution for static discharge. You can use antistatic spray to treat carpets, which is a very good short-term solution, but is probably the least effective long-term solution because it requires constant treatment. Grounding straps go around an operator's wrist and attach to a static pad under the equipment. The last solution for static is touch pads that sit on the desk next to the equipment. The operator touches the pad to discharge static before touching the equipment.

Surges & spikes

Surges and spikes are momentary increases in voltage. They can be from a few volts to over 1,000 volts. Figure 7-7 shows an example of a surge. Surges of 50 volts or more are common, sometimes occurring several times per hour, while surges of over 1,000 volts are infrequent. Surges occur as often as 750 times per month. They attack on three pathways: between hot and neutral wires, between hot and ground wires, and between neutral and ground wires.

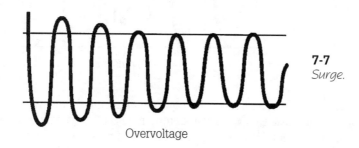

7-7
Surge.

Surge suppressors are the most widely used type of power-protection device. Without surge suppressors, you are playing with fire. Suppressors sit between the power supply and the device and protect against momentary voltage surges and spikes. Figure 7-8 illustrates a spike. Surge suppressors divert high voltage (generally over 200 to 250 volts) to ground. New surge suppressors feature built-in alarms, so when a gap exists in the surge protection, you will be warned at once. You should ensure that the surge suppressor you buy protects on all three pathways, and not just the hot and neutral path, as do cheaper

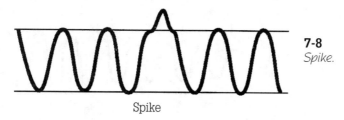

7-8
Spike.

models. Three-circuit protection devices catch the leading edge of the surge in the first circuit. If there is a stronger and longer surge, the device normally blocks the surge in the second circuit. If a really big power surge tries to sneak by, say, along the neutral-to-ground wire, it gets absorbed in the third circuit.

Even without surge suppressors, most computer equipment can handle low-voltage surges by design. Higher voltage surges, however, definitely cause damage to computer equipment. In fact, some surges are so intense they can burn right through the single-stage protection circuit common to many surge suppressors.

Noise Noise caused by copiers, air conditioners, refrigerators, fluorescent lights, and power supplies can cause sporadic disturbances in your computer, such as incorrect characters appearing on the screen. Figure 7-9 illustrates noise. In LAN environments, intermittent problems or glitches such as a workstation losing communication with the file server for no apparent reason have been blamed on noise.

7-9
Noise.

Transient

An isolation transformer isolates equipment from the power lines, eliminating much of the noise that occurs in commercial buildings. Power-line filters remove extraneous low-voltage impulses and noise. Some three-circuit surge suppressors also filter noise to prevent data errors from these unwanted signals.

Blackouts, When power dips below normal, you have suffered a brownout, dip, or sag.
brownouts, Figure 7-10 illustrates a dip or sag, while FIG. 7-11 shows a brownout.
dips, & sags Persistent brownouts can cause corruption and loss of data, and a brownout can cause a computer's internal power supply to overheat and ultimately burn out. A blackout is when the power goes out entirely. Blackouts can cause data loss and physical damage. Most operating systems are susceptible to blackouts because the operating system updates directories in memory.

7-10
Dip or sag.

Undervoltage

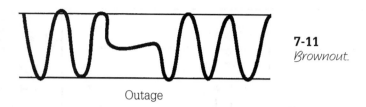

Outage

7-11
Brownout.

Backup power systems provide emergency power in case of commercial power outage or interruption. These systems are either uninterruptible power systems (UPS) or standby power systems (SPS). Generally, people refer to both these two as uninterruptible power supply.

A standby power system contains batteries and a power inverter, which can take the batteries' direct current input and convert it to 120-volt alternating current output. Figure 7-12 illustrates an SPS. Under normal power conditions, an SPS delivers power from the incoming main power. If incoming power drops (usually below 100 volts), the SPS switches from the main to the batteries and inverter, supplying power to the devices plugged in to it. The transfer switch senses a power failure and turns on the inverter, which converts direct current into alternating current. The alternating current then runs the microcomputer. When power returns, the transfer switch returns the microcomputer to normal power. A standby power supply stands by and continually recharging its batteries.

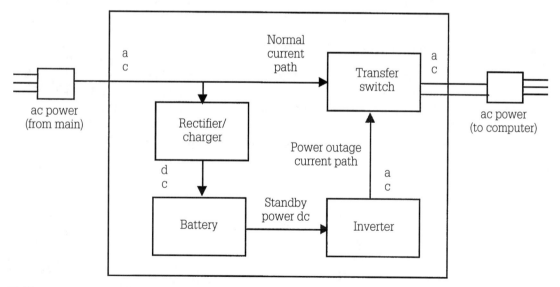

7-12 *Standby power system.*

A UPS differs from the standby system in that its battery and inverter are constantly powering the attached equipment. Figure 7-13 shows a typical UPS. Sometimes a UPS is called an *online power supply system*. The rectifier

Applying controls to hardware

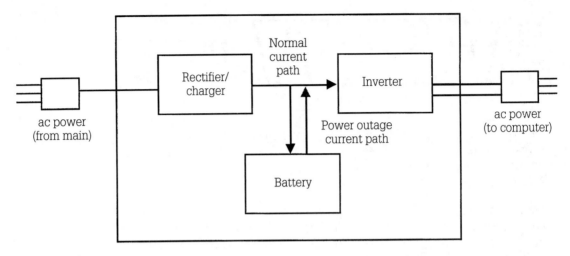

7-13 *Uninterruptible power system.*

is constantly changing alternating current from the wall to direct current to charge the batteries. The inverter then takes the direct current from the batteries and changes it back to alternating current to power the microcomputer or server. A UPS only resorts to the incoming power when the battery power is uninterruptible or fails. The benefit of UPS over SPS is zero delay when power fails; however, a UPS usually costs twice as much as a similarly rated standby system. Although UPS batteries are recharged continuously, they do not last as long as SPS batteries.

Many backup power systems can send messages to attached equipment, such as the file server, to indicate when commercial power is interrupted or the batteries are low. This monitoring function allows a file server or workstation to shut down gracefully. The monitoring hardware sends a message to the file server when commercial power is interrupted. The server then sends a warning message to users and the server closes open files and shuts down. Users are thus alerted to pending shutdowns in time to save their files.

8

Applying controls to software

If we continue our analogy of using the body to discuss parts of the LAN, software is the brains of the operation. Software sends messages to other components, telling them what function to perform, just as a human brain sends electrical current to our limbs. Server and local software provide the capability to transmit data, send electronic mail, type letters, perform calculations, and prepare mailing lists. There are many different types of software products, and the list grows longer every day.

It takes all types All types of software are available on the LAN; there is software for one user, and software for many users. Some software enables users to work simultaneously on a single document. Others operate the microcomputer or the network. Some software packages are shrink-wrapped, while others are available from bulletin boards. Application software runs the gamut from accounting to word processing. Power on a LAN is unleashed when the right software for the right task is given to the right user.

Single-user software By design, single-user software is used by a single user on a single computer. Although single-user software is not designed to allow for data or file sharing, most can be installed on LAN file servers. Licensing issues aside, single-user software usually can be used by multiple users simultaneously, but the data files cannot. Most network operating systems allow you to prevent multiple users from concurrently accessing files that should not be shared using file locking techniques.

Some single-user software provides a simple encryption feature for protecting files. Commercially-available software can decrypt files so encrypted, however, so relying on this feature would be foolhardy.

Multiuser software Multi-user software provides for concurrent sharing of data files by multiple users where appropriate. Multiuser software provides simultaneous shared access to the user while maintaining data integrity using file, record, or field-level locking. Software of this type includes multiuser database and accounting systems software.

Groupware A relatively new category of software called *groupware* is emerging in the LAN environment. Although definitions vary, groupware is essentially software that enables individuals to work together as a group, or software that facilitates group goals. The definition stretches as vendors try to position themselves under the groupware umbrella. For instance, many vendors are now trying to position their multiuser software as groupware.

As mentioned in Chapter 1, companies are moving toward workgroups. The growth of groupware parallels this trend within organizations. Members of workgroups might work in the same department or be engaged in a particular project. For example, there is markup software that allows one or more individuals to edit a manuscript simultaneously. Figure 8-1 illustrates the principles of markup software; the different editors are recognizable by their different marks. Other groupware software might include electronic

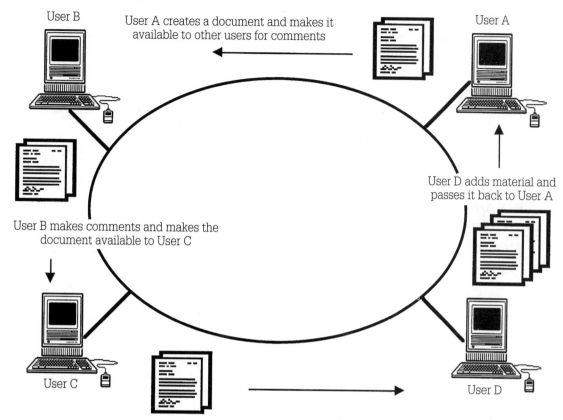

8-1 *A groupware example.*

mail, electronic meetings, group scheduling and calendaring, and project management tools. The success of even the best designed groupware products depends on user acceptance, and the commitment of the organization must be strong enough to ensure that users continue to use the product during the early stages.

Shareware and public-domain software circulate among computer hobbyists and gain wide acceptance because they fill a particular void. Publishers distribute shareware on a trial basis, and users pay the publisher if they decide to keep it or throw it away if they do not. Public-domain software is free software from the author as long as the user does not gain financially from it. The most common sources of shareware and public-domain software are computer bulletin board services (BBS).

Shareware

Shareware and public domain software are usually widely distributed, somewhat ensuring the integrity of the program. Still, it does not hurt to protect yourself. By following a few common sense guidelines, such as only

Applying controls to software 145

downloading software from known sources, avoiding the loading of new shareware directly onto your LAN until it is thoroughly tested, and performing regular rotational backups, you should avoid or prevent most problems.

Password grabbers and other hacker programs are readily available from any BBS. You would be wise to browse these bulletin boards occasionally to see what is offered. In my experience, security and audit professionals do not use bulletin boards to the extent they should. Bulletin boards provide interesting information on the security of different products, as well as handy utilities for everyone.

Network operating system

A major software component of LANs is the network operating system (NOS). There is a glut of contenders; however, only a few are serious contenders for the crown of the network operating system. Certainly, I could not mention all the different LAN operating systems in this book. From time to time, for the sake of illustration, I refer to Apple's AppleShare, Artisoft's LANtastic, Banyan's VINES, IBM's OS/2 LAN Server, and Novell's NetWare for examples. This mention is not an endorsement of these products, but these products do represent the most popular products for the Disk Operating System (DOS) and Macintosh platforms.

The network operating system can be thought of as the central nervous system of a PC LAN. This nervous system manages shared LAN resources, such as file service and print service, and provides security by controlling access to the shared resources. In a typical LAN, the network software allows a computer with a hard disk to make space on that disk available to others. Other users can then access files in that area, store their files there, and load files from that area to their PCs. This disk is clearly a security risk. You must decide who can authorize the sharing and who can share the disk. You must set boundaries on the shared area to ensure users cannot break out of the shared area and into other areas on the shared disk of the file server. All users want these assurances before they agree to place their data on the network. The network software must control what part of the disk is made available to users. Those parts not available should be provided protection.

An essential service of network operating systems is a name or directory service. Without directory services on the network, communicating with other users or using network resources is difficult. Directory services allow a network manager to alter the physical network without the user even being aware of the change. Each computer on the network must have a unique name to distinguish it from the others. Directories also provide a wealth of information about your system and its users, and you must adequately protect it.

Network operating system software must display a trophy to users attempting access. The trophy should warn users at logon attempt that the computer is a private network and illegal access will be prosecuted. The message should also declare that progress beyond this point is not permitted to unauthorized users. Many judges have ruled that you must show your intention to protect your network. If you have a tempting logon screen that says "Welcome to the Network," you could be inviting trouble. While the advisory notice is essential, you must ensure that it also does not provide too much information to a would-be intruder. The network operating system should provide the following security options:

- Account
- Password
- Directory
- File
- Communications
- Logging

AppleShare security

As previously mentioned, Apple's Macintosh microcomputer comes network-ready right out of the box. Consequently, thousands of AppleTalk LANs are in existence. These LANs are easy to install and maintain. As these LANs grow larger, however, and are incorporated into the enterprise-wide network, the network administrator must account for files and users.

AppleShare is Apple's answer to accounting for users and resources. Apple's network operating system is file server software that uses the AppleTalk Filing Protocol (AFP). AFP is a Presentation-Level protocol governing remote file access. AppleShare once used the dedicated network file server model. With the latest release, AppleShare 3.0 now operates in either dedicated or nondedicated mode. AppleShare is a network product using LocalTalk cabling and the AppleTalk protocol. AppleTalk also runs on other media, such as unshielded twisted-pair, coax, and fiber.

AppleTalk works with most network types, including LocalTalk, Ethernet, and Token Ring. The network type affects data transmission speed, maximum size of individual network segments, and network setup costs.

The security administrator must address two areas on a network. First, the administrator must address network management, restricting LAN access to network managers for activities such as configuring routers and assigning file server passwords. Second, the administrator must address the security of the users and their data. AppleShare provides facilities to help administrators with their network.

In AppleShare, the security facility is implemented as a small special-purpose database called the Users & Groups Data File. Every server, whether dedicated or nondedicated, has its own file that is used to administer the security of local resources, services, and accounts. The data file and other parts of the AppleShare software work together to provide the basis for the security options.

AppleShare includes simple security provisions, such as passwords for user accounts. Perhaps AppleShare security is simple because of the history of the Macintosh. The first users of Macintosh were not corporate users. They tended to be in more visual fields—for example, desktop publishing and CAD/CAM—and thought nothing of sharing their resources. Notwithstanding the Macintosh's genesis, several user account and password controls do exist.

You can define user privileges by assigning only the minimum access rights to users and deny network management rights to all users. Users are owners of either the disks or the folders constituting the file server. Unfortunately, the security of the data is only as secure as the passwords. If the security administrator wants a secure server, users must guard their passwords—and it is never a good idea to assign blank passwords for anything. The security of resources and services rely on AppleShare's three access privileges:

See Folders   Allows a user to view the contents of a folder or see a folder within another folder.

See Files   Allows a user to see and open documents or applications within the folder.

Make Changes   Allows a user to modify the folder's contents, including moving icons and creating or deleting files.

You can assign these privileges in any combination to achieve the desired effect on folders and files. These privileges allow the network administrator to adapt security mechanisms to the needs of the organization, tailoring security for each user and workgroup. The administrator can also lock folders, files, and programs. When locked, they cannot be moved, renamed, or deleted, even by their owner.

Thus, the network administrator can provide more or less security based on the data and the user. Again, the network administrator must understand the value of the data and the organization's access policy. With Apple's new System 7 file sharing, users must now take more responsibility for creating accounts and passwords for people with whom they want to share data. Thus, your users will need adequate education and training to appreciate the value of the data and to understand the organization's protection requirements. Users should know the dangers of using file sharing and allowing users access to their files. They should only implement file sharing when they have a real need to share with another user or group of users, and they should keep the number of users with access to their files to a minimum.

Account   AppleShare also provides access control. File server access is controlled by a registered user name and passcode. The system keeps a security profile of every user and only allows access to file servers based on privileges assigned by the system administrator or owner of the file server.

To log on to an AppleShare file server, a person must correctly enter a valid account (user name) and a corresponding password. If the person enters either incorrectly, access is denied. Alternatively, AppleShare allows a user to log on to a guest account that does not require a password. Administrators must ensure that the guest account cannot access confidential information. AppleShare allows the following logon-related restrictions to be put on a user's account:

Login enabled	Allows a user to connect to a server. Disabling this option still allows file service to others. You can exclude a user from access without deleting the name.
All privileges enabled	Turns a user into a superuser. Superusers can override the access privileges set by users and modify those set by themselves. They also can see the contents of all storage devices, not just the shared portions.
Program linking enabled	Allows a user to create a link between a program on the server and the workstation. Users with linking enabled can access data on the file server that is not necessarily shared.

Users can be assigned to groups to limit the use of folders and files on the network to a subset of users. Users in a group can share folders and documents.

Password AppleShare allows the following password restrictions to be put on a user's account:

Existence of passwords	Users either enter a password or they do not. Common sense suggests all users have passwords assigned.
Change password enabled	Allows a user to change passwords from a workstation. You can decide whether passwords are administered centrally or distributed. In a distributed environment, users set their own passwords.
Require new password on next login	Requires users to change their password the next time they log on to the file server.
Minimum password length	You can set the minimum length of passwords for users. Passwords should be at least 6 characters in length to provide good security.
Password expiration date	You can age passwords and require users to select a new password after a set time period.

These password features are not rich, and miss the password repetition, logon grace period, and periodic password changes provided by other network operating systems. Table 8-1 provides a summary of AppleShare password features. Note that passcodes on AppleShare file servers are not encrypted. Wherever possible, you should not enable guest logons under System 7 File Sharing, particularly for your entire disk. If you do, anyone who logs on can delete any or all of your files.

Table 8-1
AppleShare password summary

Feature	Yes / No
Force password use	Yes
Users can change passwords	Yes
Require password on next logon	Yes
Set password length	Yes
Expire password	Yes
Allow logon grace period	No
Force periodic password changes	No
Prevent password repetition	No
Set minimum password age	No

File File sharing before System 7 was straightforward. With the inclusion of the File Sharing feature in System 7, users can now make their workstation a distributed file server and share their files. Users must understand the dangers of unlimited file sharing and of allowing other users access to their files. You should minimize the number of users accessing a user's workstation. If most people require access to files, you should put them on a central file server controlled by a network administrator.

It is critical that you not enable guest logons under System 7's File Sharing. Again, this is most likely an application for a central server. You must also ensure you have not given guest access to your hard disk, or anyone can access your data. Third-party add-on products can inform you when a remote user accesses files under File Sharing. Most also maintain an activity log. Entries in the log provide information about the user attempting to connect, as well as the time and date of the attempt.

Communications An effective method of managing network security is to restrict certain areas of the network. As mentioned earlier, not all users need to know or need to access all network files and resources. Filtering limits the access of certain users and hardware filters are discussed in the next chapter. Software filters are discussed now.

A GetZoneList filter restricts users from accessing your network. This feature is helpful if you frequently have guests on your system. You can set up a GetZoneList filter to restrict the zones available to these guests. A *zone* is a collection of networks on an AppleTalk internet. A secondary reason for breaking your network into zones is to reduce the amount of searching a user does to find a network resource; for example, users only see those printers intended for their use.

How does GetZoneList filtering work? When users boot their Macintosh, a GetZoneList packet is sent to the router to obtain the internet zone list to display in the Chooser. The router returns a filtered zone list, and the Chooser displays available zones. Because users only see the filtered zone lists, they do not usually try to get to other zones.

Accounting and auditing AppleShare networks   If you have a large network, perhaps one comprising several workgroups, then you might want to implement accounting management software relating to network usage. Using accounting management software, you can provide usage statistics on file server, printer, network modem, or facsimile modem use. By auditing usage of these components, you can catch potential trouble spots on your network and avert future downtime by reacting quickly. Unfortunately, no AppleShare accounting management software exists. You can do several things, however.

The easiest device on which to monitor usage is the printer. You can keep track of type of output, number of pages, and the person who submitted the print job. AppleShare's Print Server software does not provide much statistical information. If you need this level of information, you need to dedicate a server to print spooling. Specialized print spooler software can provide information on jobs sent to network printers. Spool software provides an audit trail as well as a calculation of printing costs per job.

For the file server, you might want to track the amount of disk storage used. Tracking disk storage could free up space and help develop a realistic backup plan. Unfortunately, AppleShare provides little help with monitoring files on the server, as is the case with current shared asynchronous communications devices for AppleShare networks.

LANtastic by Artisoft is a peer-to-peer network operating system. *Peer-to-peer* means that every machine on the network can offer the same services to network users. For example, a user on one workstation can print files using a printer connected to any other workstation. LANtastic can do this because it runs NOS concurrently with the application software. In this mode, the workstation acts as a nondedicated server; however, LANtastic is configurable with a dedicated server. (The different types of servers were discussed in the previous chapter.)

LANtastic security

LANtastic is a bus network, which means that workstations attached to the network transmit data whenever they want. They construct a data packet and then attempt to transmit it, rather than use an existing packet circulating on the network.

Artisoft's NOS runs on all versions of DOS operating systems. In truth, LANtastic relies heavily on DOS to conduct operations such as disk file reading and writing and supports IBM's NetBIOS networking standard. The LANtastic package is complete, with network operating system, network adapters, cabling, and other NOS utilities, and programs.

LANtastic has four distinct network software layers:
- Network applications
- Network operating system
- NetBIOS
- Network device driver

Each software layer only communicates with the layer immediately above or below it in the system. For example, the network operating system layer only talks with the NetBIOS and network applications layers. Each layer performs specific functions, and communication between the layers is controlled by standards.

The three major components of LANtastic are the redirector, the server and LANBIOS. The *redirector* is responsible for intercepting requests made to DOS by application programs and redirecting them to the network. For example, when you request a file from another machine on the network, the redirector makes that request to the remote machine with the data. The *server* is the software component that services network requests for file access, printers, or other networked devices. *LANBIOS* or *AILANBIO* (adapter-independent LANBIOS) are extended network versions of NetBIOS that support Artisoft's networking products. Every workstation and server must have a copy of the redirector and LANBIOS actively running, but only machines offering network resources, such as files and printers, must have the server software. DOS SHARE must also be loaded on any server to control record and file locking.

Account LANtastic recognizes users by means of a user account or login account. The account is information that identifies the user to the NOS. Account names for each server must be unique. LANtastic keeps a security profile of every user and only allows access to valid accounts. To log on to the file server, a person must correctly enter a valid account and, possibly, the corresponding password. If the person enters either incorrectly, access is denied.

LANtastic's NET_MGR utility allows the following logon-related restrictions to be put on a user's account:

Account disable   This function provides the ability to temporarily suspend a user's account without deleting the account. LANtastic retains all account information, but does not allow a login against that account. This feature is useful when you have determined an intruder is trying to use the account or an employee goes on extended leave. Users can disable their own account using this utility.

Expiration date   Expiration allows an administrator to set an expiration date on any user's account. This feature is useful when consultants are providing periodic work.

Limit time-of-day   This function offers the ability to restrict the hours of day
connections   and days of the week a user can access the network.

Unfortunately, LANtastic does not prevent concurrent logons. Therefore, more than one person can log on to the same account with the same password. This feature makes accountability difficult to prove, and should be prohibited within your organization. You can, however, limit how many times a user can log on to the server with an account name. You can thus prevent concurrent logins by keeping the number set to the default: 1.

With LANtastic version 4.0, group accounts were added, allowing several users to share an account name and thereby share resources or limit the use of programs and files on the network to a subset of users. You can define a standard set of network resources and privileges for several users and assign them to the same group. For example, accounts receivable clerks could share an account name that provides access to the customer database. You also might want to use groups to administer print queues by allowing every user to log on using the group account to spool print files. You should not use the group account, however, in any way that negates the accountability principle, that is, that every user on the network is responsible for his or her actions and is held accountable for those actions.

Each account also can have privileges associated with it that allow the user to override access rights specified in the access control lists (ACLs). You might want to configure a resource so no user can write to the resource, yet you could set an access privilege on an account that allows the user to write to the files. LANtastic defines five access privileges that can be set using NET__MGR. These access privileges are described as follows:

Super ACL (A)   This privilege allows a user access to all shared resources. Users with this privilege can override all access controls on shared file resources. Only the network administrator should have this privilege.

Super Queue (Q)   This privilege allows the user to administer the printer queues. The user with the Q privilege can see all the print jobs in the queues, stop and start all printer queues, and delete jobs from the print queues.

Super Mail (M)   This privilege allows the user to administer the electronic mail queues. The user with the M privilege can see all messages in the mail queues. Anybody with this privilege can read everybody's mail!

User Audit (U)   This privilege allows the user to add entries to the server's audit log. The user with the U privilege can issue a command that places a note in the server's audit log. If logs are not enabled for the server, this privilege is meaningless; therefore, ensure that logging is turned on. You might want to allow ordinary users to mark the server's log files. For example, if you want the operator to add an explanatory note at the start and end of a system backup.

System Manager (S) This privilege allows the user to issue the NET RUN and NET SHUTDOWN commands. Only the network administrator should have this privilege because it allows the user to execute remote commands and close down the network servers.

The combination of privileges provides an override to all network resource access controls. All these privileges should be set for the system administrator account. With all privileges, the administrator can configure and maintain the network properly. Having said that, I also caution you about providing these privileges to more than one account. Users with the A privilege can read any file or message as well as make changes to those files or messages.

Password LANtastic allows the following password restrictions to be put on a user's account:

Existence of passwords Users either need to enter a password or they do not. If the user is set up with a password, then the user must provide the correct password to use the network.

Minimum password length The minimum length of a password is set at five; you can set the maximum length to eight for users. Passwords should be at least six characters in length to provide good security.

Periodic password changes You can specify that the user must change the password regularly. LANtastic displays a warning message advising the user of password expiration. Users can use the NET utility to change their passwords.

Table 8-2 provides a summary of LANtastic password features.

**Table 8-2
LANtastic password summary**

Feature	Yes / No
Force password use	Yes
Allow users to change passwords	Yes
Require password on next logon	No
Set password length	Yes
Expire password	No
Allow logon grace period	No
Force periodic password changes	Yes
Prevent password repetition	No
Set minimum password age	No

Directories and files LANtastic uses the DOS file system. Its file resources are either a single file or a collection of files and directories. No practical limit exists to the number of shared files you can have on your network; these files can exist on any disk partition on any server on the network. Any server can offer access to its disk file resources to any machine on the network. These files, and the underlying disk partitioning structure, are those supported by DOS. Each resource identifies a new root directory on the referenced disk partition. You can specify files below that point in the directory tree by using a DOS path name, similar to specifying a path name of a file on your local disk.

You can protect every shared file by an ACL that specifies the type of access allowed for every user on the network. The list of users and their access privileges is literally attached to the shared resource. ACLs apply to each type of shared resource: files, printers, and mail queues. The ACL defines the type of access allowed to the resource for each network user. For example, an ACL on a file determines whether a user can read it, write to it, or load and execute it as an application program. If the shared resource is a directory, the same access controls apply to all files and subdirectories within the directory. When LANtastic receives a request for access, it begins a search at the top of the list. The search ends as soon as it can determine whether to allow or deny access.

Access to shared resources is controlled by restricting access to the three different network resources: shared files, shared printers, and mail queues. Access control allows you to specify exactly who gets what resource and under what conditions. Twelve access types are used by LANtastic for protecting network resources:

Read (R)   Allows a user to view the contents of a file, read mail messages in the mail queue, and examine the contents of files in the print queue.

Write (W)   Allows a user to change the contents of a file, send messages using that mail resource queue, and print using that printer.

Create file (C)   Allows a user to create new files within the directory identified by the shared resource, send messages via this mail queue, and create a file in the printer spool area. The Create File access differs from Write access because Write allows a user to change the contents of existing files.

Make directory (M)   Allows a user to create a subdirectory within the specified directory.

Lookup (L)   Allows a user to list the contents of directories within a specified directory, examine the list of held mail messages for a mail queue and examine the list of files held in the printer spool area.

Delete file (D)	Allows a user to delete existing files, mail messages from a queue, or jobs from the print queue.
Delete directory (K)	Allows a user to delete a subdirectory.
Rename file (R)	Allows a user to rename existing files.
Execute file (E)	Allows a user to execute the print spooler program or a program held as an executable or batch file within a specified directory
Attribute (A)	Allows a user to issue ATTRIB or disallow the use of this command.
Indirect (I)	Allows a user to create indirect files within a specified directory. Indirect files have no content, but are pointers to another file. Indirect files are also known as an alias.
Physical (P)	Allows a user to access the shared file resource directly, that is, a user can write directly to a diskette drive without the LANtastic server's control. Granting this privilege can severely degrade the system.

The abbreviations of the access privileges are shown in parentheses next to the name. These options allow the network administrator to adapt security mechanisms to the needs of the organization, tailoring security for each user and workgroup. The ACL for a resource allows you to either grant or deny any of the twelve access privileges for the resource. Again, the network administrator can provide more or less security based on the data and the user. Again, the network administrator must understand the value of the data and the organization's access policy to provide proper access. The network administrator then uses the NET__MGR utility to create the ACLs. Following are samples:

```
SYSOP      RWCMLDKNEAIP
DAVISP     R------L-----E-----
```

In the first example, SYSOP has all rights to the resource. Putting the specific letter of the type of access in the ACL grants the access, while a dash (–) denies the access. Therefore, the account DAVISP can read, lookup, and execute the resource. Normally, the R, L, and E rights go together because they imply an ability to read data. The R right allows the reading of data files, the L right allows the reading of directories, and the E right allows the reading of application programs for batch files.

One last word about protecting resources. LANtastic, especially the NET__MGR utility, uses a special directory, called the *network control directory*, which contains information about network configuration and all the shared resources and their ACLs. You must protect this directory from users. Because of the importance of the directory, LANtastic allows an additional password for the directory—in addition to the password for the network administrator's account. Without the second password, nobody can use the NET__MGR utility to access or change the network configuration. Naturally, once you have set a NET__MGR password, you must enter the correct password every time you use the utility. If you do not enter the correct password, the utility terminates immediately with an error message. Should you forget the password, you must restore an unprotected copy of the network control directory to the network.

Communications LANtastic Z provides remote access via dial-up. It also allows machines without slots to join the network and enables the copying of files to laptop or portable computers. LANtastic Z has the same functions as LANtastic, but it does not require network adapters. Understandably, this limits speeds between the workstation and the server.

LANtastic Z has a facility similar to NET__MGR known as Z__MGR. Z__MGR's role is to set up and use a personalized phone book and manage connections to the machine listed in the phone book. On the calling machine, use Z__MGR to list every server you intend to call. Likewise, set up a phone list of machines that call in to prevent the server from calling out. It is important to remember not to use a " * " in the phone list for the server; otherwise, any machine can call the server.

Artisoft's Network Eye is a network management product designed to work on any NetBIOS LAN. When run on LANtastic, it allows the network administrator to control a remote network host. This feature allows you to run diagnostic programs on the remote or reboot the remote host.

Artisoft is provided with a remote boot feature. Remote booting allows a machine to load DOS and the network software from another machine onto the network, as long as the workstation you want to boot has the appropriate Artisoft ROM chip installed on its network adapter. Remote booting allows you to use diskless workstations and thus provide better control over remote users.

Even though a single microcomputer can have more than one network adapter, no bridging mechanism presently exists for LANtastic. Thus, a machine that has an Ethernet and a 2-Mbps adapter installed cannot bridge the two networks; the user connected to the Ethernet network cannot access resources located on the network servers connected to the Mbps network. Users on both networks can, however, share files located on the shared host.

Security logging LANtastic supports audit trails. You can record all network logons as well as logouts and any logon attempts. LANtastic enters all audit trail entries in a file called SYSTEM.NET\LOGS. This file is found in the LANtastic network control directory of C:\LANTASTI.NET (default). The LOGS file is a plain text file that can be used with NET__MGR or any text editor. Because you can use a text editor with LOGS, you can manipulate the data using spreadsheet or database software.

The administrator decides whether logging is kept for all accesses, failures only, or not at all. Several good reasons exist for recording events. First, you can record attempts to access network resources where the user has no rights, that is, access-denied events. The access denial occurs when a user did not have the necessary privileges to use the resource. You also can monitor network usage by reviewing the logs. This information helps the system administrator decide whether a printer should be moved to another network to balance the workload. Finally, you can use the log to implement a network accounting system. The audit log holds enough information for developing an accounting management system to determine resource use by users. Table 8-3 lists network events, their identifying prefix, and reason for recording them in the LOGS file.

Table 8-3
LANtastic audit log entries

Identifier	Event	Reason
*	Server up	Enabling the server up field causes the server to record two events: the date and time the server starts, and the date and time it shuts down.
!	Server down	Enabling the server down field causes the server to record two events: the date and time the server starts, and the date and time it shuts down.
I	Logins	Enabling the logins field causes the recording of each login to the server.
O	Logouts	Enabling the logouts field causes the recording of each logout to the server.
Q	Queuing	Enabling the queuing field causes the recording of an audit log entry whenever a print job or mail message is added to a server queue.
S	Printing	Enabling the printing field causes the recording of an audit log entry when the server has finished printing a print job.
U	User entry	Enabling the user entry field allows the recording of user-generated entries in the audit trail file.
A	Access allowed	Enabling the access allowed field causes the recording of an audit record when access is given to a shared resource. You can set the auditing for any of the 12 access rights.
D	Access denied	Enabling the access denied field causes the recording of an audit record when access is denied to a shared resource. You can set the auditing for any of the 12 access rights.

The LANtastic NET utility has several security commands, described in TABLE 8-4. Because of the implications of using NET, you should determine whether all users need NET or whether they can use LANPUP, a subset of NET.

**Table 8-4
LANtastic NET security commands**

Command	Action
ATTACH	Connects logical disk drives on the workstation to all available shared resources on a server.
AUDIT	Adds an entry to the server's audit log. User must have the User Audit (U) privilege.
CHANGEPW	Allows a user to change a password.
DETACH	Disconnects all the drives that were redirected to shared file resources on a server.
DIR	Allows a user to get a directory listing for the resource.
DISABLEA	Allows a user to disable his/her account.
LOGIN	Allows a user to log in to a server.
LOGOUT	Allows a user to log out from a server.
LPT COMBINE	Combines multiple printed files into a single print file.
LPT FLUSH	Forces the completion of a print job.
LPT SEPARATE	Makes each print command produce a separate print job.
LPT TIMEOUT	Sets the job timeout period for a printer.
MAIL	Allows a user access to E-mail.
MESSAGE	Enables or disables the network message service on the user's workstation.
PRINT	Prints a file.
QUEUE HALT	Halts a print queue immediately.
QUEUE PAUSE	Pauses a print queue during a print job.
QUEUE RESTART	Restarts a stopped or paused print queue.
QUEUE SINGLE	Prints one job from the queue and halts the queue.
QUEUE START	Starts a print queue.
QUEUE STATUS	Displays the status for a print queue.
QUEUE STOP	Stops a print queue.
RUN	Allows a user to run a command on a remote server. User must have the System Manager (S) privilege.
SHOW	Displays the current network status of the workstation.

continued

SHUTDOWN	Allows a user to initiate the orderly shutdown of a network server. User must have the System Manager (S) privilege.
STREAM	Enables or disables a logical printer stream.
UNLINK	Breaks the connection with a server after a remote boot operation.
UNUSE	Breaks a network resource connection.
USE	Establishes a network resource connection.

NetWare security

Novell NetWare software was the first true file-server system available for PC LANs. Accordingly, Novell has a very large share of the LAN market. Originally, NetWare ran on proprietary file servers and network interfaces. NetWare now runs on most PCs, including any IBM XT, AT, PS/2, or compatible microcomputer. NetWare will work with most network interfaces including ARCnet, Ethernet, and Token Ring. In addition, NetWare supports DOS, OS/2, and Macintosh workstations. (Operating system support is discussed in more detail under operating systems software.)

In NetWare, the security facility is implemented as a small special-purpose database called the Bindery. Every server has its own Bindery for administering the security of local resources, services, and accounts. The Bindery and other parts of NetWare work together to provide the basis for the security options. Depending on the version of NetWare, the Bindery is implemented in the SYS:SYSTEM directory as one of the following files, which are not available to users and are nonshareable, meaning that the operating system keeps them locked and constantly open.

- NET$BIND.SYS (NetWare 2.x)
- NET$BVAL.SYS (NetWare 2.x)
- NET$OBJ.SYS (NetWare 3.x)
- NET$PROP.SYS (NetWare 3.x)
- NET$VAL.SYS (NetWare 3.x)

Bindery objects are the actual users, groups, and other named resources. Each object has a name, type, identification number, static/dynamic flag, and security byte. The identification number uniquely identifies one object from another. It is not easy to remember identification numbers, so objects are also assigned names. The object type specifies what the object is. Some common object types are *user*, *group*, and *print queue*, which are known as static objects because they must be physically removed. Dynamic objects include objects added or deleted without any user intervention, such as file servers tracked by the internal routing mechanism. The object security byte has two parts. The high-order nibble controls Write, and the low-order nibble controls Read. A nibble is 4 bits, or half a byte.

The Bindery's security mechanism allows access to its functions. The five levels of Bindery security are:

Anyone — Any program, including a NetWare shell, can access the Bindery information regardless of who is logged on to the server. For example, you could run SLIST without being logged on to the server because you can see the SYS:LOGIN directory.

Logged — A program can access the Bindery information only if the user running the program is logged on to the file server.

Object — Only the object itself can access its Bindery information. For example, during logon, the LOGIN program reads the account restrictions in the LOGIN_CONTROL property. The LOGIN program cannot read anyone else's account information because the property's read security is set to Object.

Supervisor — Only the supervisor or equivalent can access the Bindery information. For example, only a supervisor can set Intruder Detection and Account Lockout parameters.

NetWare — Only the operating system can access the Bindery information. For example, the operating system is the only one that can read or write the PASSWORD property.

The SYSCON and PCONSOLE programs are text editors for maintaining the Bindery. SYSCON is primarily for maintaining users and groups, while PCONSOLE is primarily for printing-related Bindery objects, such as print servers and queues.

The security of resources and services relies on various combinations of NetWare's eight rights:

Read — Allows a user to view the contents of a file, see a record in a database, and run commands in an executable file.

Write — Allows a user to change the contents of a file or a record in a database and write configuration information to an executable file.

Open — Allows a user to open a file.

Create — Allows a user to create new files or subdirectories in a directory.

Delete — Allows a user to delete existing files or subdirectories in a directory.

Parental — Allows a user to change his or her access rights to the directory and subdirectories and to control other user's rights to resources where the user is the parent.

Search — Allows a user to list the contents of a directory or subdirectory.

Modify — Allows a user to modify information, but not the contents, for a file, including the name, attributes, and last access date and time.

You must combine rights in many cases to achieve the desired effect on files within a directory. Table 8-5 shows the effect of combining rights. These options allow the network administrator to adapt security mechanisms to meet the needs of the organization, tailoring security for each user and workgroup. Thus, the network administrator can provide more or less security based on the data and the user. It is important that the network administrator understand the value of the data and the organization's access policy.

**Table 8-5
NetWare rights combinations**

Activity	Rights
List files in a directory	Search
Read file	Open + read
Write to file	Open + read + write
Create file/subdirectory	Create
Delete file/subdirectory	Delete
Rename file/subdirectory/directory	Modify
Modify file attributes	Modify
Alter extended information of subdirectory	Parental + modify
Alter extended information of directory	Supervisor
Set directory attributes	Modify
Assign trustee rights in subdirectory/directory	Parental
Modify maximum rights mask of subdirectory/directory	Parental

Account NetWare provides high levels of security and access control. File server access is controlled by a user name and passcode. The system keeps a security profile of every user and only allows access to directories at security levels assigned by the system supervisor. NetWare provides status that the administrator can give to different users as follows:

Supervisor — This is a user name with special rights. The purpose of the supervisor account is to manage accounts on the file server. The supervisor sets up the security system and creates users and groups. Because of its special rights, the supervisor has ALL rights on the system and can read or write to any directory, file, or data.

Security equivalence — Users assigned security equivalence are given rights equal to that of another user. In addition, users who belong to a User Group account get the rights of the User Group.

Console operator	Users assigned console operator status can monitor and control file access through FCONSOLE.
Queue operator	Users assigned queue operator status can edit print queue files, delete any file from the print queue, modify the queue's status, and change the priority of jobs in the print queue.
Network user	Users who are assigned access rights by the network Supervisor or security equivalent.

To log on to a NetWare file server, a person must correctly enter a valid account (user name) and its corresponding password. If the person enters either incorrectly, access is denied.

NetWare provides for workgroup management, and uses three types of users to facilitate this concept: supervisor, workgroup manager, and account manager. The supervisor is omnipotent and can access anything. Workgroup managers are omnipotent within their sphere of influence; that is, the supervisor delegates some account management responsibilities to the manager. In turn, workgroup managers can delegate responsibilities downward to account managers. It is important to note that workgroup managers cannot give rights to account managers or users not already possessed by the workgroup managers. Account managers can control accounts assigned to them. The supervisor or workgroup manager can create user accounts using the following programs:

- SYSCON—creates and deletes accounts and changes passwords.
- MAKEUSER—creates and deletes more than one account using scripts.
- USERDEF—similar to MAKEUSER, but allows the administrator to create print job configurations.
- NWSETUP—sets up a NetWare file server.

When the system is installed, NetWare automatically creates the users supervisor and guest and the User Group Everyone. A User Group account provides a single identity for a collection of users who have a common bond. Users can belong to more than one group and any number of user accounts can belong to the group. A group cannot belong to another User Group account. New users are automatically created as a member of the group Everyone. When you want everybody to have access to software or data, then you grant access to the group Everyone. Never delete the group Everyone!

You cannot delete the supervisor account. As mentioned, the supervisor has rights to all directories and all files within those directories. The supervisor account can perform the following:

- Create and delete user and group accounts.
- Create and delete workgroup managers.
- Create and delete print queues.
- Assign console operators.
- Create and modify the system login script.

- Set system defaults, including account restrictions and intrusion detection parameters.
- Set a password for the server.

Because of the power associated with the supervisor account, you should control its use. There are two ways to control the supervisor account. One, give the network administrator a working account to monitor network use and run applications but that does not have all the rights of the supervisor. Two, do not give the supervisor account a home directory, an application menu, or a mailbox, so that the supervisor must log off to send mail and run jobs as a user.

Originally, Novell included the guest account to simplify printing to print queues on other file servers using NPRINT and CAPTURE. The guest account has its own mailbox and is security-equivalent to the group Everyone. Therefore, it also has rights to the SYS:PUBLIC and SYS:MAIL directories. The user name *guest* can and should be restricted. Unless you have a verifiable need for this account, you might want to delete guest using the SYSCON program because guest is the first account unauthorized users try when attempting to access your system. If you do not want to remove the guest account, you can delete it from the group Everyone. However, should you want guests to print, you must add guest as a queue user to the print queues using PCONSOLE. This program also can add a password to a print server account. When the printer is started, NetWare will prompt you for the password to establish a connection with the file server. Only the supervisor can add a print server account to the Bindery and assign the print server account a password.

NetWare allows the following logon-related restrictions to be put on a user's account:

Account disable	The ability to temporarily suspend a user's account without deleting it. This feature is useful when you have determined an intruder is trying to use the account.
Expiration date	Provides the ability to set an expiration date on any user's account. You can use this feature when you have consultants working for a specified period of time. The default is no expiration.
Create home directory for user	When a user is added, the administrator can assign a home directory with access rights to keep the user's files safe from access by others.
Limit concurrent connections	Gives the ability to limit the number of sessions a user can have at once, that is, you can prevent a user from logging on more than once. You can use this feature to limit account sharing. Because only one user can log on at any time, users cannot simultaneously share an account. The default is two concurrent connections.

Limit time and station connections — The ability to restrict the hours of day a user can access the network. For instance, you can set the hours from 9:00 AM to 5:00 PM and users can only use the network between these hours. You can limit the days of the week a user can log on. For example, you can prevent users from accessing the network on Sunday or during system backup. In addition, you can restrict the user to specific workstations on the network to ensure the network administrator uses secured workstations only.

Group trustee rights limit the use of programs and files on the network to a subset of users, such as payroll employees. You can limit access to employee payroll records by group trustee assignments by defining a group called Payroll and attaching all the payroll clerks. These clerks then all have the rights associated with the Payroll group.

Password NetWare allows the following password restrictions to be put on a user's account:

Existence of passwords — Users either enter a password or they do not (default is yes). All users (including the guest account) should have passwords assigned.

Minimum password length — You can set the minimum length of passwords for users. The default is five characters, but, as already discussed, passwords should be at least six characters in length to provide good security.

User password changes — You can decide whether passwords are administered centrally or distributed. In a distributed environment, users can set their own passwords.

Periodic password changes — You also can decide how long passwords exist before they expire (using Force Periodic Password Changes). Typically, network users should change their passwords every 30 to 60 days, depending on their authorities. The more authorities an account has, the shorter the period should be. The default is 40 days between forced password changes.

Password repetition — You can prevent users from reusing passwords by tracking the last eight passwords using the Require Unique Passwords option. Some users alternate between two or three easily remembered passwords, a practice that compromises security. The default is to require unique passwords. (For those of you who think you can defeat this rule by writing a script that changes the password nine times, you should note that NetWare only moves one password to the Bindery each day. Because the Bindery is where the eight

	previous passwords are kept, you must keep a new password for at least one day.)
Logon grace period	You can set the number of times a person can use an old password after expiration before changing it. The default is one grace login. Allowing an unlimited number of grace logons defeats the purpose of forcing password changes.
Password expiration date	You can invalidate passwords on a specific date.

Table 8-6 provides a summary of NetWare password features. These password features are fairly rich, matching those provided by mainframe access control packages. Note that passcodes on NetWare file servers can be encrypted, allowing a user to have the same logon name and passcode on different servers (with different supervisors) without compromising security.

Table 8-6
NetWare password summary

Feature	Yes / No
Force password use	Yes
Allow users to change passwords	Yes
Require password on next logon	Yes
Set password length	Yes
Expire password	Yes
Allow logon grace period	Yes
Force periodic password changes	Yes
Prevent password repetition	Yes
Set minimum password age	No

Directory At the user level, you provide access to a directory by assigning users or groups a combination of rights to that directory. These are *trustee rights*, because you implicitly make the users trustees over the files in the directory. When deciding the rights to assign, consider the files within the directory and the authorities users need. For example, in a directory containing executable files, users need only the Open, Read, and Search rights. For directories with data files, users probably need at least the Open, Read, Write, Create, and Search rights.

Remember that trustee rights flow down to any subdirectories of the directory where you originally assigned the rights, unless they are redefined at a lower level. Because of the flow-down effect, never grant trustee rights at the volume level, since everything on the volume would then have the same rights. This rule is especially true for the system volume. Mail directories reside on the system volume, for example, and when you grant access at the volume level, users have sufficient rights to read other user's mail!

The Maximum Rights Mask option can restrict the rights any user has in a given directory. The mask supersedes any trustee rights assigned to users (except for the supervisor). By default, all rights are available in a directory.

Later versions of NetWare allow the assignment of various attributes (using the FLAGDIR command-line utility) to a directory. These attributes include the following:

- Normal is the default attribute, indicating that no attributes have been set. Administrators can use normal to cancel any attributes previously assigned.
- Private prevents users from seeing the contents of a directory unless they have Search rights for the directory.
- Hidden prevents a directory from showing its contents in a directory listing.
- System is used to flag a system directory. A system directory does not show in a directory listing.

Never delete or rename the SYS:PUBLIC, SYS:SYSTEM, SYS:LOGIN, or SYS:MAIL directories; these are critical network operating system files and essential to the operation of the network. As such, you also should ensure these four files are adequately protected.

File In addition to directory-level security, there is file-level security that applies to even the supervisor. You can assign the following attributes (using the FLAG command) to protect files on a NetWare server:

- Read-only file attribute prevents users from writing to the file, renaming it, or deleting it, regardless of rights in the directory.
- Read-write file attribute allows users to change the contents of or rename the file.
- Shareable file attribute allows users to work simultaneously on the file.
- Nonshareable file attribute allows only one user at a time to work on the file.
- Transaction tracking system attribute allows NetWare to start tracking files flagged with this attribute.
- Indexed/non-indexed file attribute is used for files in excess of 2 MB to keep an index of the file in memory on the server, thus providing faster access to larger files.
- Execute only file attribute allows the file to be executed or deleted, protecting the file from being copied.
- System file attribute allows only NetWare to execute these files.
- Hidden file attribute ensures files with this attribute cannot be seen in a directory search, nor can they be deleted. These files can be seen, however, with the NDIR command or by a user with the right using Filer.
- Modified file attribute indicates if the file has been changed since the last backup.

Applying controls to software **167**

The Transaction Tracking attribute is worth discussion. Because transaction control is necessary for any operating system sharing data, NetWare has it built in. The Transaction Tracking System (TTS) is part of NetWare's system fault tolerance. TTS protects the integrity of data files by controlling how files are modified. TTS also attempts to recover from system crashes and data errors by restoring affected files to their original state before the error.

Speaking of system fault tolerance, Novell provides backup and fault tolerant features to improve the availability of the network. In 1985, Novell announced systems fault tolerant (SFT) NetWare. Novell offers three levels of fault tolerance with SFT NetWare. Level 1 is available with Advanced Level NetWare and NetWare ELS 2.0. Level 2 is available with SFT NetWare. Level 3 is available in NetWare 386.

Level 1 NetWare provides a relatively low level of fault tolerance, focusing on disk fix functions rather than data mirroring. Level 1 systems are more concerned with ensuring data remains uncorrupted than with keeping the system running continuously. While Level 1 does nothing to ensure the system will continue to run in the event of a disk failure, it does protect the data.

Level 2 includes mirroring, duplexing, and transaction tracking. The TTS available with Level 2 allows any application to define a series of operations as a transaction, which is an advantage for transaction-oriented database management systems. *Transactions* are clusters of data objects and read/write instructions grouped together by the application. Every transaction consists of a beginning and ending point. The whole transaction, and all of its related operations, must be completed to be written to the disk. If services are interrupted for any reason, and the transaction has not been completed, the transaction is entirely abandoned, and the database is returned to where it was last known to be consistent. When TTS is available, NetWare uses it to update the Bindery.

TTS operation is simple. It notes the beginning of every transaction and records the progress of the transaction. Before TTS allows a process to write data to the target file, TTS reads the existing data from the target file at the start of the impending write. After reading the existing data, TTS writes the data to the TTS log file. Upon completion of the write to the log file, TTS allows the process to write data to the target file. After successfully writing data to the target file, a process can end a transaction. If the transaction progressed normally, TTS erases the data from the log file and forgets about the transaction. Should the transaction not progress normally, however, TTS restores the data from the log file. Ideally, NetWare does this immediately; however, in the event of a fatal error, TTS restores the data file to its pretransaction state when the system is brought up.

Level 3 includes the features of Level 1 as well as 2, plus mirrored servers. All data written to one server can be duplicated on a second server. The servers are completely synchronized and communicate with each other. One server is designated as the primary, and if it fails to respond, the mirrored, or secondary, server assumes the first is down and takes over. When the primary is repaired, the servers are resynchronized and the secondary server backs off to allow the primary to take over again. Level 3 fault tolerance is designed for mission-critical applications and environments.

Security utility: detecting wormholes and other security exposures   NetWare provides a security facility located in the SYS:SYSTEM directory. The Security utility is most useful as a supervisor command. Briefly, the utility checks for any potential breaches in security. It prints details according to user to the screen, file, or printer, including the existence of login scripts, grace login status, password changes, password length, existence of passwords, and rights in root directories of volumes. The utility checks for the following deficiencies:

- Accounts with no passwords assigned. All users should have a password; otherwise, anyone can log on as the user.
- Accounts with insecure passwords, such as accounts equal to password, passwords less than five characters, accounts that are not required to change passwords at least every 60 days, accounts with an unlimited number of grace logons, and users who do not require unique passwords.
- Accounts with security equivalence of supervisor that have access to everything on the system.
- Users with directory rights at the volume level. Noting who has volume directory rights is important because security rights flow down, and anyone with volume rights has the same rights to every directory and file in the volume. Anyone with Parental rights in a root directory can grant anybody, including themselves, all rights to the volume.
- Accounts without a logon script. If a user does not have a logon script, it is possible for another user to create a "Trojan Horse" logon script for the user.
- Accounts with excessive rights in certain directories, such as, the system directory. For example, the utility points out any users possessing rights greater than Create or Write in a user's mail directory.

Table 8-7 provides a list of NetWare security commands. In addition to those commands, NetWare provides an optional intruder detection and lockout function. The supervisor can enable intruder detection using SYSCON. Intruder detection is set for incorrect login attempts; when a specified number of incorrect logon attempts are made with a given user name, the user account is flagged. You also can set the Account Lockout option, which locks any account where an intruder is detected. You can specify the time that must then pass before the account is unlocked.

NetWare, like LANtastic, also supports diskless workstations. When the workstation boots, it loads DOS from a boot file located on the server disk. To accomplish this boot, a Remote Reset or Boot PROM chip is usually installed on the network interface card in the diskless workstation. Unfortunately,

Table 8-7
NetWare security commands

Command	Action
ALLOW	Sets the inherited rights mask.
CAPTURE	Redirects LPT ports to a print queue.
DOSGEN	Creates a boot file for use by diskless workstations.
FLAG	Sets file attributes.
FLAGDIR	Sets directory attributes.
GRANT	Gives trustee rights to users and groups.
MAP	Assigns DOS drives to directories.
NPRINT	Spools a file to print queue.
PURGE	Deletes permanently erased files.
REMOVE	Removes a user or group as a trustee of a file or directory.
REVOKE	Takes away rights from a trustee.
RIGHTS	Reports on effective rights in a directory.
SECURITY	Reports on possible security problems.
TLIST	Lists trustees for a directory.

diskless workstations are useless when the server fails. If downed file servers is a serious concern, you might want a backup file server.

One last word about NetWare: it offers commands that can be issued from the file server known as console commands. Examples of NetWare console commands are ENABLE LOGIN, MONITOR, DISK, CLEAR STATION, and DOWN. These last two commands are potentially dangerous if improperly used. Any time a user is disconnected or the server goes down unexpectedly, data can be lost. Because of these powerful console commands, NetWare 3.x provides server password protection using a NetWare loadable module (NLM) program called MONITOR. This utility offers the following useful options for the performance of the network:

- Connection information.
- Disk information.
- File open and lock activity.
- LAN information.
- Lock file server console.
- Resource utilization.
- System module information.

OS/2 LAN Server security

OS/2 LAN Server runs on any IBM PS/2 or compatible microcomputer. The OS/2 LAN Server works with Token Ring network interfaces.

OS/2 provides a default userid for the security administrator. The security administrator's default userid USERID uses the User Account Subsystem

(UAS) to update the domain control database. Administrators can then perform the following functions:

- Add, delete, and change userids and passwords.
- Control groups and user membership in those groups.
- Define, view, and change user's access rights.
- Determine audit logging.

The security of resources and services rely on various combinations of LAN Server's eight rights, which are described as follows:

None	No access allowed.
Execute	Allows the owner or administrator to restrict copying of one file and to control the number of users sharing a common program.
Read	Allows a user to view the contents of a file, see a record in a database, and run commands in an executable file.
Write.	Allows a user to change the contents of a file or a record in a database and write configuration information to an executable file.
Create	Allows a user to create new files or subdirectories in a directory.
Delete	Allows a user to delete existing files or subdirectories in a directory.
Attributes	Allows a user to issue ATTRIB, or disallow the use of this command.
Permissions	Allows other people PERMISSIONS authority to change an ACL for a file, directory, or domain.

You can combine rights to achieve the desired effect on files within a directory. These options allow the network administrator to adapt security mechanisms to the needs of the organization, tailoring security for each user and workgroup. Thus, the network administrator can provide more or less security, based on the data and the user. Again, the network administrator must understand the value of the data and the organization's access policy. Access is controlled by restricting subjects and objects.

Account As with NetWare, file server access is controlled by a userid and password. The system keeps a security profile of every user and only allows access to directories at security levels assigned by the system supervisor.

To log on the file server, a person must correctly enter a valid account (userid) and its corresponding password. If the person enters either incorrectly, access is denied. The administrator can, however, enable the guest account. Whenever an unknown user tries to log on, the system assigns the user to the guest group. LAN Server allows the following logon-related restrictions to be put on a user's account:

Expiration date	The ability to set an expiration date on any user's account. You can use this feature when you have consultants working for a specified period of time.
Limit concurrent connections	The ability to limit the number of sessions a user can have at once; that is, you can prevent a user from logging on more than once. You can use this feature to limit account sharing. Because only one user can log on at any time, users cannot simultaneously share an account.
Limit time and station connections	The ability to restrict the hours of day and days of the week a user can access the network. In addition, you can restrict the user to up to eight specific workstations on the network. You can use this restriction to ensure the network administrator uses secured workstations only.

Group trustee rights limit the use of programs and files on the network to a subset of users, such as payroll employees. You can limit access to employee payroll records by group trustee assignments by defining a group called Payroll and attaching all the payroll clerks. These clerks then all have the rights associated with the Payroll group.

Information about the user's last logon is available to an application programming interface (API). You can provide this information in a trophy on logon so that the user can verify that only authorized logons took place. Similarly, the number of failed logon attempts is available to an API. Using the interface, you can temporarily suspend a user's account without deleting it. This feature is useful when an intruder is trying to use the account. The system does not force users to reboot after three failed logon attempts. It does delay each logon for several seconds as a deterrent, however.

Password LAN Server allows the following password restrictions to be put on a user's account:

Existence of passwords	Users either enter a password or they do not. All users (including the guest account) should have passwords assigned.
Minimum password length	The minimum length is set at five characters and can be set to the maximum length of eight. Passwords should be at least six characters in length to provide good security.
User password changes	You can decide whether passwords are administered centrally or distributed. In a distributed environment, users can set their own passwords. You can prevent users from changing their passwords through an API.
Periodic password changes	You also can decide how long passwords can exist before they expire. As already stated, network users should change their passwords every 30 to 60 days, depending on their authorities.

Password repetition   You can prevent users from reusing passwords by tracking the last eight passwords.

Password age   You can specify the minimum age of passwords. This facility prevents users from rapidly changing passwords to keep their existing password.

First use expiration date   You can immediately expire a password so the user must change it on first use.

Password expiration date   You can invalidate passwords on a specific date.

Table 8-8 provides a summary of OS/2 LAN Manager password features. These password features are fairly rich, matching those provided by NetWare and mainframe access control packages.

Table 8-8
OS/2 LAN Server password summary

Feature	Yes / No
Force password use	Yes
Allow users to change passwords	Yes
Require password on next logon	Yes
Set password length	Yes
Expire password	Yes
Allow logon grace period	No
Force periodic password changes	Yes
Prevent password repetition	Yes
Set minimum password age	Yes

Passwords are one-way encrypted on a global basis. The system also uses different session keys during logon, preventing unauthorized users from masquerading as authorized users. In addition, the system encrypts stored passwords, preventing users from copying the password database and deriving legitimate password/userid combinations. OS/2 LAN Server 3.0 has a utility to change passwords across domains. Examples of domains are midrange IBM systems and LAN segments.

Object control   Administrators control access to objects by ACLs, which are a bit map of allowable accesses. Discrete resources, such as files, print queues, and OS/2 objects, are protected. OS/2 objects include serial ports and named pipes in the UNIX environment. Generic resources, such as files in a directory or domains, are also protected.

Directory   At the user level, you provide access to a directory by assigning users or groups a combination of rights to that directory. These are trustee rights, because you implicitly make the users trustees over the files in the directory. When deciding the rights to assign, consider the files within the directory and the authorities users need. For example, in a directory containing executable files, users need only Read and Execute rights. For directories with data files, users most likely need at least Read, Write and Create rights. Remember that trustee rights flow down to any subdirectories of the directory where you originally assigned the rights, unless redefined at a lower level. Because of the flow-down effect, never grant trustee rights at the volume level, because everything on the volume would have the same rights. This rule is especially true for the system volume.

File   There is no universal access concept where all users have access to the file. However, the same access is accomplished by creating a group called   Users. You can then add everybody to the User group and give the group access to files.

OS/2 LAN Server 3.0 also provides peer services, or ACLs on workstations, to protect the workstation's hard disk. Peer services were discussed under AppleShare and LANtastic, so refer back to those sections if necessary.

Security logging   Rich logging features are available with the OS/2 LAN Server. Each server does its own logging, so different rules could exist for different domains. The administrator can turn logging on or off. Records are logged for logons, resources accessed, logoffs, and changes to access lists. The administrator decides whether logging is kept for all accesses, failures, or not at all.

In addition, the system provides event alert notification. For example, the system can notify the administrator of the number of log on failures per minute or the number of repeated access failures per minute.

VINES security

A Banyan VINES network has several components, usually computers and peripherals, connected to at least one VINES server. A VINES server is any computer running VIrtual NEtworking System (VINES) software. Figure 8-2 illustrates the VINES server components.

VINES software has two components: system software running on the server and network software running on a PC. The system software consists of programs for sharing printers and disks attached to the network. The server provides services to users. These services are programs that run on a VINES server and perform functions for users. Resource sharing services available are as follows:

File services	Allows users to share information by using the full-function, multiuser file system on server disks.
Print services	Allows users to share printers connected to servers by providing print queues.
NetBIOS services	Allows users to run application programs requiring the NetBIOS interface. A NetBIOS service consists of locally

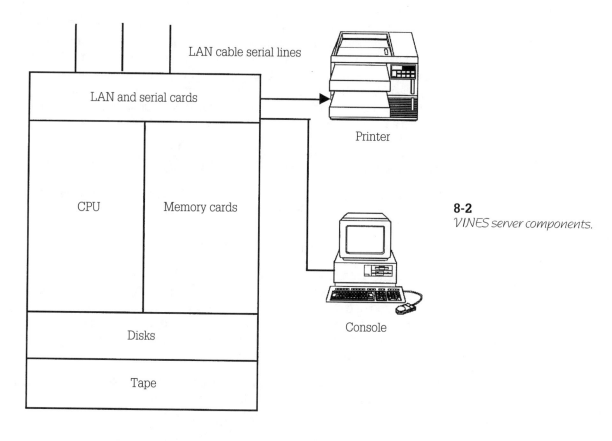

8-2 VINES server components.

	resident NetBIOS emulation software and a service on the VINES server.
Semaphore services	Allows users to share files requiring semaphore services. PC-resident semaphore software works with the semaphore service on the server to provide synchronization and record-locking functions for application programs that call for them.
Mail services	Allows users to have a mailbox and to receive mail routed to them.

Other optional services also exist, including asynchronous terminal emulation, 3270/SNA, 3270/BSC, and network management services. Each service has two parts: service software running on the server and corresponding client software running on the PC. To access a service, the user runs the client program locally. In a VINES network, users gain access to the server when their StreetTalk names are added to the AdminList. Banyan uses a distributed database called *StreetTalk* to identify all users and resources on the network through the following naming convention:

Item@Group@Organization

AdminLists control system and security administration functions. They are special StreetTalk lists that contain individual names or lists of names of individuals who can modify the StreetTalk catalog and manage specific parts of the network. Whenever a new group is created, VINES automatically creates an AdminList for the group. The security administrator manages AdminLists like any other list; however, unlike other lists, AdminLists are created automatically and cannot be manually created or deleted.

The AdminList that a user belongs to dictates the scope of an individual's administrative authority. There are three levels of Admin Lists as follows.

First, VINES automatically creates the group SERVERS@SERVERS when the first server on the network is started. Consequently, the following AdminList is created:

AdminList@SERVERS@SERVERS

On networks with more than one server, this AdminList exists only on the first server. StreetTalk names on this AdminList identify those individuals who can add and delete organizations on the network. By default, this AdminList contains a StreetTalk name entered during startup (normally the name of the administrator who installed the software). Version 4.0 no longer creates the group SERVERS@SERVERS.

Secondly, the software creates the group Server-Name@SERVERS at creation of a new server. Consequently, VINES creates the following:

AdminList@Server-Name@SERVERS

StreetTalk names on this AdminList identify individuals who can add other servers to the network or services to the server identified by the server-name.

Finally, VINES creates an AdminList when a group is created within an organization as follows:

AdminList@Group-Name@Org-Name

The StreetTalk names on this AdminList identify people who manage and add items within the group, Group-Name. VINES provides high levels of security and access control. File-server access is controlled by a StreetTalk name and passcode. The system keeps a security profile of every user and only allows access to directories at security levels assigned by the system supervisor.

In a VINES network, you become an administrator when another administrator adds your StreetTalk name to an AdminList. Two types of AdminLists exist within VINES: group administrator lists and server administrator lists. Group administrators appear on the AdminList of a specific group. They manage the resources of the group, including users, lists, nicknames, and services. Group administrators also can create subordinate groups.

Server administrators appear on the AdminList of a particular server. Like group administrators, server administrators manage the resources of the server, such as services, servers, and organizations. Contrary to other network operating systems, there is no super user or other global administrator who can override access control. You could simulate such a user if necessary by putting a user with maximum rights on every AdminList.

The VINES structure of AdminList membership controls what individuals can do based on their StreetTalk names. Within that structure, you can separate responsibilities based on your security policy.

Account   In VINES, every network user or service is an item, and each item belongs to a group. Groups consist of items with something in common and include users, services, and lists. An example is all the employees working in the Human Resources department. Each group also belongs to an organization. An organization consists of related groups and are the highest levels of names on the network. Like group names, organization names refer to structural areas of the business. A user can have one or more StreetTalk nicknames or aliases. Following are two examples of valid StreetTalk names:

>Peter T Davis@Systems@Home Office
>
>PeterFiles@Systems@Home Office

To log on to a Banyan server, a person must correctly enter a valid StreetTalk name and its corresponding password. If the person enters either incorrectly, access is denied. VINES allows the following logon-related restrictions to be put on a user's account:

Account disable	The ability to temporarily suspend a user's account without deleting it. This feature is useful when an intruder is trying to use the account.
Expiration date	The ability to set an expiration date on any user's account. You can use this feature when you have consultants working for a specific period of time.
Limit concurrent connections	The ability to limit the number of sessions a user can have at once, that is, preventing a user from logging on more than once. You can use this feature to limit account sharing. Because only one user can log on at any time, users cannot simultaneously share an account.
Limit time connections	The ability to restrict the hours of day a user can access the network. The administrator can set the system to request the user to log off if logged on at an unauthorized time, or it can force the user to log off.
Limit link and station connections	The ability to restrict the link and workstation a user can access within the network.

Applying controls to software

Password VINES allows the following password restrictions to be put on a user's account:

Existence of passwords	Users either need to enter a password or they do not. Common sense suggests all users have passwords assigned.
Forced password change	You can specify whether the system should prompt users to change their passwords at the next logon. This feature is useful to force users to change their password from the one selected by their network administrator.
Password expiration date	You can invalidate passwords on a specific date. Invalidating passwords is useful when you know the user only needs access for a short period of time, such as a consultant.
User password changes	You can decide whether passwords are administered centrally or distributed. In a distributed environment, users can set their own passwords.
Force password change on expiration	You can force the user to change the password following the expiration date.
Minimum password length	You can set the minimum length of passwords for users. Passwords should be at least six characters in length to provide good security. The maximum length for a password is 15.
Password life	You also can set the number of weeks a password can exist before expiring.

Table 8-9 provides a summary of VINES password features, and TABLE 8-10 shows the default settings for the password features. These password features are fairly rich, matching those provided by NetWare and mainframe access control packages.

Table 8-9
VINES password summary

Feature	Yes / No
Force password use	Yes
Allow users to change passwords	Yes
Require password on next logon	Yes
Set password length	Yes
Expire password	Yes
Allow logon grace period	No
Force periodic password changes	Yes
Prevent password repetition	No
Set minimum password age	Yes

**Table 8-10
VINES default security settings**

Setting	Default
Minimum password length	No minimum
Password life (in weeks)	Never expires
Force users to change password on expiration	No
Allow users to edit their profiles	Yes
Allow users to change their passwords	Yes
Maximum number of concurrent logons by a user	No maximum
Limit time of connections	No
Limit workstation connections	No

Directory A directory can be created within a particular file service by an individual who is on the AdminList for the group. At the user level, you provide access to a directory by assigning users or groups a combination of rights to that directory. For users, network volumes are assigned the letters *A* through *Z*. For example, when you set drive H: to the file volume USER FS 1@Data@CC, all operations involving drive H: use files on that volume.

VINES provides an access rights list (ARL) facility to enable or restrict file access at the directory or subdirectory level. Administrators can set access rights via the SETARL command by specifying the directory for protection. Four levels of directory access exist as follows:

Null   Restricts access to a file or subdirectory. Any user not included in the directory's ARL has null access to the directory.

Read   Allows a user to read and copy the contents of files and subdirectories and run commands in an executable file.

Control   Allows a user to control access rights for a directory or subdirectory, to create, delete, or modify new files or subdirectories in a directory and to delete directories.

Modify   Allows a user to read, create, delete, or change files or subdirectories.

These four levels are trustee rights, because you implicitly make the users trustees over the files in the directory. When deciding the rights to assign, consider the files within the directory and the authorities users need. You must remember that trustee rights flow down to any subdirectories of the directory where you originally assigned the rights, unless redefined at a lower level. Because of the flow-down effect, never grant trustee rights at the volume level, because everything on the volume would then have the same rights. This rule is especially true for the system volume. Mail directories, for example, reside on the system volume, and if you granted access at the volume level, users have sufficient rights to read other users' mail!

On the network, *drive designators* refer to network file volumes, not physical disk drives. Drive designations are set via the SETDRIVE command to refer to particular file services. A server disk can contain several file volumes. Each file volume is one VINES file service, or network drive.

File In the Banyan environment, VINES file services manage DOS file storage on server disks. Files volumes, which are large areas on the VINES server, store files. A file volume is similar to a diskette because it contains applications and data. Users can share a file volume.

The administrator sets up access rights to a file volume for a group and assigns StreetTalk names to them. When a file volume is created, it has a single area, called the root directory, that contains the files. Users can create subdirectories and assign the access rights shown above to the subdirectories. Subdirectories can contain files and other subdirectories. It is very important to group similar files within subdirectories. As you can see, granularity with VINES file control is difficult to achieve.

Under VINES, every file has a sharing attribute describing whether file locking is ignored. The sharing attribute is important for files written to by application programs, including print queues and user data files. You should only use the sharing attribute when the application cannot work without it.

Communications VINES allows an organization to interconnect two or more VINES networks via serial communication lines. The administrator decides the amount of information that these interconnected networks can exchange. On each server, there is an internetwork access list. VINES consults this list whenever a serial link between two networks is established. Lists on both the sending and the receiving network determine how the networks exchange information.

These lists must contain the names of remote servers that can connect to the server. Associated with each name is an internet password and a parameter that specifies how much information is exchanged if there is a password match. The access is as follows:

Unrestricted access	The networks act like one network. Users on one network can access information as if they were local users, subject, of course, to access rights associated with the resource. In effect, the StreetTalk names on the networks merge. Network mail flows freely between the networks.
Restricted access	The networks only exchange Network Mail. The StreetTalk names on the networks do not merge, but remain separate.
Secure	The networks exchange nothing.

When two networks connect and disagree on the exchange level, the software defaults to the lowest level specified by the two networks. You also should understand that the level of access specified for another server applies to all information that reaches that server. If the server is attached to a third server, you could receive mail from the third network if you allow mail from the second network.

Security logging The server logs information on system and service activity, including security violations. To specify the volume and types of messages recorded, the administrator uses the OPERATE command and sets the log level, which can range from 0 to 3. Increasing the log level increases the volume of messages recorded. A service always logs Level-0 messages, which include security violation events such as failed logon attempts and fatal errors.

The administrator can generate log reports using the MANAGE Server Logs function of OPERATE and view them online or in a file. VINES records logs for each service and includes basic operating system logs, operating system option logs, and user-defined logs for file and print services.

Table 8-11 summarizes the security features of the major LAN network operating systems discussed in these sections.

Operating system

Unlike mainframe computer operating systems, PC operating systems were not developed with security in mind. Most PCs, in fact, were not built to ensure adequate protection. Microsoft DOS, for example, used by AT, XT, EISA, and PS/2 hardware, provides the means to set file status to Read Only, System, and Hidden. This feature is intended to supply a small measure of discretionary access control. Apple's Macintosh operating system provides the means to lock files to prevent their deletion. The switches controlling these states are not protected, however, and can easily be changed.

Most PC operating systems cannot be trusted because certain commands do not function as reasonably expected. For example, the MS-DOS ERASE command does not erase files—it merely releases the file space and leaves the data intact. Similarly, emptying the trash on a Macintosh does not remove a document from the system—only its pointer. The latest version of Macintosh does not even remove the pointer when a document is moved to the trash; rather, the trash is just like any other folder on the system.

Vendor manuals offer a look at security weaknesses. The most comprehensive books on operating systems are the manuals accompanying the system when purchased. Most hacker software thus exploits known features of operating system software. For instance, the previously mentioned GETIT.COM, which actually exists, exploits a documented feature of DOS. Default passwords provided with software and documented in the manual are the first passwords attackers try, and users should change these defaults immediately. They

Table 8-11
LAN NOS summary

	Apple AppleShare 3.0	Artisoft LANtastic	Banyan VINES	IBM LAN Server 3.0	Novell NetWare 3.0
GENERAL					
Operating system	MAC	DOS	UNIX	MAC, OS/2	DOS, MAC, OS/2
SECURITY					
User groups	✓	✓	✓	✓	✓
Require regular password changes	✗	✓	✓	✓	✓
Restrict logon time	✗	✓	✓	✓	✓
Restrict workstation permitted	✗	✓	✓	✓	✓
Prevent concurrent connections	✗	✗[1]	✓	✓	✗[1]
Disable accounts	✓	✗	✓	✗[2]	✓
Limit subdirectory/folder to one user at a time	✓	✓	✓	✓	✓
Restrict individual files	✓	✓	✓	✓	✓
Provide distributed name service	✗	✓	✓	✓	✗
Offer security utilities and routines	✗	✗	✗	✗	✓
BACKUP					
Server-to-tape backup	✗	✓	✓	✓	✓
Disk mirroring/duplexing	✗	✗	✓	✗	✓
Fault-tolerance	✗	✗	✗	✗	✓

1 Concurrent connections can be set to 1.
2 Accounts can be disabled using the Application Programming Interface.

usually do, but many network system administrators forget or do not understand the risks. Systems people participate in active experimentation, or learn by doing, and only read the manual when faced with unsolvable problems. The attackers, therefore have, in many cases, more information than the system administrator.

Proper network management is becoming more and more crucial because of the increasingly important roles networks play. Some organizations simply cannot afford to have their networks go down, or can tolerate only short breaks in service delivery. These organizations need some method of keeping tabs on network performance, not only for detecting, but for anticipating problems.

Network management software

Most network operating systems have built-in management capabilities, but these are usually not sufficient for today's networks. Administrators are faced with combinations of different hardware and software that might, or might not, exchange the information needed for management. Again, standards are needed to ensure network management can be accomplished across different operating systems, cablings, and network topologies. The standards must bring the different technologies together to provide an overall picture of the network's status. Current standards are the Simple Network Management Protocol (SNMP) developed in 1987 and International Standards Organization (ISO)'s Common Management Information Protocol (CMIP). SNMP has gained momentum over the last few years. It represents the most widely available technology for managing large networks. Its simplicity is exactly the characteristic that has made it so successful. The ISO has listed six key areas of network management, which are shown in TABLE 8-12.

**Table 8-12
ISO network management architecture**

Accounting management	Establishes charges for the use of managed objects and identifies costs for the use of those objects.
Configuration and name management	Exercises control over, identifies, collects data from, and provides data to managed objects to assist in the continuous operation of services.
Fault management	Detects, isolates and corrects abnormal operation of the OSI environment.
Performance management	Evaluates the behavior of managed objects and the effectiveness of communication activities.
Security management	Addresses aspects of OSI security essential to the correct operation of OSI network management and protection of managed objects.

Accounting management

In many organizations, projects, cost centers, or divisions are charged for the use of network services. OSI standards call for internal accounting, if not chargeback, so that the network manager can track resource usage. Tracking usage allows the network manager to detect abusers and inefficiencies and plan for growth of the network. The network manager must specify the accounting information to be maintained and control access to the information and the accounting algorithms themselves.

Configuration & name management

Configuration and name management handles network initialization and shutdown, as well as the maintenance, addition, and update of relationships among components and the status of components themselves during network operation.

The network manager needs the capability to identify the components that compromise the network and to define the desired connectivity of the components. In addition, the network manager needs the capability to reconfigure the network when users' needs change or when problems need resolution. Reconfiguring a network often is called for in response to a performance evaluation or in support of a network upgrade, fault recovery, or security checks. The network manager must specify the configuration information to be maintained and control access to that information.

Fault management

Proper operation of a network requires care be taken to ensure systems and their components are functioning. When a fault occurs, fault management must determine the exact nature of the fault, isolate the network from the failure, reconfigure the network to minimize the impact, and repair or replace the failed component.

Users expect fast and reliable problem resolution. Most end-users understand the occasional outage, but they do not tolerate excessive downtime. Users expect immediate notification and problem correction without delay. Users also expect the network manager to track and control problems to prevent any repetition of faults. (The benefits of problem tracking were discussed earlier under software metrics.) To meet these goals, the network manager needs prompt and reliable fault detection.

Dozens of ills can afflict a LAN or bring it down completely. A LAN manager need not rely on trial and error to locate problems, however. LAN analyzers can help troubleshoot LAN bugs, monitor network traffic, analyze network protocols, capture data packets for analysis, and assist with LAN expansion and planning. These analyzers also can perform one function not necessarily planned—they can read plain text passwords.

Performance management

Performance management of a network ensures that the varied components work together. *Monitoring* and *controlling* are the two broad categories of performance management. Monitoring tracks activities on the network, while controlling enables adjustments to improve performance.

Performance management calls for associating the appropriate metrics with components and monitoring the many resources to provide information to assess network operating levels. Network managers need performance data to help them plan, manage, and maintain their systems. By collecting and analyzing this information, the network administrator becomes more adept at troubleshooting the network. This information helps the administrator recognize potential bottlenecks before they cause problems to the end-users. End-users expect their networks to be managed in such a way as to consistently provide good response time.

Security management

Generating, distributing, and storing encryption keys and passwords is part of security management. Security management also includes the collection, storage, and review of audit records and security logs, as well as the enabling and disabling of logging facilities. Users want assurance that proper security policies are in place, they are effective, and management of the security facility itself is protected.

Application software

The last category of software is broadly referred to as *application software*, which is what empowers the user. Most people are familiar with electronic mail. While electronic mail is an important tool to emerge from LAN technologies, the exchanging of messages between users is not its only implementation. Every organization's complete strategy must be based on commitment to a set of core applications, the most common being electronic mail and database systems. Both applications hinge on standards.

The wide range of applications for LANs is shown in TABLE 8-13. Most applications are complex in nature and are the subject matter of their own articles and books. For the purposes of this book, I highlight those that cause businesses security nightmares.

Electronic mail

Electronic mail is a powerful tool. The electronic mail industry has experienced tremendous growth, as shown in FIG. 8-3. Applications such as interpersonal messaging, workflow management, and electronic data interchange are furthering the interest in electronic mail in the business community. As standards for electronic mail develop and vendors deliver products that meet the standards, we rapidly reach a point where almost any computer user with a modem or LAN connection can talk with any other user.

Many organizations are developing comprehensive plans for the use of electronic mail. The Ontario Provincial Government plans to connect every ministry to every other ministry, and eventually to every one of its over 85,000 employees. Likewise, Nestlé plans a seamless, corporate electronic mail system to connect its 60,000 employees located in 80 countries. Organizations send billions of messages annually. The benefits of electronic mail include the following:

Accessibility   Users can (with obvious limitations) access their mailboxes from anywhere in the world.

**Table 8-13
LAN applications**

Data processing	Batch processing
	Data entry
	Enquiry
	File transfer
	Transaction processing
Energy management	Heating/ventilation/air conditioning
Factory automation	CAD/CAM
	Inventory control/order entry/shipping
	Process control
Fire and security	Sensors/alarms
	CCTV
Office automation	Calendaring/scheduling
	Electronic mail
	Project management
	Word processing
Telephones	Messaging systems
Television/visual arts	Off-the-air
	Video presentations

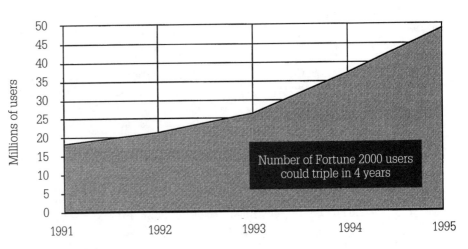

8-3
Growth of electronic mail.

Fortune 2000 and equivalent enterprises in the U.S. and Canada
(revenue > $500 million)

Data: Electronic Mail Association

Reliability	The service is quick, dependable, and perhaps more accurate than conventional mail and telephone.
Accuracy	Messages are stored more accurately and for longer periods than telephone or personal messages.
Coverage.	Messages can reach almost anyone in hours or days.
Productivity	Electronic mail reduces the need for face-to-face meetings and telephone tag.
Flexibility	Unlike telephone calls, electronic mail can be sent and retrieved at the convenience of the sender and recipient, which is especially important where time zones are involved.
Speed	Electronic mail sends information faster than any printed document or message delivery system, and almost as fast as a telephone call.

These benefits are, however, counterbalanced by drawbacks—some of which derive from the nature of the network. Figure 8-4 shows several threats to your electronic mail network. Some people equate the informality of electronic mail messages with low information sensitivity. Most people do not stop to think about the messages they are transmitting—personal, marketing, financial, and technical data. Our organizations depend on this information. Naively, most mail users believe that only the addressee can read the mail. They also assume the message is intact and has not been altered in any fashion, and, that the sender is the person who really sent the message. These are not always safe assumptions.

Neither case law nor etiquette has dealt with the ethical and legal issues of electronic mail. In 1989, Alana Shoars, a system analyst specializing in electronic mail at Epson America, Inc., confronted her boss with the suspicion he was reading employees' mail. She was later terminated for gross misconduct and insubordination. The company used as evidence information that Shoars claims her boss misinterpreted while reading her mail without permission. Shoars sued the company for wrongful dismissal and invasion of privacy.

Corporate invasions of privacy create distrust and suspicion between employees and managers. A policy should allow management to monitor mail only under strict controls that respect an employee's right to privacy. The morale of a company, and its ethos, is too precious to jeopardize in an effort to prevent electronic gossip! Corporations should have an explicit policy for electronic mail. Informing staff of the policy solves most problems beforehand and could forestall litigation.

A closer look at electronic mail helps us understand some of the risks and compensating controls. Electronic mail means different things to different people. For our purposes, electronic mail refers to the *store-and-forward* transport of electronic messages between two or more communicating

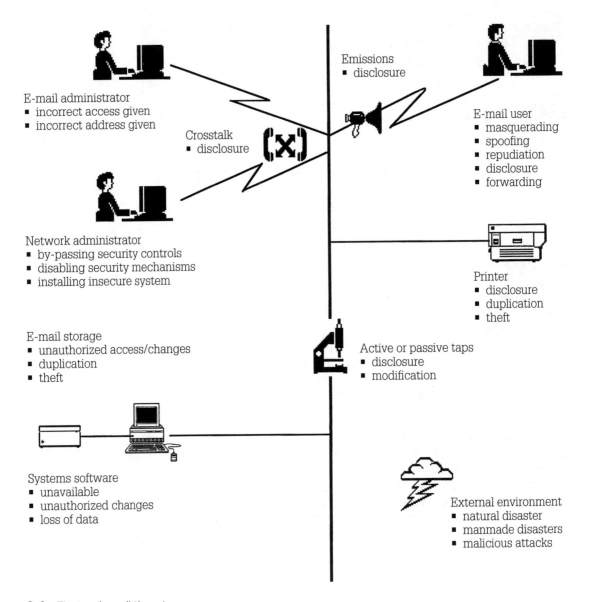

8-4 Electronic mail threats.

parties. Although some LAN databases require high-speed, constant, and immediate communications, such contact can be expensive and is not always necessary. An alternative is a store-and-forward scheme where messages are not sent until someone is ready to accept these messages. Messages could be sent when data is ready to transmit, when a certain amount of data exists to transmit, at intervals, or at any other predetermined conditions. With store-and-forward techniques, senders and recipients operate asynchronously.

Because many people use electronic mail to replace telephone communications, they fail to recognize the inherent risks in store-and-forward communications. Electronic messages are stored records of communications, whereas telephone communications are not normally stored nor recorded.

Electronic messages often consist of electronic files; that is, they can be used to transfer any type of computer-readable information. Message systems are combining the previously separate voice, facsimile, and image technologies into an integrated environment. Because of this, messages can be person-to-person, computer-to-computer, person-to-computer, or computer-to-person.

As our reliance on electronic mail and networks grows, so does the requirement to understand and address security. Electronic mail has unique security requirements. Seven distinct broad security services are defined in the CCITT X.402 *Message Handling Systems* standard and are as follows:

- Origin authentication services provide the means by which one party can validate the identity of the other party.
- Secure access management services protect the resources of the message-handling network from unauthorized access.
- Data confidentiality services ensure the contents of a message are known only to the sender and the intended recipients.
- Data integrity services protect against message and sequence modification.
- Non-repudiation services provide irrevocable proof to a third party that a message was sent by the sender or received by the recipient.
- Message security labeling services indicates the authority required to access a message.
- Security management services defines authorization and labels to the access management and labeling services.

Message content confidentiality and integrity and nonrepudiation of origin are the most critical of the services. All three can be implemented by the use of encryption. Obviously, the message contents can be scrambled so that the contents are unintelligible to anybody but the holder of the right key for decryption. Encryption also provides integrity and nonrepudiation of origin services because information encrypted can only be decrypted with the right key. If the message decrypts properly, the recipient can conclude logically that the message was generated by the indicated originator. The operation of signing or verifying electronic signatures is independent of whether the message itself is encrypted for confidentiality. A message need not be confidential to be signed. The signature also proves the origin of the message to a third party—the characteristic that qualifies an electronic signature for use as a nonrepudiation of origin service. Table 8-14 illustrates control objectives for electronic mail.

Two other problems of electronic mail are worth mentioning. Users generally can send messages to anyone on the mail network. Many a person has been

Table 8-14
Electronic mail control objectives

Control	Objectives
Message origin authentication	The recipient of a message can verify the origin of the message.
Content integrity	The recipient of a message can check whether the message was altered during transmission.
Content confidentiality	The recipient of a message is the only person who has read the message.
Message security labelling	The message is provided with a machine-readable classification to control access rights.
Message sequence integrity	The sequence of the message is preserved on receipt, and messages are neither lost nor duplicated.
Proof of delivery	Electronic acknowledgement is provided attesting to the fact the recipient received the message in readable form.
Proof of submission	Electronic confirmation is provided attesting to the fact the message was sent.
Non-repudiation of origin	The recipient of a message can verify the origin of the message and prove the origin to a third-party.
Non-repudiation of delivery	The sender of a message can verify the receipt of the message and prove the receipt to a third-party.
Non-repudiation of submission	The recipient of a message can verify the message and prove the submission to a third-party.
Message flow confidentiality	Traffic analysis of message transmission is distorted by additional security measures.

tempted to log on as someone else and send a nasty message to the boss. One partner where I worked used to send messages to another partner on behalf of a senior manager. As your connections to the outside world grow, you might want to consider the use of a filter to screen unwanted junk mail. Otherwise, you could suffer from a real information glut that you are incapable of handling.

Another interesting dilemma is the forwarding of mail. I sent a message to one of my managers regarding the work of one of his staff. He promptly forwarded my message to the individual. Now, you probably question his wisdom—I know I did—but he saw absolutely nothing wrong with what he had done. I am faced with two possible courses: do not send the message, or automatically prevent the message from being forwarded. Until proper electronic mail etiquette is developed, we must meet with these issues whenever we transmit messages.

File transfer

File transfer was one of the first applications supported on networks. Figure 8-5 shows how it works. File transfer is an extension of the file management system found on single-computer systems. Sometimes these facilities move a complete file across a network without even knowing the use for the file.

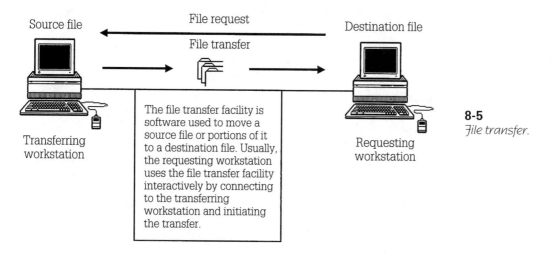

8-5
File transfer.

Typically, the online user uses the file-transfer facility interactively. Another application program could also trigger the file transfer. For example, a store could call headquarters every night and download sales data. Again, it is important to control who and what can transfer files across the network.

Database systems

LANs have extended the usefulness of database software by allowing a workgroup to access the same data concurrently. The design of such a system can change the work flow in a group, so the stakes are high. For example, centralized systems are easier for users to access all data. Standards and security are also easier to enforce on a centralized system. A more distributed system encourages people to manage the information relevant to their jobs. These systems give remote users more immediate access to the microcomputer as a dynamic tool of use to them in accomplishing work, rather than as a system for reporting work already done. So, what is a database?

A database is essentially an automated recordkeeping system. The database itself can be regarded as a kind of electronic filing cabinet, a repository for the collection of computerized records. This comparison is a rather simplistic definition, but it captures the essence of a database systems and its components. Its two components include a file management system, and an interface to the filing system, often including application development tools.

Currently, file service is the standard for retrieving data from a database. With file service, a database program running on a work station requests data from the file server. With most database files, only the requested data is provided, and that data is then locked to other users. The workstation can modify the locked records, and then update the server, at which time the record is unlocked to other users. With file service, database processing occurs at the workstation.

Workstations run the user interface software, while another machine on a network processes the database requests. This processor is the database engine, or database server. A database server can be implemented in several ways:

- A separate, secondary process on a network file server. The database runs under the network operating system.
- A value-added server process. The process performs tasks that are integrated with the file server tasks.
- Application coprocessor in the file server system. The file server has a separate processor board installed, which processes all database requests.
- Dedicated database server. The database runs on a separate personal computer.
- Background database server on a workstation. Under multitasking operating systems, the database runs as a background task.
- Application coprocessor in a workstation. The database runs on a separate board on the workstation.

Figure 8-6 illustrates a variation of a secure database management system. A serious potential problem with distributed database processing is that each of the workstations has the power to corrupt the entire database. Figure 8-7 illustrates this and other threats to your database. With database service, all database processing is handled by a single dedicated computer, resulting in less chance of file corruption.

Transaction and concurrency control are other potential database problems. *Transaction control* preserves the integrity of the database from errors when writing data to data files. It ensures the system never writes partial records to the database; the system either writes the entire record successfully or none of the record is written—original record remains untouched. Transaction control is a necessary component of a database system because it ensures the integrity of the record by ensuring its completeness. If the transaction fails, the application need not worry about where the operation failed.

Concurrency control became important when applications moved from batch processing to multiprocessing because it became possible for two users to request the same data at the same time. This concurrent request raised

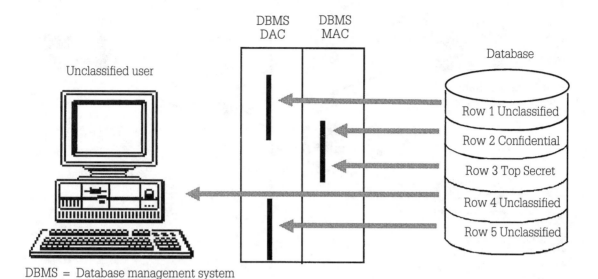

DBMS = Database management system
DAC = Discretionary access control
MAC = Mandatory access control

8-6 *Secure database management system.*

conflicts between users and created a race condition—users wanting access or update records concurrently. Concurrency, as stated previously, is achieved through locking the database or portions of it. A file lock protects an entire file, whereas a record lock protects only a portion of the file. These locking mechanisms are granted as either exclusive (other users cannot read or write to the locked entity) or shared (other users can read the entity but cannot write to it). Database applications must run on operating systems that provide these locking mechanisms as an integral component. Most database systems, however, offer some level of concurrency control independently of the operating system. Distributed databases enable you to retain central control and empower remote users and offices.

For database applications, standards issues revolve around client-server solutions, the foremost being the Structured Query Language (SQL) standard. While many database server systems have been announced, few are available for PC LANs. The new era of LANs, database servers, and distributed databases is foreign to many information systems professionals. They also see these developments as a threat to stability—in production systems and their careers.

A growing shift from host-based systems to client-server applications is occurring, as shown in FIG. 8-8. Client-server applications are forms of distributed processing. Rather than having a server responsible only for file and peripheral sharing, the server now acts as a computer that runs sophisticated network applications.

Client-server applications

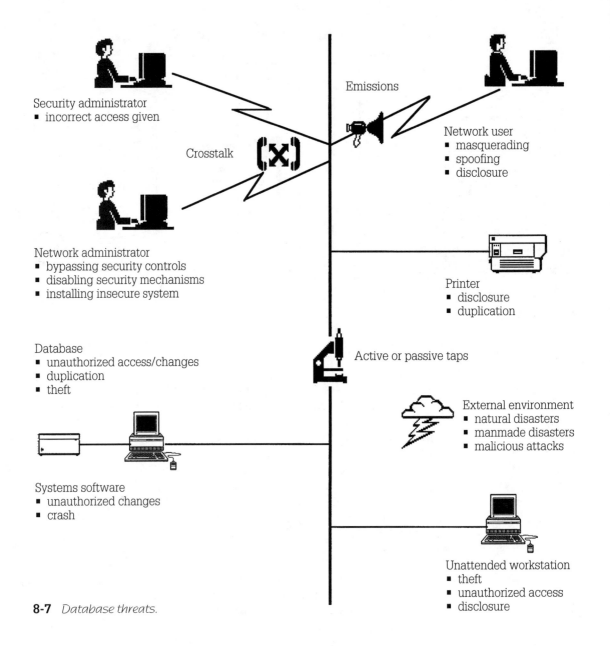

8-7 Database threats.

The client-server architecture makes possible the distribution of processing functions between the workstations and the server. The server now does data handling functions as well as common file server functions, such as returning files to the workstation.

Thus, the server is an intelligent server. It handles the customary high-level requests for data, but only returns the data needed to satisfy the request. The client-server must understand more than the raw data; it also must know

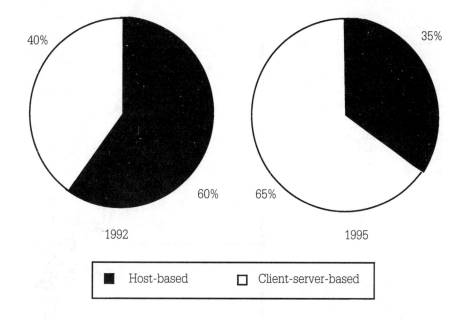

8-8
The shift from host-based to client-server applications.

how to process the high-level requests. Such a server is a database server, and the most common is the SQL server. SQL is fast becoming an industry standard for data retrieval.

Client-server computing overcomes many problems of typical client-based computing. By separating processing functions, the transmission of unnecessary data is reduced because only the requested data is sent, freeing bandwidth for use by other workstations. Because the database server's primary task is to process requests for data, it can thus be optimized for the task.

Figure 8-9 portrays a client-server application. Client-server applications combine the benefits of centralized mainframe and minicomputer database systems with the user-friendliness and user orientation of microcomputers. In fact, some software suppliers have developed a graphical query language that is icon-based and helps create SQL commands, further simplifying data requests.

The client concentrates on application processing functions, such as the user interface and reporting, while the server concentrates on data definition and handling, security, backup and recovery, concurrency, and transaction management. Client-server applications provide the following benefits:

Centralized security administration	A database server enables centralized security administration because all data is managed and accessed by the server, also simplifying data backup, concurrency, integrity, and recovery because they all can be centralized.

Applying controls to software

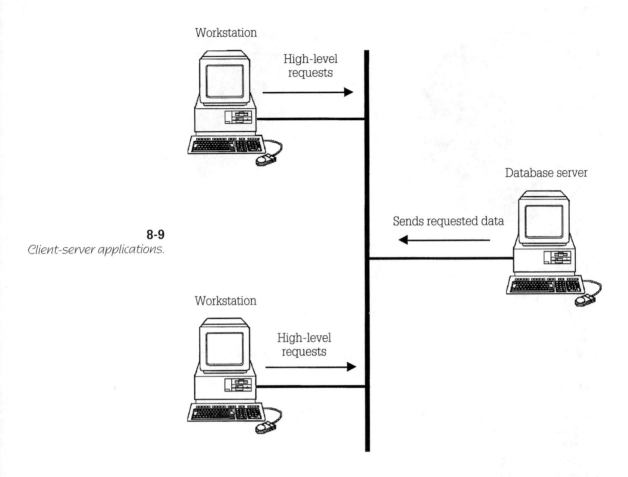

8-9 Client-server applications.

Improved performance	A database server significantly cuts traffic and, as a result, improves system performance. Because database functions are clearly allocated to different devices, each can be optimized for their tasks. For example, the client computer can concentrate on the user interface while the server can concentrate on data recovery and concurrency.
Open system	Most database servers have published interfaces for application development.
Scalability	Because the processing of application and database functions is separated, you can replace or upgrade the backend database server without touching the user's frontend. Consequently, user productivity is not affected.
Flexibility	A client-server application not only allows users to manipulate data quickly and easily, but provides flexibility in rapidly assembling information for complete decision-making.

Economy   Smaller computer platforms are less expensive. For example, the cost per instruction on a microcomputer is about 3 percent of the cost of an instruction on a mainframe.

Risks are associated with client-server applications, however. First, the technology is relatively new, so it is less stable than mainframe and minicomputer technology. There are many successful implementations, but they need uncommon effort and care. Second, it is difficult to piece together the disparate incompatible components of a system, including components from the same vendor but on different platforms. Much time is spent trying to solve these problems. There are also serious security considerations.

In any database environment, security is an important parameter. The database can provide security facilities independent from those of the operating system for restricting access to all or parts of it. Database servers control access at two levels. At the server level, the software only allows access to valid users. At the database level, the software allows the assignment of privileges to users.

The database server calls for every user to have a valid logon code and password. Moreover, every valid user code must be defined as a valid database user name for every database the user needs to access. Within the database, the user must have the necessary permission to conduct operations and access data.

Every user wanting access needs a database logon account for the server. The logon account has three components: a server logon code, an associated password, and a default database. The default database for a logon account is the database the user automatically connects to when first logging on.

The ability to perform operations on a database object and to create and drop database objects is controlled by special privileges. A *privilege* is permission to perform an operation on some object. The database administrator must grant all privileges explicitly—a user has no permissions by default. Even the owner of the database must be granted the privilege to use it. The software allows the definition of groups within the database. Privileges can be assigned collectively to groups. Every user within the group inherits the group's privileges.

In addition to the granting of permissions, the database administrator can further control security by limiting access by views and stored procedures. A *view* is a derived subset of the database, a window into the underlying data. Only data viewed through the window is available to the user. You can independently define permissions to view the underlying data. By defining the appropriate permissions for the view and revoking all access to the underlying data, you can limit a user's access.

You also can improve security through stored procedures. The user can specify explicitly legal operations on the data. For example, a stored procedure can retrieve employee information while omitting salary data. By granting users permission to execute stored procedures and denying access to underlying data, you can again control user's access.

I feel compelled to say one final thing about databases. These databases are time bombs. Users are creating little data havens. To paraphrase an old saying, "To a man with a computer, everything looks like data." Because we can store data better, we feel obliged to store that data. Likewise, we can crunch numbers better, so we feel bound to crunch numbers. Lamentably, most users cannot appreciate the value of the data or the serious implications of its disclosure. Repeatedly, I find microcomputers with sensitive personal information available to all users on a LAN. Confidentiality is important, but so is availability and integrity. Increasingly, users rely on the availability of data on the network to do their job. Unavailability of the data, therefore, adversely affects their productivity. Likewise, users depend on the spatial coherence of data to make decisions. When we remove these databases from the controlled mainframe environment, the reliability of the data becomes more suspect. Organizations must wrestle more with these problems as LANs become epidemic.

Application passwords Programs like WordPerfect, Microsoft Excel, Lotus 1-2-3, and Quattro Pro all offer password file protection to stop the casual reading of documents. On the surface, this seems like a good idea. But what happens if the person with the password dies suddenly, forgets the password, or is fired? You could be locked out of your files because of employee spite or negligence.

One vendor now sells a program that recovers the password using the encryption process available in many commonly used software packages. The program recovers documents that use the application's password scheme. This fact seems to suggest that you should not rely primarily on password schemes provided by application software. These password schemes can, however, complement other, more secure methods.

Applying controls to communications

Just as software is the brains and hardware is the brawn, cabling and communication devices are the circulatory system of a network.

Internetworking & connectivity

A LAN, like a standalone PC, can communicate with other networks. These other networks could be other LANs, or they could be Metropolitan Area Networks (MANs) and Wide Area Networks (WANs). LANs can be attached to mainframes as well. Many companies have found that attaching LANs through gateways is cheaper than using local controllers.

Consider a large LAN installation with terminal and microcomputer access to files and client-server applications distributed over several remote computers and other LANs. The LAN can provide access to long-distance voice networks through a modem server, and other data networks through routers and bridges. Providing security over the LAN is clearly complex.

Communication security guidelines

Communications security can be improved by the following:

- Restricting users from routinely using certain output devices, such as high-resolution imagesetters and slide makers.
- Subdividing the network so one workgroup cannot access another workgroup's resources, such as files and documents.
- Controlling access to special services, such as network modems, facsimile devices, and external mail services.
- Limiting dial-in access to the network.
- Controlling user privileges on shared workstations.
- Applying passwords to file, print, database, and mail servers.

An effective method for managing security involves restricting certain areas of the network. Just as certain areas of an organization are restricted, areas of the LAN must be offlimits. If one LAN application is really sensitive, you should disconnect that LAN entirely from other LAN segments. For most applications, however, a filter is all you need. You can get filtering through network software.

Network components

Networks, and network segments, are interconnected in various ways at different layers, as shown in TABLE 9-1. Traditionally, LAN interconnection devices (LIDs) are repeaters, bridges, routers, brouters, and gateways.

**Table 9-1
Network interconnections**

Interconnection device	PROTOCOLS		
	Physical layer	Data link layer	Network layer and higher
Repeater	Same	Same	Same
Bridge	Different	Same	Same
Router	Different	Different	Same
Gateway	Different	Different	Different

Understanding these network components provides insight into appropriate security countermeasures. Let's look at the more common network components.

Repeaters

The simplest LID is a repeater. Figure 9-1 shows the use of a repeater. *Repeaters* are simply devices that amplify and reshape the signals on one LAN and pass them to another, as shown in FIG. 9-2. Repeaters can also be used to extend LAN cable distances. Because most LAN architectures call for a limit on the number of repeaters placed in sequence, a limit also exists to the usefulness of repeaters in extending LANs.

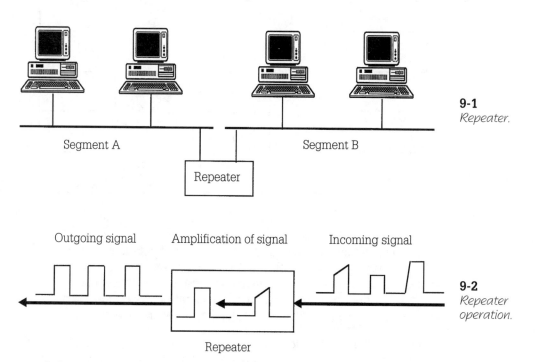

9-1 *Repeater.*

9-2 *Repeater operation.*

Because repeaters simply repeat signals and do not provide any filtering capability, all traffic on all LANs connected by one or more repeaters propagates to other LANs, which can have a negative effect on LAN performance and security. Repeaters do not, in themselves, provide any security features.

Bridges

Bridges, like repeaters, connect LANs together at the hardware level. Figure 9-3 provides an illustration of how a bridge works. While repeaters connect LANs at the lowest physical hardware level, bridges connect at the higher hardware level, the Media Access Control Level are a combination of hardware and software.

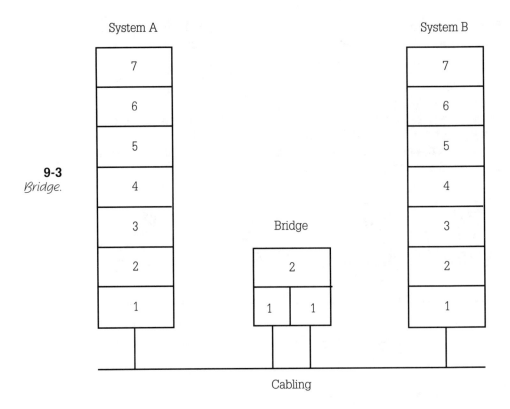

9-3 Bridge.

Bridges help overcome distance and station-count limitations and filter traffic. Bridges use routing tables to decide which traffic to forward to the devices across the bridge. Thus, local traffic stays local, while other traffic can cross the bridge. Figure 9-4 shows the operation of a bridge. Local network traffic on one LAN does not affect security on another bridged LAN.

To function properly, a bridge must know the addresses of devices to which it can forward packets. With early bridges, network administrators manually had to build a routing table to tell a bridge what addresses were on which side of the bridge. Most bridges today are learning bridges and can build

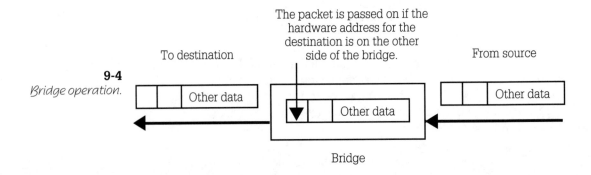

9-4 Bridge operation.

their own tables. Learning tables learn the locations of network devices that send and receive packets.

When used properly, bridges can increase network performance and security. By sectioning a large LAN into smaller ones linked together with bridges, local transmissions can be kept in the local area, and only traffic addressed to a remote LAN will cross the bridge. The establishment of multiple LANs can improve the security of communications. It is desirable to keep different types of traffic that have different security needs, such as accounting and personnel, on physically separate media. At the same time, different types of users with different levels of security need to communicate through controlled and monitored mechanisms.

Installed improperly, bridges can impair the security of LAN communications. Bridges call for special considerations when they extend LANs. Particularly, Ethernet LANs should not be connected so that data must flow across more than seven bridges. As previously mentioned, Ethernet uses CSMA/CD. Before sending a message, Ethernet listens to the line to determine whether anyone is broadcasting. If the line is quiet, the station sends the message. After sending, the station listens for a collision and resends the message if necessary. The message must reach its destination within a predetermined period of time, which is sometimes not possible over several segments. The station might not be able to detect collisions then, and data could be lost.

Routers

Routers determine paths through the network and transmit data packets. They operate at the Protocol Level, and are therefore hardware-independent. Instead of forwarding packets, routers forward the data in the packets. Routers provide more robust error recovery, better congestion control, and more segregation of network resources than bridges. Figure 9-5 illustrates how a router works. Routers are protocol specific; a router must know the protocol used for the forwarded data. Because routers operate at the Protocol Level, they can be used to link dissimilar LANs. Some routers support multiple protocols. They have the advantage of supporting connections between multiple protocols on multiple types of LAN hardware.

Figure 9-6 demonstrates router processing. Like bridges, routers only forward traffic addressed to the other side, which means that local traffic on one LAN does not affect performance and security on another. Again, like bridges, routers can be proprietary devices, or they can be software and hardware residing in general purpose computers, such as a microcomputer. Routers are useful for interconnecting similar and dissimilar LANs, as well as limiting LAN traffic.

Routers usually have filtering software for controlling cross-domain resource access. Filters are further subdivided into one-way and two-way access restriction. One-way access restricts either incoming or outgoing access.

Applying controls to communications **203**

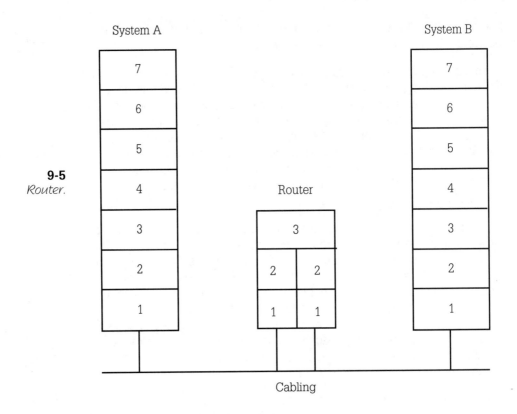

9-5 Router.

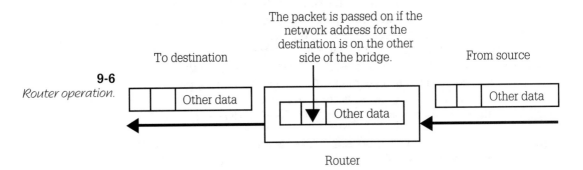

9-6 Router operation.

For example, users of one network segment cannot access any network services outside of their segment. The filter does, however, allow incoming traffic to the segment. With a two-way access filter, users from one network are restricted from accessing services in a second network, and users from the second network are restricted from accessing services in the first. A full fault tolerance router is already on the market to meet the demand for highly available networks.

A *brouter* is a hybrid router and bridge. Brouters link LANs together remotely through a variety of means. They can link at the protocol or media access level, depending on the traffic. This linkage is accomplished by software and hardware. A brouter provides all the advantages of routing over bridging where possible, but still provides connectivity using bridging where necessary. Like bridges and routers, brouters can provide additional security by isolating certain workstations or networks.

Brouters

A *gateway* is a device that connects different network architectures by performing a conversion at the application level. It maps from an application on one computer to an application that is similar in function but different in detail on another computer. The gateway itself uses all seven layers of the OSI model, plus any layers of any proprietary architectures being connected.

Gateways

There are three different types of gateways: LAN to LAN, LAN to WAN, and LAN to host computer. The called network must be capable of authenticating the caller before granting access to the network. Figure 9-7 illustrates some examples of LAN interconnectivity.

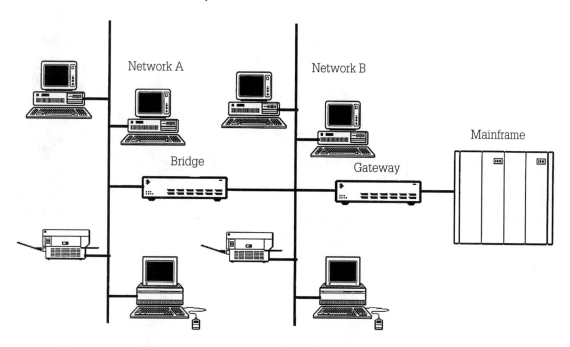

9-7 *LAN interconnectivity.*

LAN to LAN   LAN-to-LAN gateways, like routers, work at the Protocol Level. Unlike routers, gateways provide protocol conversion. Gateways allow users to route data from PCs, say on an ARCnet LAN, to a UNIX computer on Ethernet.

Applying controls to communications 205

LAN to WAN Like LAN-to-LAN gateways, LAN-to-WAN gateways provide routing and protocol conversion. The most common LAN-to-WAN gateway allows users to route data from PCs to packet-switched networks like Tymenet, Telenet, and Datapac. Most gateways for WANs are microcomputers, a wide-area communications board, communications software, and a high-speed synchronous modem. Usually, the microcomputer is dedicated to the gateway task, but some gateways can be nondedicated.

LAN to host computer A LAN-to-host computer gateway allows multiple microcomputer users on a LAN to communicate with a mainframe or minicomputer not locally connected to the LAN. There are gateways to connect LANs to an IBM mainframe, IBM midrange, Unisys, DEC, or other computer. Figure 9-8 illustrates some of the ways that LANs can interconnect to an IBM systems network architecture (SNA) network. Figure 9-9 provides a comparison of SNA and OSI network models. Usually, a host gateway needs a PC on the LAN that is dedicated to the job. This connection is still cheaper than the controllers needed for most dumb terminals.

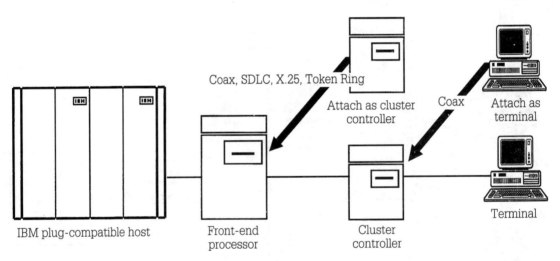

9-8 *LAN connectivity to an SNA network.*

You must consider the effect on the host when connecting LANs. For example, printing on PCs is different from printing in a mainframe environment. Traditionally, the standard network attached printer was a dot-matrix with lots of buffer space. Between the controller and the printer, there was usually enough memory. The laser printers that are attached to most LANs have limited buffer space. They also require considerable mainframe programming to use. Consequently, they are used for basic printing. Most microcomputer-attached printers are quite sophisticated. A single page of formatted text and graphics take thousands of bytes of data. The implications on network volumes could be catastrophic!

OSI	SNA
Application	Transaction services
Presentation	Presentation services
Session	Data flow control
Transport	Transmission control
Network	Path control
Data link (HDLC)	Data link control (SDLC)
Physical	Physical control

9-9
Comparison of OSI and SNA models.

The gateway computer usually contains a special communications board and runs special communications software that allows it to communicate with the host computer, as well as with other PCs on the LAN. Microcomputers that want to use the gateway must run special software to communicate with the gateway as well as terminal-emulation software to talk to the host computer. The terminal-emulation software must work so that the host computer thinks the microcomputer is one of its standard terminals.

The terminal-emulation software allows the user to store frequently used information, such as modem speed and terminal type. Additionally, you ordinarily can find all the information required to access computer systems over telephone lines, including phone numbers, user names, and passwords. These systems could include mainframe computers, minicomputers, and other microcomputers.

Many dial-up computer systems rely on passwords to restrict access. Failure to protect passwords is a serious breach of security that could lead to the unauthorized disclosure of personal or corporate information, unauthorized changes to information, or the destruction of information.

A growing menace to LAN security is backdoor dial-up, which occurs when a user installs special communications software and a modem on his or hers workstation. The software allows users to operate the workstation remotely as if they were seated at the keyboard. In this way, they can access mail or database applications from their homes, hotel rooms, or wherever. This back entrance clearly is a problem to security-conscious organizations. I suggest you search out these modems before they contribute to a breach of security. Figure 9-10 presents an example of modem operation.

Modem

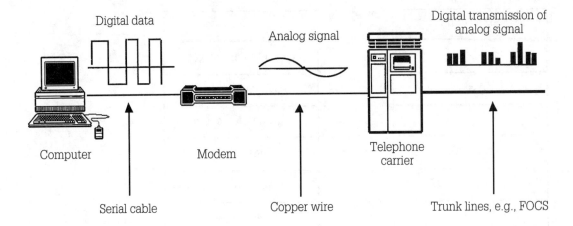

9-10 *Modem operation.*

Part four
The future

In guessing the direction of technology it is wise to ask who is in the best position to profit most.
— **Ben H. Bagdikian**

The science of today is the technology of tomorrow.
— **Edward Teller**

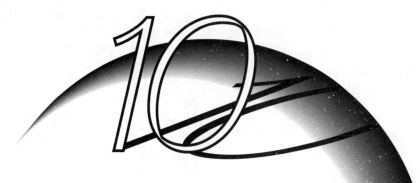

Future LAN security issues

In the first chapter, we talked about a major paradigm shift in the economy—the movement from an industrial-based society to an information-based one, as shown in FIG. 10-1. To understand the future, we must look for paradigm shifts as they occur. A *paradigm* is a set of rules describing boundaries and norms within those rules that must be followed for success.

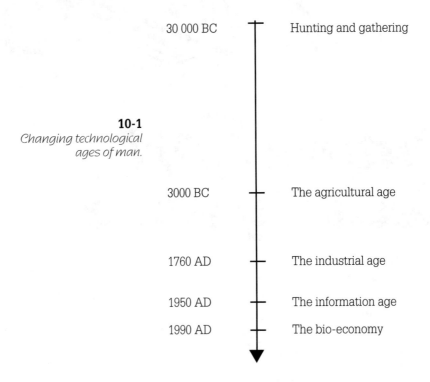

10-1
Changing technological ages of man.

A paradigm shift occurs when the rules change, thereby changing how one acts. To not understand how to act causes a state of anomie or technostress. By understanding the dramatic shifts and knowing how we are expected to act, we can better anticipate the future. A paradigm is really a framework for perception. It is how we view the world. For example, we expect gravity to control our lives and the sun to shine. Paradigms make us comfortable, allowing us to get on with our business. Paradigms do not last forever, however. Here are a few of the dramatic changes since the 1960s:

- Emergence of information as a critical resource.
- Growth of flatter, more participatory organizations.
- Widespread use of microcomputers.
- Development of LANs linking these microcomputers.
- Terrorism as an everyday activity.

We have seen quite a few changes in a relatively short time. As John Naisbitt (1982) writes at the end of *Megatrends*, "My God, what a fantastic time to be alive!" It also is a time of tremendous change, though.

During our discussion of LANs, we have touched on these paradigm shifts. In this chapter, I attempt to look at future paradigm shifts. It is important to look at paradigms because they influence our perceptions of the world. As history has shown us, we resist changing our present paradigms because we are good at using them. People who are on the outside of the existing paradigms are the ones who usually create the new paradigms because they have the least to lose by changing them.

Those who change to a successful new paradigm gain new vision and new approaches for problem-solving. James R. Beniger (1986) opens *The Control Revolution* with the following:

> One tragedy of the human condition is that each of us lives and dies with little hint of even the most profound transformations of our society and our species that play themselves out in some small part through our own existence.

Those who recognize and exploit the shift early can gain a competitive advantage. Those who do not might not survive economically the 1990s.

Many people have tried to predict the future with varying degrees of success. Nostradamus supposedly predicted world wars and the death of President Kennedy. Leonardo da Vinci predicted manned flight long before it happened. Sir Francis Bacon's predictions of scientific achievements, published in his 1627 book *New Atlantis*, have proven remarkably accurate. His vision that these inventions would lead to a scientific Utopia, however, has not. Sir Bacon predicted telephones for communicating and amplified light for traveling over great distances. I doubt that I can better those predictions, but I can make some of my own. As I do not have a crystal ball, I shall rely on educated guesses, just as do futurists John Naisbitt, Faith Popcorn, Jeremy Rifkin, and Alvin Toffler. These educated guesses come from a review of announced products as well as futurist literature. My predictions are as follows:

- The 1990s will see a tremendous growth in the use of wireless LAN technologies.
- LANs have facilitated and contributed to the growth of cooperative processing, which will continue to grow in the 1990s.
- Telecommuting will become a way of life for many workers in major urban areas during the 1990s.
- Image processing systems will proliferate on LANs in the 1990s.
- Rightsizing will continue as companies move from mainframes toward smaller systems.
- A major disaster will occur on a LAN involving mission-critical applications.

While these predictions are hardly earth-shattering or without basis, they do have serious security implications. We should look at these predictions and develop our plans now, before we are forced to react in haste. The major events that affect organizations in the future are not extrapolations of the past. They are paradigm shifts. Let's look at some of these shifts.

Wireless technology

A fast-growing area of telecommunications is wireless services, collectively known as personal communication networks (PCNs). The acceptance of a wireless world will come after quality cellular phones fit both the pocket and the pocketbook. The use of a personal communications number allows anyone to send data from anywhere in the world. These personal communications numbers will be as ubiquitous in the future as social security or insurance numbers are now. Voice and data traffic will eventually travel along wireless PBXs and wireless LANs. The systems of the future, described in the following subsections, all create new security problems for organizations, too.

Mobile communications

With every passing day, our society becomes more and more mobile. How many corporations have embraced cellular telephone technology for employees? Right this minute, thousands of people outside your window are making calls over the airwaves. Are these people aware that anybody with a frequency scanner from their local radio store can eavesdrop on their conversation? Prince Charles obviously was not! In early 1993, English tabloid newspapers published transcripts of a racy cellular conversation between Prince Charles and his old flame Camilla Parker-Bowles. In most jurisdictions, listening to conversations is not even a crime! Acting on information gained from eavesdropping or interfering with a conversation is, however. Most cellular phone manufacturers realize the problem and now offer scrambling options.

It is just not portable cellular phones! Today, businesses have an increased demand for fast, accurate information. These demands signal the need for ubiquitous access and availability to the latest information, regardless of a user's locale. To date, mobile radio communication has been limited largely to voice, because of market considerations and technical constraints. Vendors are now overcoming these constraints, and mobile access is becoming a reality. Increasingly, the term *mobile communications* describes a variety of mobile services that can be of use to such industries as trucking and railway firms, for example, as a means to increase efficiency and effectiveness. At this time, it is possible to access information from a mobile terminal miles from the nearest telephone line. The advantages of the wireless data network are similar to those of the wireless voice network, that is, portability, mobility, and economy.

These advantages create almost endless possibilities for applications. Typical users might include auditors, traveling salesmen, real estate agents, and insurance adjustors. Mobile data networks allow mobile users to exchange data, text, and voice messages with their dispatch centers and with each other in areas such as truck fleet control, taxi dispatch, warehousing operations, public safety service, and maintenance operations. Anyone presently using a modem can find uses for wireless modems, just as users found uses for laptop, notebook, and palmtop computers. Users can always process data and use information in remote environments.

Economically, advantages do exist to the wireless data network, particularly in communicating without the expense of landlines. Wireless networks eventually access the existing telephone network, but users do not have to extend the wire network or conform to its physical constraints. Rather, airwaves become the transmission medium. As we see in the next section, wireless LAN technology already exists for intraoffice networks, reducing the wires between offices. Even greater economic advantages are found when a radio frequency network is used to reach the office by a salesman in a car miles from the home office.

There are two emerging technologies in wireless data networks—direct modulation and cellular. Presently, these mobile data networks are just as susceptible to message interception as cellular phone calls. As business users become more mobile and access voice, data, and images through wireless networks, the need for improved communications security increases.

Wireless LANs

The wireless office is now manifesting itself in LANs. It is currently a small market, but will grow in this decade, according to a report by Market Intelligence of Mountain View, California. The report—*The Wireless Office: LAN, PBX Users Cut Cables, Eye Integration*—says the U.S. wireless office market will approach $500 million in 1993, $1 billion in 1994, and $3 billion by 1997. Figure 10-2 demonstrates this growing trend. Even though the experts might not agree on the size of the market; wireless is hot!

When wireless first emerged, everybody wondered whether it was a niche market or whether the market would grow to challenge cable-based LANs.

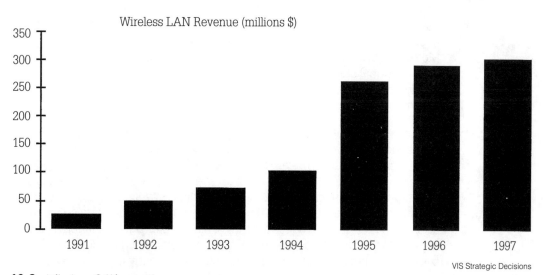

10-2 *Wireless LAN growth.*

Industry watchers think wireless LANs will challenge. Their slow initial growth was due partly to the low capacity of wireless when compared to their cabled competition. The impetus for future growth comes from less-expensive products, looming standards, and the growing mobile communications market. Until the time of this challenge, pioneers will choose wireless LANs if they frequently move their LAN, or they cannot cable the building. A primary incentive for wireless LANs is the reduced cost of installing, moving, and changing these networks.

Local area wireless networks (LAWNs) currently exist and require no wires. LAWNs use frequency transmissions to perform the functions of conventional networks, including peripheral sharing, file transfer, and electronic mail. The transmissions can travel through walls, floors, and other barriers. Figure 10-3 illustrates a radio wireless LAN. NCR markets WaveLAN, which can transmit data at a rate approaching 2 Mbps.

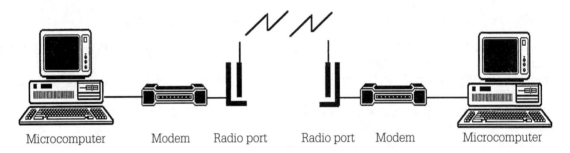

Microcomputer   Modem   Radio port   Radio port   Modem   Microcomputer

10-3 *Wireless LAN.*

Other wireless LANs use microwave transmissions. These transmissions, however, require line-of-sight view to work. Anything, even a single piece of paper, that blocks the beam between two nodes brings the node down. Motorola's WIN (wireless in-building network), however, which uses nondirectional microwave technology, overcomes infrared's line-of-sight problems and handles 4-Mbps and 16-Mbps Token Ring and 10-Mbps Ethernet.

Unencrypted, wireless LAN transmissions are easier to eavesdrop than conventional networks. Therefore, it could be necessary to encrypt them. Some vendors argue, however, that it is easier to intercept the electromagnetic fields around cables than it is to pick up a few microwaves. On top of that, they argue, the wireless transmission is encoded. If you intercept the signal, you still need the encoding scheme to understand the data. Wireless vendors also argue that their networks are more reliable than cabled networks; any administrator can tell you that the majority of networking problems are traced to wiring problems. Radio transmitters presently are expensive, however, which make them a popular target of thieves.

Like the LAN itself, wireless LANs will change the way people work. We will no longer need buildings in which to work. Truthfully, we only came together to work because the information and tools we needed to do our jobs were centralized. Home offices now have microcomputers, modems, facsimile machines, and laser printers. Soon, we will be able to access the information from anywhere, and wireless LANs are an enabler in this future. Individuals will use wireless communications to access people and information anytime, anywhere. The only question is how quickly this will happen.

Cooperative computing

In the years preceding the turn of the next century, organizations will be forced to develop products and make decisions faster to remain competitive. They must adopt structures that can change with the business. New software types and networks will be driving forces, shaping structure and strategy as these organizations fight for survival. Modern software will facilitate the sharing of information and cooperation between people with less hierarchical control. We have seen already the development of several new types of software to support this, including workflow and groupware. This software will increase in power as the development of new hardware, such as ensemble processors and hypercomputers, also facilitates cooperation.

Workflow software

The 1990s will see an explosion of workflow software capitalizing on the power of the electronic mail networks. *Workflow software* takes advantage of the electronic mail already in place in an organization to move data. Workflow software automates the processing and routing of data in an organization via mail, replacing the handling of large amounts of paper with the automated movement of data.

The most common example of workflow processing is expense reports. How does your corporation currently process an expense form? Probably the same way most do. First, employees fill out their reports, including attaching all receipts. They verify the numbers and pass the paperwork on to their supervisor. The supervisor reverifies the numbers and recommends approval of the expense. The supervisor then sends the report on to the person authorized to approve the expense. These people reverify the amounts, check recommendation for approval, and approve the payment. The supervisor then sends the report with all its approvals to accounting, where it reverifies the amounts and produces a check.

There is a better way. Rather than filling out an expense form, employees fill out an expense report electronically. The software verifies and cross-checks the amounts. When completed, the form is processed by the workflow software, which determines the next step after reviewing it. The next step could be to route all expenses over $500 to an employee's supervisor, or all expenses over $1,000 to the division head for approval. The software knows where the form should be sent based on predefined rules.

The person receiving the form via electronic mail approves or rejects the expense. If that person grants approval, the form is forwarded to accounting for disbursement. If the expense is rejected, the originator gets the form returned with an explanation, and the cycle starts again.

Workflow software is one of those products that promises to reduce the amount of paper generated by an organization. The software is only the start. The restructuring of the office, resulting from the use of LANs and other technology, must also be completed. An organization must look at how it pays expense reports and re-engineer the process, or the organization will have *electronic varathane*. Electronic varathane is when fancy new technology is used to gloss over the same old, inefficient, uneconomical, and ineffective systems. Simply, it is paving over the old cow pastures. Automating the existing paper flow will not provide an organization with the maximum return on investment. Re-engineering is not a trivial task and is fraught with dangers. Implementation of workflow software requires attention to accounting system internal controls, including checks and balances, verification, approval, authorization and audit trails.

The security concerns are also significant. How do we ensure the forms are complete and accurate? How do we verify approval and authorization? How do we prevent one employee from seeing the information of another employee, say an executive? Who will maintain the database of departmental authorizations? Who will ensure the changes made to the authorization tables are authorized, accurate, and complete? Who will change workflow programs? As the examples show, the initial purchase price for workflow software will be small compared to the time and money needed to rework the internal systems.

Groupware

A fundamental aspect of business practice, perhaps more basic than sharing information, is manifesting itself in a new class of software engendered by the LAN environment itself. Called *groupware*, this software enables groups to coordinate their actions to work together effectively toward group goals. Some groupware software allows users to integrate different products into a cohesive set of interoperating software, in effect a *cobbleware* approach. Other software tries to build total functionality into a single, unified product, while still others provide built-in functionality and the ability to integrate external functions or replace built-in functions with other products. Groupware software includes electronic mail, group scheduling and calendaring, project management, and electronic meetings. These groupware products provide more than sharing of information; they provide a structure to facilitate how people naturally work well together.

For example, groupware enables people to work closely together from separate places and at different times. Software of this kind can enormously impact where and when people work, which can then affect who can work together, and where they can live. It also can enormously impact the existing control systems. The questions we asked for workflow software also need answering for groupware.

Networks are dynamic, not static. Because results at work inevitably derive from the give and take of people working together, information seeks always to be shared. At the same time, information is a valuable commodity that companies look to protect. LANs are the corporate lifeline, providing effective paths for sharing and protecting information. These lifelines will need adequate policing.

It is not simply that the information sharing takes the form of text documents, spreadsheets, drawings, images, and other complex files, as opposed to a simple database record. It is also that many different group members can do many different things to these very different information objects, sometimes consecutively and sometimes concurrently. Add to that the further complication of possible wide geographical dispersal—including group members who travel and use notebook computers to connect to the group—and soon you realize this is not a simple problem. Just as important is the need to understand the specifics of the internal workings of a group.

There are major issues when considering groupware. First, because groupware entails supporting more than a single user, it must foster easy communication among all members of the group. Communication must be immediate and asynchronous. Immediate means users can transmit thoughts when created; asynchronous is the user's ability to send information without knowing the intended recipient's availability or locale. Second, groupware software must balance concurrent access with the management of conflicting updates. Without this balance, the integrity of the data is jeopardized.

Third, groupware must conform to the way the group works and not vice versa. Some groups are hierarchical and are thus closely controlled through well-defined chains of command, that is, the military's model of command and control. By contrast, other groups are open and loosely structured with vague lines of responsibility. These groups dispense with hierarchies and allow for virtually any communication path. A prospective groupware product must conform to both these differing arrangements and work cultures without losing functionality.

Fourth, even with relatively small groups, there are differing levels of authorization for access to shared data. Hence, groupware must provide ready, credible, and ongoing assurance that only properly authorized users can read or change data for which they actually have the authority. Once users are identified and their authorizations confirmed, security restrictions and authorizations should automatically be replicated in every action and function of the groupware product. Properly authorized users should experience no perceptible obstacle to accessing needed information, while unauthorized users should be able to make sense from their attempted access. All authorized users should be confident that the information they share is stable and complete. Notwithstanding the hazards of the network, information should stay where it is put until it is duly modified. Groupware should contain within its infrastructure all the implicit functionality of information integrity.

Lastly, good groupware should ignore platform and application differences and deliver a standard set of functions everywhere in the group. This requirement implies cross-platform and cross-application interdependence. These platforms and applications must interoperate regardless of the topology, protocol, network operating system, bridge, or gateway.

The process of selecting and installing groupware products helps an organization understand the real workflow processes in effect, and this understanding often provides insight in simplifying the workflow. Between the facilities of groupware and the new process simplifications, organizations find they can work faster, better, and cheaper.

Ensemble processing   Alvin Toffler in *The Third Wave* talks about the organizations of the future. In his book, he quotes advertising man Lester Wunderman as saying, "Ensemble groups, acting as intellectual commandos, will . . . begin to replace hierarchical structure." Toffler also quotes Tony Judge as saying, "The network is not 'coordinated' by anybody; the participating bodies coordinate themselves so that one may speak of 'auto-coordination.' " A new type of processing being developed in universities, *ensemble processing* will emerge to serve these new organizations. Ensemble processing differs from groupware in concept but provides similar results. When a user requires extra processing, the user sends out a task on the network. Any machine with excess or idle capacity picks up the task and processes it. When the user needs the result, the machine looks on the network for the result placed there by the other machine.

Ensemble processing effectively uses the full power of all the machines on the network. Idle machines can work on tasks for other machines and in turn provide tasks for other machines to work on. One hundred information machines working on the same problem form an ensemble—an entity that is more, in some sense, than the sum of its parts. These machines communicate and coordinate with each other to make progress as a group on the same problem.

Hypercomputers   Roping together networked computers creates a *hypercomputer*. These hypercomputers will be joined with fiber-optic cable and will process today's problems at the speed of light. The combined power of the microcomputers on the network will be greater than the sum of its parts.

Telecommuting   In *Entropy: A New World View*, Jeremy Rifkin and Ted Howard (1980) talk about the decay of the infrastructure of modern cities, citing New York and Cleveland as examples. They contend that large cities are unsustainable and will inevitably collapse. The flooding of downtown Chicago in 1992 supports their theory, as does the same-year gas explosion in Guadalajara, Mexico . More energy is expended moving supplies into and out of these large urban centers than on creating the supplies themselves. The authors conclude that self-supporting centers of about 100,000 people are the answer. Perhaps telecommuting is an answer as well.

Twice daily people get in their cars and everybody in the east end heads west, and everybody in the west end heads east. In the future, this daily odyssey will be curtailed. The information revolution opens the way for transferring millions of jobs from centralized offices and factories into neighborhood work centers and even homes. Society has found that shuffling people around for 3 hours every day is not supportive of productivity or conducive to good health. Some people believe telecommuting will not work because humans are social by nature. There are, however, viable alternatives to satisfy both concerns.

Offering an alternative to 3-hour roundtrip commutes to Orange and Los Angeles counties, California's largest telecommuting work center provides all the amenities of the office without going to the office. Strategically placed near the intersection of three major highways, the work center offers 250,000 commuters an alternative. The work center is a joint initiative of public and private sectors financed with state funds.

These work centers will appear more and more as governments and businesses see the benefits of telecommuting. This trend is a direct reversal of a basic trend of the industrial revolution, which saw a shift from the countryside to the cities as society moved from an agricultural-based society to the industrial revolution.

Some people think the trend will not happen because of the loss of close supervision and control. Studies show, however, an increase in productivity for workers who telecommute. Their supervisors also reported a significant increase in the worker's commitment to the organization, improved service to customers, less stress, and greater job satisfaction. Moreover, cost savings are likely with telecommuting.

Costs for centralization go up while costs of computers and communications drop. Work at home, or telecommuting, will thrive when these cost curves intersect, as already demonstrated in Southern California. Note that employees working in these environments do create new security concerns for organizations. Employers will face tough issues around ownership of data, workers' accident and disability insurance and compensation when this shift occurs.

In early September 1992, officials held the First Southeastern Telecommuting Conference in Atlanta after threats of reduced federal transportation funding for the region. The region is required to reduce ozone levels by 15 percent. With an estimated 5.5 million Americans presently working at home or in satellite offices, and with rapid advances in technologies like fax, electronic mail, and local and wide area networks, along with the growing concern for the environment, there is strong evidence that telecommuting will double by 1995.

Imaging: the last frontier

Judges are doing it. Insurance brokers are doing it. The government is doing it. Even dressmakers are doing it. It seems like everybody is doing it. Doing what? Imaging! Judges want to review case evidence in their chambers before entering a decision. Insurance brokers want to see police reports and accident-scene photos while processing a claim. Government employees want to call up a birth certificate and print it out while the customer waits. Dressmakers want to see designs on their terminals before cutting. These people are some of a growing number of businesses and governments who are turning to low-cost, document-imaging systems to work on everyday tasks. There are several intertwined reasons as to why organizations have zealously taken up this technology.

Over the next decade, North American businesses will fill an estimated 8 trillion pieces of paper with information, and in the process will lay to rest the notion that the paperless office is just around the corner. Technology, as it turns out, may staunch the flow of paper, but it will not eliminate it. Everything from insurance forms, canceled checks, and legal documents to interoffice memos, requisition forms, and invoices must be stored somewhere for future retrieval.

Each of these documents, along with every piece of paper with writing, drawings, photos, graphs, or charts on it, represents an individual image. The need to manage these images—to be able to find and use the information they contain—has created the electronic imaging industry. What is an image processing system (IPS)? The answer depends on who you ask and how old they are. Older folks might answer computer-output microform (COM), whereas younger folks might suggest geographical information systems. *Electronic imaging* is one of those generic technology terms that can refer to a number of things—micrographics, document imaging, geographical information systems—but it typically relates to the capturing and storing of images.

The medical community uses imaging tools such as X-ray machines to look inside the body. Engineers, architects, and scientists use imaging tools to look at the various structures they work with, such as, CAD/CAM systems. The biggest and most immediate use for imaging, however, is in helping deal with the more than one billion pieces of paper business creates every day.

Imaging technology facilitates decentralization: imaged files are easily shared and cross-referenced, unlike paper files, which are more restrictive. Imaging also can reduce the time workers spend filing and retrieving documents, and by that reduction enable them to spend more time interpreting the information, thus serving the customer. Eliminating paper records and paper record storage facilities generates marginal savings.

Banks, insurance companies, and governments tend to be the biggest producers of images, about 95 percent of which are in the form of paper records. In this information age, just 1 percent of all business information is stored in computers; the remaining 4 percent is stored in magnetic archives or on microform. Wang Laboratories, Inc., of Lowell, Massachusetts, says its research suggests that the average executive spends three hours per week looking for lost information, and administrative assistants spend three to five hours per week looking for the same information. Meanwhile, the paper mountains expand, covering desk tops, filling file cabinets, and piling up in warehouses, where the paper doubles every four years.

Three or four years ago, as the technology for electronic imaging started making its way to the marketplace, industry gurus predicted the paperless office—a workplace where all business is transacted electronically. These must have been the same pundits who predicted that electronic document interchange would have the same effect!

Despite the many benefits of electronic imaging—cost and space savings, faster document retrieval—commercial organizations that, in other times, might enthusiastically embrace such technology, are hesitating. The reason is cost. Electronic imaging systems can cost anywhere from $135,000 to many millions of dollars. Imaging systems actually take and store electronic photographs of documents, which, under the best of circumstances, requires 10 times more memory than simple text to store.

To paraphrase an old Chinese proverb, "One image is worth more than a thousand words." Today we must ask, "Is a picture worth a million bytes?"

In some ways, information technology specialists see every new product as their own personal Mount Everest—conquering it because it is there! Nat Goldhaber, Chief Executive Officer of Kaleida, the Apple-IBM joint venture, recently said, "In multimedia we're willing to accept unbelievably low production values, but that's only because we're computer nerds. Any normal person wouldn't feel that way, and that's why normal people don't find it very enticing." Nothing elicits "oohs" and "aahs" from computer nerds faster than image processing.

Technology is the enabling device, making possible the connectivity and creating compatibility of previously incompatible parts to create new wholes. A typical imaging system includes the following components:

- A scanner for digitizing images.
- A database server for indexing.
- Workstations with high-resolution monitors.
- A high-volume storage medium called an *optical disk storage system*.
- A laser printer.
- A network system for sharing images.

The components of imaging systems are not new, but their compatibility is. The development of imaging systems was akin to the explosion of LANs when vendors made the connectivity of the components economical.

Imaging systems can improve security over access to information—risk of losing or misfiling a document can be reduced with imaging. Some companies have quantified the cost of replacing a lost paper document to justify image technology expenditures. Installing an IPS, however, does not guarantee that information is adequately secured.

The growing problem of managing paper and data is precisely why imaging is crucial. We need document storage and retrieval systems that capture external documents, create retrievable digitized images, and link them with data output. These digital document image and data systems can be used for departmental and enterprise-wide applications. Image processing systems can provide significant added value to available products, cut the cost of operations, increase productivity, improve customer service capability, and improve cash flow by speeding the collection process. The net result can be a significant strategic competitive advantage.

Converting externally generated paper source documents to a digital record requires creating document-digitized images with a bit-map scanner and then keying the cross-reference index data into the magnetic index database. The system flow begins with the receipt of external source documents. The paper is scanned, index fields are keyed, and an optical disk image is automatically assigned to each document. This address is then incorporated into the online magnetic index for later retrieval of the optically stored image by the system. Because long-term legal or audit requirements often exist for storing paper documents, the systems must be capable of accessing the index for as many as 5 to 7 years. The ability to manage large magnetic disk databases is therefore a key ingredient of optical systems.

The document management software controls the index data located on the magnetic disk and the retrieval of optically stored images. The software provides direct access to an unlimited number of images, or documents. This combination of magnetic database indexing and optical-image retrieval provides an access time of 4 to 30 seconds to any document image in the file. Although this access time might seem slow compared to an online system, it is extremely fast compared with the traditional sorting, filing, and retrieval of paper document files.

When the integration of the computer data and paper document image-delivery systems is complete, the result is a database system that contains all of the common index data necessary to link computer data with the related source document image. For example, a computer-generated customer statement can be automatically tied to all of the supporting source documents, such as the credit application, credit card drafts, and customer correspondence.

Optical disk-based image and data applications use a digital optical disk for storage and retrieval of paper documents and computer output. Image systems can digitally capture images on paper with a document-digitizer scanner; store the image on the optical disk; index and retrieve the image using application specific indexing and retrieval software; and display, print, or transmit the retrieved images to the required user location. Data systems similarly provide access to computer information now stored on paper, magnetic tape, or computer-output microfiche (COM).

Image-processing systems bridge the gap between existing paper document files and computer data. The ability to create electronic images of paper files means that the integration of paper document management into other mainstream information systems is now possible. These systems process two primary applications: paper documents that are received from outside the organization and stored offline in file cabinets and computer data that is stored online or offline on paper, COM, or magnetic tape.

Currently, paper and computerized data storage function as separate systems with little or no link between media or information. In most business systems, however, both of these sources must be accessed to respond properly to a request for information. Because each of these methods independently stores and retrieves information, problems are becoming more pronounced as the demand increases for immediate information access and response.

The methods of storing and accessing information have evolved as independent solutions to what is actually a central information file problem. A brief explanation of these information sources is important to understanding their relation to optical systems.

Paper documents are now a major management concern. These source documents cause filing requirements to grow by 25 to 30 percent annually. Other factors fueling interest in digital optical systems to handle the paper storage problem are the following:

- Ubiquity of paper documents in the office—paper is not going to disappear in the near future. Currently, less than 2 percent of all corporate data is in digital form.
- Labor shortage—it is no longer easy or sometimes possible to hire or retain qualified file clerks.
- Demand for instant information—the storage and retrieval of external documents is becoming mandatory for corporate decision making and for handling customer service and collection functions.

In the current information environment, offline, manual systems are not integrated into the computer information transaction cycle. The lack of integration of computer data, microfilm, and paper files creates an extended information search process usually measured in hours or even days. Recent studies show that almost all information is still contained on paper, which is a major barrier to using computers strategically and responding to customer needs quickly.

Microcomputer-based imaging system configurations can be standalone workstations, dedicated networks, or image servers to company-wide systems. Options include optical character recognition, facsimile capabilities, links to other software applications, and integration with micrographics.

Technology is advancing rapidly, and industry standards are emerging for operating systems, interfaces, file formats, optical storage, and communications protocols. The processing power of microcomputers is increasing, while optical storage is decreasing in cost and increasing in capacity. New developments have risen in networks, notably the use of fiber. As the market matures, vendors are responding technologically with the following:

- Increasingly nonproprietary platforms and protocols.
- Compliance with industry standards.
- Multivendor connectivity.
- Faster processing and throughput speeds.
- Increased optical character recognition (OCR) and fax support.

As previously stated, an IPS converts a paper document, photograph, or other representation into a digitized and compressed image. The image is then indexed and stored so that it can be retrieved and viewed at a workstation and, if necessary, sent to a printer. The process enables users to manage images in ways not possible with conventional media. Image processing systems allow compression, decompression, rotation, and scaling of images and photographs.

OCR software converts digital data into characters that can be incorporated into an information management system without manual re-entry. Emerging technologies include intelligent and handwritten character recognition software. For example, Apple is developing NEWTON, a handheld scratchpad for notetaking and drawing.

Imaging components

Although numerous mainframe optical systems are on the market, the most popular are microcomputer-based systems because of the departmental nature of most of the early applications, as well as the lower cost of implementation. As previously noted, the growth in the use of microcomputers created the need for personal computer networks. These networks led to the adaptation of software and hardware originally developed for larger computers and networks. Today's image processing systems comprise several major components, illustrated in FIG. 10-4 and listed below:

- Workstations with high-resolution displays.
- Digital scanners for handling the image entry.
- High-capacity mass storage, such as optical disks with storage capacity from 800 MB to more than 4 GB per disk.

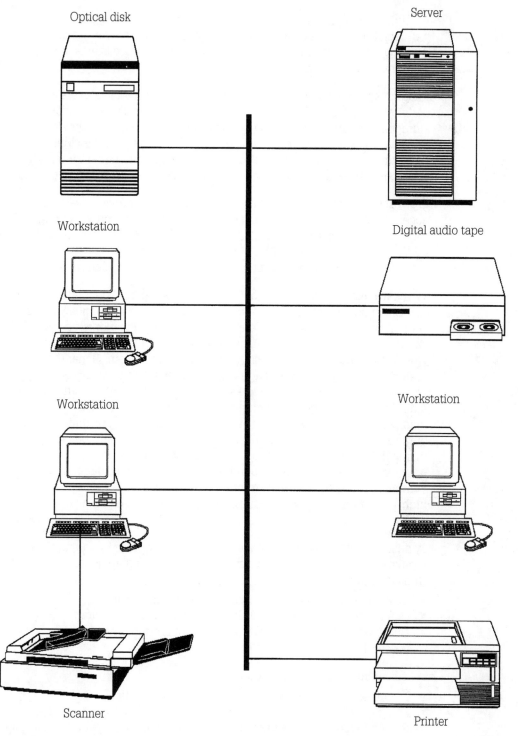

10-4 *Image processing system.*

- High-resolution output devices, such as a printer
- Specialized software, including image application software, database software with document retrieval, and workflow processing software
- Communications software and hardware

Imaging systems are increasingly configured with multiple servers, with each dedicated to a particular task: image input, display and manipulation, storage, or output. High-end imaging systems often maintain the database and image management on a minicomputer or mainframe. Intelligent workstations manipulate images under a microcomputer operating system, and optical storage is handled by specialized software on a dedicated server.

Operating systems Standard operating systems provide users with access to other applications. Operating systems supported by imaging systems are as varied as the platforms and include MS-DOS, Macintosh/OS, OS/2, UNIX, and Digital's VMS. Multitasking operating systems allow workstations to manage data processing applications concurrently.

Workstations The number of workstations supported depends on the number of document servers or host processors; some high-end systems can support thousands of workstations. The total number of workstations supported, however, does not necessarily reflect the number of image workstations that can operate simultaneously on a system. Generally, imaging systems can support fewer imaging workstations than nonimaging workstations. Image-capable workstations are used for display and the manipulation of images. In document image-processing systems, manipulation generally refers to such functions as scaling (zooming in and out), panning, rotating, enlarging, and reducing, rather than the bit-by-bit manipulation of graphics applications. Workstations are often microcomputer-based, even when the imaging system is mainframe-based. Features in workstations important for image processing are large-screen, high-resolution displays and compression/expansion boards.

Scanners Scanners are the primary input device on document imaging systems. They translate the image on a sheet of paper or other surface into a digitized image that a computer can understand. All graphic images fall into three categories:

- Line art, which is white and black text or illustrations.
- Continuous tones, which are shades of gray, as in photographs.
- Color, which is typically not a requirement for document imaging processing for business applications.

All scanners have four basic components:

- Document feeder system—usually flatbed or sheetfed.
- Sampling device—usually a charge-coupled device (CCD) or a laser. Sampling devices detect the light reflected from the page and convert it

into digital data by dividing the page into a grid of dots. More dots per inch means higher resolution and a finer image.
- Controller—converts the voltages emitted by the sampling device into a digital signal comprising binary bits and then passes the stream of bits to the computer, along with instructions for where one row ends and the next one begins.
- Software—scanner software acts as a bridge between the scanner and application programs.

Optical character recognition There are two main reasons for OCR in document imaging systems: text input and indexing. Text stored in a file created by word processing, database, or spreadsheet programs can be integrated with images to varying degrees, dependent upon system image management software. Some systems support cut-and-paste applications between windows, allowing the user to add text that has been scanned and optically recognized into a scanned image file. Automatic indexing is important for OCR in document imaging systems. All images must be indexed in a database for later retrieval.

Mass storage While image compression can considerably reduce the required storage space for digitized documents, the sheer volume of documents encountered in the average office still creates a storage problem. Magnetic disks are quickly filled to capacity and subject to data loss through operator error or system failure.

Optical disks, with storage capacities measured in gigabytes, make document retrieval systems practical. Optical disks can be write once, read many (WORM), rewritable (erasable), or CD-ROM. Each type has advantages and disadvantages that make it appropriate for different applications. Industry-standard (ANSI XB311) WORM and rewritable drives allow disks to be read using the products of different vendors; with each type, products conform in varying degrees. Both WORM and rewritable drives have slower access times and are more expensive than magnetic media. CD-ROM drives, practical only for volume production and distribution, are not as useful in document-imaging systems. Optical disk drives are available as standalone devices or as jukeboxes. Disks are manually inserted and removed from standalone drives—a time-consuming and inconvenient process. Jukeboxes insert and remove disks automatically and generally support multiple drives.

Printers Most imaging applications require printed output at some stage. Page printers are used for image printing and use different technologies. Most common of the technologies is electrophotography, which encompasses laser, light-emitting diode (LED) and liquid crystal shutter (LCS) printers. Page printers produce hard copy in three stages.

The first stage is *processing*, where the printer controller converts text and graphic images into a raster pattern, or a grid of dots. The host computer transmits the text or graphic data as a stream of ASCII or EBCDIC codes, allowing the printer controller to translate these codes into font patterns or graphics. The translation requires a raster image processor (RIP) that resides inside the printer, in the host computer, or in a separate housing. When the printer controller has received and processed a page of text or graphics, it sends the pattern to the imaging device.

The second stage is *imaging,* where the imaging device writes the raster image onto the electrographic drum or belt. The process requires a light source that selectively exposes the drum or belt under the control of the printer controller.

The third stage is developing and transferring the image, where the light-exposed areas of the drum attract positively charged toner particles and print black. Unexposed areas repel toner and print white.

Important issues for printers used in imaging systems are resolution, speed, and capacity. Requirements for each depend on the application. Printers can be attached to workstations or to dedicated servers and can be either distributed or centralized.

Image management software Document-imaging software remains a small niche in the overall imaging market. Nonetheless, this segment is experiencing resounding growth, and its importance continues to increase. Imaging software unbundled from hardware is the future. With the growth of more-powerful microcomputer systems and networks, and the growing demand for imaging systems, imaging software vendors face a vast opportunity.

Document imaging has come into its own as an important, albeit niche, market. User interest in imaging systems is soaring, paralleled by vendor interest and activity. Bolstered by price decreases in imaging system peripherals (such as optical storage and laser printers) and by rapid advances in computer performance, each part of the imaging puzzle has fallen into place to make imaging more attractive to a critical mass of end users.

This market is distinct from earlier generations of imaging systems, where the software was developed to run on specific hardware systems that served as the vendor's primary focus. This hardware-focused approach was dictated primarily by the state of the technology at that time and that so little expertise existed for specifying the appropriate components for imaging systems. The concept of single-vendor, proprietary hardware or software imaging solutions developed in an environment where only large sites were targeted for imaging implementations.

The additional expense associated with proprietary approaches shielded early developers from competition and was absorbed by early adopters as the cost of being a pioneer. This pattern traces the beginnings of the market, when only minicomputers and mainframes had the computing horsepower to handle document imaging. As technology at the desktop level continued to accelerate, implementing a document imaging system for smaller workgroups and departments became feasible. At the same time, developers recognized that implementing software-only solutions on widely available and competitively priced hardware was a strategically sound approach.

Workflow software, now a component of full-featured integrated image management software was originally a separate standalone application, and some vendors still market it as such. Because the concept of integrated workflow and image processing is spreading, most important developments in this area will result from developments marketed by the vendors for complete image-management systems.

Modeled on the software components of proprietary imaging systems, image-management systems are complex, typically modular software applications that facilitate document-image throughput. Usually running on industry-standard microcomputer hardware or popular minicomputer platforms, image-management software represents the core of the imaging-software market. These integrated and full-featured packages are shifting the document imaging market into broader applicability by virtue of their lower prices and appropriate scale for workgroups and departments.

Vendors must provide a fully functional basic system for users that tries not to contain too many unneeded or unwanted features. Taking a modular approach, vendors are providing a basic level of functionality and adding advanced features as users require them. Striking this balance, and educating potential users about the various capabilities and processes that image management software handles, are the challenges facing vendors.

Imaging applications

Before we can decide why we need an image-processing system, we should look at the information architecture. Aristotle once remarked that architecture consists of form and function. Information forms are quite straightforward—data, text, sound, and image. Function is similarly straightforward—creation, processing, storage, and transmittal of information. Most of us are familiar with the concept of data, the numbers, letters, and symbols processed or produced by a computer. Data always existed, even before the computer. The computer only made the handling of data easier, which in turn, spawned information technologies.

Text also is a simple concept for most of us: it is prose, the written language. Text is either written by hand or reproduced by mechanical means, such as a typewriter. Sound is what we hear, and takes the form of either voice or music. Radio, telephone, compact discs, and tape recorders all handle sound.

Finally, we have images. They are visual forms. They can be a photograph of your car or my daughter's drawing of our house. Charts, diagrams, and paintings are all images. Images can be artistic or pedestrian, realistic or imaginative. They also are either presentations or representations, expressions or impressions. Some are black and white, some color. The scanned image of a page of data and text is treated as a single image, although they were created separately. Thus, the copier, fax, printer, and scanner, which all handle images, are likely to merge completely in the near future.

Because this section deals with images, we use images to look at the functions of information. A scanner takes information in one form, such as data or text, and captures it for presentation in another form, an image. Creating information does not typically imply intellectual inspiration, but rather the preparation of information into a form readily understood by the user. Essentially, this means digitizing it and arranging it into machine-readable information (bits) that a machine can use. Depending on the medium, bits are either magnetized spots, electronic impulses, or magnetically charged cores. Once information is digitized, it can be easily handled in subsequent information functions.

Processing is how the computer makes its greatest contribution, starting with data processing, then word processing, and now voice and image processing, thus covering all forms of information. The processing function analyzes, combines, computes, converts, edits, and synthesizes, that is, manipulates and transforms, information.

The third function, storage, takes information in one of the four forms and saves it for later use. The storage function is essentially the creation of a memory bank where information is filed and collated for later use. As already observed, books, and even whole libraries, are stored on computers, saving vast amounts of paper and space.

The last function, transmission, involves sending and receiving all forms of information from one point to another at the speed of electromagnetic waves on copper or the speed of light on fiber. Transmission moves information through space; contrast this to storage, which moves information through time. Transmission involves the broadcasting, switching, networking, reception, signal processing, collection, and display of information. Computers have dominated the first three functions, while telecommunications dominates the fourth.

Imaging is therefore the integration of all forms and all functions. The main technology trend for document imaging is the increasing ability of computers to handle the image as any other data type. This trend will pervade product development and user applications in the coming years.

Traditional computing disaggregated form and function through software design, but new approaches, such as object orientation, takes images and reaggregates them, simplifying their use. Combining more forms and more functions equals added value and more business.

Multimedia processing As the market for departmental and enterprise systems widens, the emphasis is less on imaging and more on multimedia processing. Imaging systems technology will be expanded to include support for video, voice, and sound processing, as well as traditional computer and text processing. The development of efficient and robust database technologies must also coincide with these developments.

Standalone systems As the imaging market shifts from micrographics to technology for electronic document-imaging processing, the market for dedicated single-user imaging applications systems wanes. Even vendors who traditionally target this segment are preparing to reach out into the other segments by focusing on industry-standard equipment and adding LAN support to their systems. In this market, purchase decisions will be based on cost and proven technology; hence, we see vendors introducing systems under $10,000. Micrographics, a proven technology, will remain a viable alternative in this market, where the functional emphasis is on storage and retrieval.

One of the obstacles vendors will face in this segment is the integration of electronic imaging with existing micrographics systems. Many organizations have a heavy investment in micrographics equipment. To protect this large investment, a standard optical-disk data file structure that enables users to interchange data stored on different platforms will be required.

Departmental systems One of the keys to success in this market is the support of widely accepted, standard user and communication interfaces and hardware. These systems must accommodate high-volume, paper-intensive workgroup imaging applications. Widely accepted standards means that users can use the computing power they already have to run imaging software, or the computing power they are adding for imaging can also run other popular software. The functional emphasis in this market will be on automated transaction processing. Hence, these systems must go beyond mere file-folder storage and retrieval operations and add support for workflow automation. Because every organization has its own way of doing things, applications must be programmable by those who manage the operations or are familiar with the end user's strategic business requirements. Applications toolkits, designed for nontechnical administrative staff, are a necessity. The key is to design systems around future applications, not around a specific technology.

Enterprise systems The dominant product strategy in this market segment is to provide images as a data type to all applications within an organization. This implies the following:

- Developing imaging capabilities for the current installed base of computing products.
- Making images available to popular workgroup programs.
- Developing application program interfaces that allow any processor in a network to obtain client service from any imaging server on the network.

- Developing standard interfaces for peripherals such as scanners and optical disks.
- Continuing the use of standard user interfaces, such as the graphical user interface.
- Developing image as an object that can be integrated with any other data type, including video, voice, graphics, and text.
- Adding rules-based workflow application toolkits designed for knowledge-based workers.

Many mainstream vendors, such as IBM, NCR, Hewlett-Packard, and Digital, have seen opportunities for developing systems that provide these necessary tools for enterprise applications. The question is which vendor's approach will arrive at the market first and thus become the imaging standard.

Imaging trends Imaging also creates novel problems for security professionals. Some image degradation is tolerable, but any change to the data is not because the data then loses its usefulness. Minor changes to an image might be imperceptible. Does this mean you have suffered a loss of integrity? This is a question your organization must ultimately face.

The main technology trend for document imaging is the increasing ability of computers to handle the image as any other data type. This trend will pervade product development and marketing strategies in the coming years in the following areas.

Integrated document management Along with the trend toward multimedia processing is the change in processing methods from index or file management to object management. Object-oriented applications can link, combine, and manipulate data forms from any source. Graphical interfaces built on desktop application tools enable users to link data forms to other application documents and programs.

Client-server computing The client-server architecture will become more prevalent as vendors develop product strategies to protect their capital investments and increase price-to-performance ratios. Multimedia processing will demand more computing power, so client-server platforms must be scalable and conform to widely accepted industry standards.

Integrated applications platforms Currently, most imaging systems are based on custom front-ends developed by the system vendor. In keeping with their investment protection strategies, vendors will image-enable widely accepted desktop applications. By giving all microcomputer users access to image data, customers will benefit from productivity gains on an enterprise-wide level.

Document-driven workflow Most image-workflow processing is applications based; that is, the workflow is determined by a program that routes (or queues) the necessary documents for a worker to complete a transaction. The trend toward object management will further the trend toward document-driven workflow whereby entering a document into a system will call up a sequence of processes based on the data within the document. Advances in compound object management technologies will play a role in application development tools, enabling nonprogrammers to build and run their own workflow processes as needed. In general, these technology trends should result in product marketing strategies for document imaging systems to become more application-oriented, more standards-oriented, and more workflow-oriented.

Manufacturing Manufacturing has always been quick to adopt new technologies, which accounts for the comparatively large productivity gains in this industry segment. It is not surprising then that in 1991, 29 percent of electronic imaging expenditures were made in this vertical market, including imaging support for engineering, parts manuals, and inventory management. The most important requirement for manufacturers will be the ability to make engineering drawing data easily available to all levels of the organization as needed.

Government In 1991, government accounted for 15 percent of electronic imaging expenditures in such applications as tax returns and legal records. As governments at all levels feel the impact of reduced spending budgets, officials look to computer automation to maintain services. Expenditures might increase as workflow technology becomes more sophisticated to meet the demands of government applications.

In May 1990, the Ministry of Consumer and Commercial Relations of the Province of Ontario obtained approval from Cabinet to implement automated imaging at the Office of the Registrar General. The Registrar maintains 18 million records of births, marriages, divorce, name changes, and deaths from 1869 to the present. It now has 11 million of these records stored as images on optical disk and will add the 500,000 records it receives each year.

The Workers' Compensation Board has 900 image processing workstations across the Province of Ontario to replace paper claim files with electronic copy, making it the largest electronic document imaging system in Canada and perhaps the world. In 1990, WCB paid $3.2 billion in benefits. It has spent an estimated $6 million to buy a mainframe computer and hundreds of PCs. The PCs and mainframe are all linked in an network. Any time a new claim for workers' compensation is made, it is recorded electronically rather than on paper. Old records are not being converted, but all new records will be stored in computers, increasing the speed and efficiency with which compensation-board employees can process claims.

In early 1993, the U.S. Internal Revenue Service awarded Grumman Data Systems an 8-year, $87.7 million contract for OCR and imaging systems for use in automated tax-form processing. The IRS will purchase two systems in 1994 and can optionally buy 11 more over the next 7 years.

The future will see a tremendous growth in governmental image processing systems. Because of legal and statutory requirements, integrity of the documents is a crucial issue for these governments.

Financial services Financial services accounted for 13 percent of 1991 IPS expenditures. Applications include loan applications, check remittance and securities processing. With continued government deregulation of the U.S. banking system, financial institutions are facing increasing competitive markets. This industry will look to system vendors to provide strategic application tools for developing competitive systems.

Wholesale and retail In 1991, the wholesale and retail sector held 12 percent of the total IPS market, close behind financial services in electronic imaging expenditure. Again, with the current shakeout in this industry segment, competitive concerns will force systems vendors to design systems to meet this segment's productivity goals.

The ultimate logic of ever-finer differentiation of the market is a market of one; that is, meeting the tailored needs of individual customers on a mass basis. Again, computers are making this concept more of a reality. An example of this trend is found in the way that mass retailers are using transactional terminals to customize their offerings.

Customers are familiar with terminals in retail stores, but it is the salesperson who usually deals with them, entering and retrieving the information. Transactional terminals, however, conduct business directly with a customer, helping to close a sale. Merchandisers are experimenting with these machines in the mass-customized marketing of everything from paint and hair coloring to shoes, clothes, and eyeglasses.

Home Hardware Stores of St. Jacobs, Ontario, uses a document imaging system to store and update the full inventory of products available to stores. In its old paper-based system, Home Hardware had to cut and paste its manual every time it added products. Now the manual is done completely electronically.

Insurance Insurance boasts many successful applications of imaging systems, accounting for 8 percent of the total expenditures. Again, because each firm within this industry has its own methods for success, the demand will be for application tools rather than "canned solutions." The need for advanced workflow applications is an important competitive factor for insurers, as is high-volume transaction processing.

Health care Health care accounted for only 5 percent of the electronic imaging expenditures in 1991, but, as health costs rise, look for an increase in demand for systems tailored to this industry segment. Applications include patient records processing, drug applications, and image-assisted diagnosis.

In a document-intensive business environment, IPS can improve information flow and handling. IPS benefits can include reduced labor and storage costs, faster document retrieval time, increased control over sensitive documents, enhanced customer service, and improved audit trails.

Managing imaging: cost-benefit analysis

Installing image technology is often difficult to cost justify, however. Installing image technology by itself does not guarantee improved office productivity. Imaging expenditures produce a payback only when organizations re-engineer their business and use document automation to improve business operations. Image-processing technology is both new and expensive. The technology is expensive because it requires a lot of storage.

Image-processing systems are a combination of an optical disk for image and data storage, retrieval software for index data management, and transmission media to send images or data to remote locations for instant access. These components provide a system that has great strategic potential. An image processing system allows users to access frequently needed computer-based information in a rapid, cost-effective, and efficient manner. These systems replace computer printouts, COM, and magnetic tape storage archival. They allow data to stay online, providing quick delivery of current as well as historical computer records at low cost. The benefits of IPS systems include the following:

- Storage systems provide extremely fast access to information, (2 to 4 seconds), resulting in a dramatic reduction in clerical functions, such as research, filing, and hard-copy reproduction, as well as faster customer service capability.
- Data is stored in printed-page format on high-density optical disks with storage capacities of 400,000 pages (on 5-1/4 inch disks) to 3 million pages (on 12-inch disks). Because the data on optical disk media is machine-readable, it can easily be restored to the host computer if necessary.
- The multilevel cross-reference index can be structured to allow retrieval of data by any desired field, such as invoice number, customer number, or date.
- Users can annotate the formatted page data with information that might be relevant to a transaction. The additional information is stored as a note and tagged to the corresponding data page, thereby providing a complete audit trail of all file-access transactions.

Many organizations will move their image processing systems from their mainframe to their LAN, which brings me to my next prediction about computing's next wave.

I predict that interconnected microcomputers will become the essential building blocks of corporate computing's next wave, that is, the foundation of such strategic architectures as client-server computing and distributed processing. Reading any trade journal or looking around your organization shows you that the role of the LAN in business is rapidly changing.

Rightsizing

When LANs first emerged, organizations used them for internal applications such as electronic mail and file transfer. The uses for LANs changed, however, as the hardware and software changed. The emergence of faster microcomputers and client-server software caused a shift in data processing applications. Organizations have slowly rightsized all their data processing functions.

Rightsizing means moving data processing applications from large mainframe or minicomputer hosts to microcomputer LANs. Organizations are rightsizing away from mainframes toward smaller systems in client-server environments. These organizations are building mission-critical applications that will run on distributed LANs. A client-server environment is really only a form of distributed data processing.

Rightsizing entails the transfer of data and programs from a single large computer to many microcomputers connected by a network. Usually, this entails splitting the application between server and workstation functions. Rightsizing also calls for the redesign of controls for managing and maintaining the data and programs as well as a paradigm shift from a centralized to a distributed environment. We previously discussed that distributed environments are inherently less secure. No longer are all the resources concentrated; they are distributed now to a few locations. Centralized systems also limit access to computing resources and data, contrasting with distributed systems that are designed to provide easy access to computing resources and data.

If these distributed systems are inherently less secure, why do organizations rightsize? Rightsizing is more than just transferring data, porting applications, and retooling management and maintenance procedures for the LAN environment. There are definite advantages to rightsizing, including increased processing power, improved network performance, shorter application development cycles, better access to data, and lower costs.

You can purchase processing capabilities in a microcomputer for $20,000 today that 15 years ago cost about $1 million in a mainframe. Yet today's microcomputer is much different than yesterday's million-dollar mainframe, including the fact that microcomputers are single-user systems and do not work well within the centralized environment.

Despite the economic benefits, rightsizing did not happen in the business world for several reasons. First, robust hardware was needed for the applications. The LAN's operating system also needed to offer services for the applications. Specifically, faster, more reliable hardware was required with large secondary storage, run by multiuser, multitasking operating systems that offered secure and reliable file sharing subsystems. This combination of requirements only became affordable in the early 1990s.

Running mission-critical applications on smaller platforms requires adherence to the same standards and requirements that escalated the costs in the mainframe and minicomputer environments. Standards for application development and secure and reliable operating systems are applicable to LANs as well.

Organizations already involved in rightsizing their operations find that moving only part of an application provides the best chance of success. The safest applications for partial rightsizing are the read-only applications, where data is read on a LAN but maintained and stored on the organization's existing minicomputer or mainframe. Because these applications are read-only, security and control requirements are less stringent. Another likely candidate for rightsizing is cooperative computing applications. For example, staff can use a LAN to perform calculations that update an application table or parameter in the mainframe production environment.

As mentioned in Chapter 1, microcomputers and LANs sprang up in corporations like wild mushrooms during the past decade—mostly shaded from the sunlight of information systems involvement. Today, low-end microcomputer LANs cannot offer the performance, reliability, stability, and security required by good data processing practices that have risen over time. This fact is especially true when these LANs are outside the management and control of traditional data processing structures. In truth, providing the required performance, reliability, stability, and security into low-end microcomputer LANs will probably make the LAN less attractive than the traditional minicomputer or mainframe system. For these reasons, many systems executives are working to spell out a LAN agenda. One issue on the agenda is support, a thorny one for LAN technology.

Support for distributed processing, that is, LANs, introduces new challenges to the organization. Application development, performance, configuration, and security management—traditionally, mainframe priorities—have not received the attention they should, and are often added as afterthoughts. Paying little attention to LAN application development, performance, configuration, and security management might be acceptable when LANs support only office automation. It is a dangerous approach, however, when downtime or poor response time affect customer satisfaction, and even profit.

Application development and maintenance should continue to operate under the complex planning and control structures of the mainframe system-development lifecycles. You cannot afford to develop mission-critical systems under any method that does not ensure the integrity of the code. Sponsoring staff must authorize changes to programs, and programming staff must test all code modifications. A change tracking system must include reasons for change for auditing purposes and problem resolution purposes.

Managing a LAN is actually not unlike managing a mainframe network. Network management involves managing many workstations, any one that is susceptible to the same problems as the host computer. To complicate matters, every networked microcomputer can be different from other microcomputers on the network. Additionally, managing a LAN includes managing repeaters, routers, brouters, bridges, gateways, hubs, and other hardware components. As previously discussed in Chapter 8, network management tools for LANs have not evolved quickly enough, making network management an arduous, but not impossible, task.

Another important area for performance consideration is capacity planning. Capacity planning for traditional networks focuses on optimizing the speed and placement of communications links to minimize recurring costs for leased lines. In a LAN environment, wiring costs are a one-time charge, and speeds up to 16 Mbps are achieved over twisted-pair wires. The more-important network components to consider for capacity planning are servers and interconnection devices such as bridges, routers, and gateways.

Capacity planning for servers involves all issues in capacity planning for any system, including memory and storage, communications interface speeds, and media. Capacity planning for LAN interconnection devices includes protocol considerations along with transmission speed and queuing delay.

The scalability and flexibility of distributed processing results in configuration management problems. Scalability is the capability to add users systematically to a network while increasing the power of the network. You add power because every microcomputer brings its resources to the network. With mainframes and minicomputers, when you add a terminal, you increase the load and thus, by definition, decrease the power of the network because you now have more users sharing static resources—either the mainframe or the front-end processor. You can add power to the traditional network by increasing memory, adding more ports, or increasing line speed.

Flexibility is the capability to add multiple-client operating systems and protocols without regard for the installed base. With distributed processing, you can isolate different operating systems and protocols, and hide their differences from the network at large while still allowing communication. Flexibility allows one user to have a powerful UNIX CAD/CAM workstation while another user has a simple DOS word-processing workstation. In this way, you can match computing resources to users and not users to computing resources, as traditionally done. Because of this flexibility, you can find almost any combination of hardware and software on the network. Thus, network administrators of LANs need to enforce standard configurations, rather than letting the system determine its own standard configuration.

The hardest part of configuration management is tracking the hardware and software of the installed microcomputers. Fortunately, specific tools allow a network administrator to determine the configuration of remote microcomputers attached to the network. The administrator's challenge is then to decide how strictly to enforce the standards.

Integrity of data is a major concern with distributed processing. Data duplication is an example of an integrity problem and occurs when there is more than one instance of the same data. Unmanaged or intentional data duplication is a potential problem. Figure 10-5 shows the four modes of distributed processing and the handling of data with each mode. With centralized processing, data duplication was not as big a problem because data was held and processed in one place. Distributed processing is an improvement over standalone microcomputers, however, where data duplication was a serious problem. Data duplication happens because any station on the LAN can create and store data. To avoid duplication, you must implement data processing applications that address the problem.

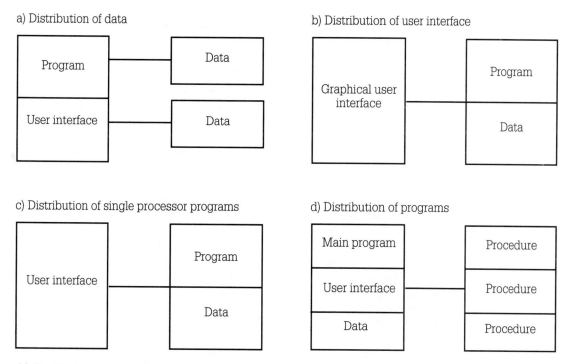

10-5 *Modes of distributed processing.*

Throughout this book, I have shown security issues associated with LANs. These issues are not insurmountable. For your reference, I have included some security LAN products in Appendix C. The issue obviously is not a lack of tools, but rather the enormity of the task in some organizations. Everybody wants to argue at the technology level rather than the business-function level. Again, security is first and foremost a management issue. It is difficult to implement security measures when dealing with multiple groups and departments in your organization when you lack the support of executive management.

An obvious concern when a LAN runs important business applications is physical security. It is easy to protect the server by putting it in an access-controlled room. The room should have smoke and water detectors and intrusion alarms. Physical access to your server is a major threat to your applications.

Rightsized applications provide easier access to data. You must strictly control logical access to data, just as you did when the data was on the mainframe. Remember, it is extremely important to value the data moved from the mainframe to the LAN and place the appropriate controls on your network. These controls could include access control software for the network and encryption for the database and transmissions.

We already discussed the effect network outages could have on your business. When the network fails and data is not available, the impact on your business and customers can be fatal. Most mainframe installations have recognized this fact and have instituted a variation of business resumption planning. Moving your applications from the mainframe environment does not dismiss the need to ensure continued availability of the data. The requirement for business resumption planning must extend to rightsized applications. These plans might include uninterruptible power supplies, backup and recovery procedures, fault tolerant software and hardware, and duplicate systems.

Rather than maintaining a single LAN, many organizations have several geographically dispersed LANs. While it is difficult to find one person with the right combination of skills and experience to manage LAN performance and security, it is virtually impossible to find someone with the right skill set for every LAN location. Not surprisingly, in many companies, the information systems (IS) group is asked either to assist with, or in some cases, take over LAN application development, performance, configuration, and security management. This is especially true for LANs supporting mission-critical applications.

Using the IS group also makes sense when you look at support from the issue of segregation of duties. When only one person is responsible for operating your LAN, your organization exposes itself to many problems, ranging from malicious mischief to theft of information assets. These situations might seem remote; however, there are well-documented cases of employee sabotage and extortion. Good internal control requires that some activities be segregated. For instance, the human resources applications programmer should not authorize program changes, nor should the programmer report to the person who authorizes the change.

These same programmers should not have access to data used by the human resource applications. Most programmers argue that they need access to production data to support the application, but I have never found this to be the case. Programmers should not use real data to test changes; rather, they should develop test files that try every possibility. Ideally, programmers should not have access to production programs. If you cannot avoid giving them direct access, their supervisor must authorize all changes, and the programmers should prepare adequate documentation for all of them.

These requirements have changed the role of information systems professionals in most organizations. Information systems professionals now are facilitators. They must help non-IS professionals select and implement LAN solutions that commonly were reserved for the centralized environment. For mission critical systems on LANs, you must implement application development, performance, configuration, and security management programs.

Your organization needs tools for tracking and measuring the reliability of the network. Without tools, your organization cannot quantify the cost of network outages. On the basis of industry averages, outages could cost your organization significant sums of money in idle time or lost business. Management must identify and track various errors. By tracking and controlling these errors during operations, your organization can improve service. Once identified, errors can be tracked and eliminated.

A valuable tool for network performance that is often overlooked is the service-level agreement. A service-level agreement describes the working relationship between the user and the supplier of the LAN. It ensures that service providers and users understand the nature and availability of the offered services. Do not enter into a service-level agreement with users until you have developed a method for tracking availability.

Your organization needs to maintain a centralized hardware and software inventory. Without a software inventory, your organization cannot readily figure out if software was licensed and still possessed by you. Without a hardware inventory, your organization cannot compute its value for risk management calculations—nor can your organization tell how many remote networks can dial up the network!

Without a proper security plan, your organization cannot readily determine if implemented security measures are cost-justified or sufficient. Your organization must value the information processed on any LAN and select appropriate security countermeasures. LAN managers must develop business resumption plans to organize a response to any unforeseen disaster, which might leave computing facilities unusable, a nice segue into my last prediction.

LAN disaster

My prediction about a major LAN disaster involving mission-critical applications is the only one I can guarantee. As shown in FIG. 10-6, your organization faces serious threats. Table 10-1 also provides some statistics on disaster incidents selected from 333 hot-site recoveries since 1982. As you

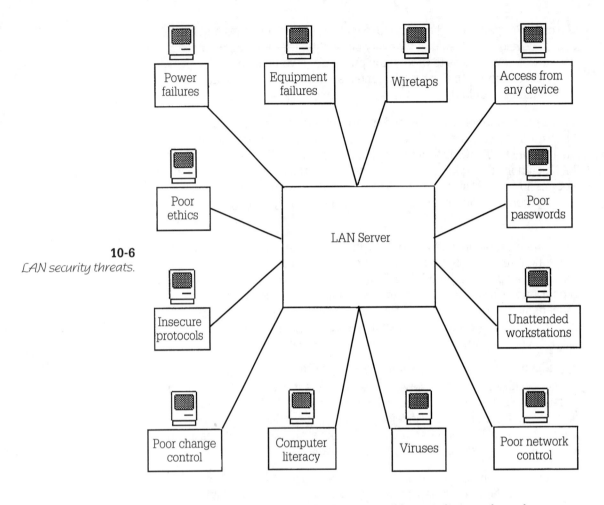

10-6 LAN security threats.

can see, the question is not whether you will have a disaster, but when. Those organizations choosing to ignore security today will be tomorrow's headlines. If you have read this far, however, maybe your organization will be one of the lucky ones who protects its network.

LANs, cooperative processing, fiber-optic networks, facsimile machines, mobile communications, telecommuting, image processing systems, and rightsizing are just some areas the new manager should be aware of. The uses made of any technology are largely determined by the technology itself; its functions flow from its form. It is not odd that LANs are used for cooperative and workflow processing.

Once a technology is admitted into an organization, it plays out its hand and does what it was designed to do. Your task is to understand this design. Alternatively, when you admit technology into your organization, you must do so with full knowledge—with your eyes wide open. A new technology does not add or subtract something to your organization; it changes

**Table 10-1
Recorded disasters**

Event	Location	Date	# Data centers affected
Rain storm	Chicago, IL	8/14/87	5
Earthquake	Whittier, CA	10/1/87	3
Phone outage	Hillsdale, IL	5/8/88	3
Hurricane Hugo	Charleston, SC	8/15/89	5
Earthquake	San Francisco, CA	10/17/89	18
Power outage	New York, NY	8/13/90	28
Utility vault fire	New York, NY	12/27/90	2
Hurricane Bob	Northeast U.S.	8/19/91	3
Terrorist bomb	London, U.K.	4/10/92	7
Flood	Chicago, IL	4/13/92	33
Riot	Los Angeles, CA	5/1/92	2
Hurricane Andrew	Southeast U.S.	8/24/92	39
Nor'easter	New York, NY	12/11/92	7
Terrorist bomb	New York, NY	2/26/93	21

Contingency Planning Research

everything. (Removing LANs from your organization will not discourage information sharing.)

We, as security administrators and managers, must grasp these new realities and realize our responsibilities to our different enterprises so that we can compete in an environment characterized by dispersal, outsourcing, and decentralization. We should understand that our solutions for our organizations must not inhibit the organization's aggressive pursuit of business opportunities. Senior executives will stop tolerating security systems that hold back the organization's progress. Information technology security professionals are advised to look at new ways to succeed.

There is an old French saying that says: "aux grands maux, les grands remèdes," which, loosely translated, means: "desperate situations, dramatic solutions." The best way to succeed in turbulent times is to anticipate the future and the best way to predict the future is to look for paradigm shifts. We can all recognize some shifts if we look for them. The more people an organization has exploring the future and looking for paradigm shifts, the less likely that the organization will be adversely affected by unexpected future events. Everyone can learn something from Wayne Gretzky, the Los Angeles

Kings' star hockey player, who once said, "I skate to where I think the puck will be."

Zig Ziglar (1988), an inspirational speaker, wrote the following:

> Whatever it is you do, there are many people in the same profession who are making significant contributions to that profession and are making a lot of money as a result. It's not the occupation or profession that makes you succeed or fail, it's how you see yourself and your occupation.

Helping your organization protect its most vital asset—information—is perhaps one way you can make your mark and help your organization succeed. It might be the only way some security administrators, managers, and organizations can survive!

	Yes	No

Access controls

1. Are access privileges controlled by
   a) Logical volume mapping? _____ _____
   b) Password recovery? _____ _____
   c) Copy protection? _____ _____
   d) Execute only programs? _____ _____
   e) User count of licensed packages? _____ _____
2. Are users provided with information about their last session on their next logon? _____ _____
3. Does the system automatically disable an account or workstation when evidence exists of repeated unauthorized attempts to access the network? _____ _____
4. If no activity has occurred for a certain period of time, does the system automatically log off the session? _____ _____
5. Are workstation identification codes used to assure that only authorized devices are using the network? _____ _____
6. Are the network banners or trophies kept to an absolute minimum, so as not to divulge information that will assist unauthorized people in attacking the system? _____ _____

Password controls

1. Is a logon procedure, including a unique individual password, required for all accesses to the network? _____ _____
2. Are passwords encrypted when transmitted across the network? _____ _____
3. Do password controls include
   a) Unique passwords? _____ _____
   b) One-way encryption? _____ _____
   c) Storage of passwords in nonplain text? _____ _____
   d) Administrative control? _____ _____
   e) Standards for length and composition? _____ _____
   f) Limited reuse of old passwords? _____ _____
   g) Forced password change? _____ _____
4. Are passwords always entered by the individual user, rather than programmed logon routines? _____ _____

LAN access to host computer

1. Do you have the following access controls to host systems:
   a) Can host identify which node is accessing it? _____ _____

	Yes	No

b) Are controls sufficient to assign user responsibility for access and modification? ____ ____

c) Does the host system authenticate itself to the user prior to beginning a session? ____ ____

d) Are controls used to authenticate host logoff to prevent line grabbing? ____ ____

2. Is encryption used to protect transmitted data? ____ ____

1. Is modem attached to LAN via
   a) modem pool? ____ ____
   b) mainframe? ____ ____
   c) file server? ____ ____

   Remote access via modem

2. Is the following type of access allowed
   a) dial-in? ____ ____
   b) dial-out? ____ ____
   c) auto-answer? ____ ____

3. Is there dial-up access? ____ ____

4. How is dial-up access controlled? ____ ____

5. Can dial-up access be used to access the host system, i.e., backdoor access? ____ ____

6. Are automatic callback devices used for dial-up lines? ____ ____

7. When dial-up users reach the network, are they met by modem tone or by a tone other than a carrier? ____ ____

8. Are high-speed modems used on dial-up lines to thwart persons using the more commonly found 300/1200/2400-baud modems? ____ ____

9. Are the telephone numbers for dial-up lines unpublished or otherwise made unavailable? ____ ____

10. Are the telephone numbers used for dial-up connections changed periodically and whenever a compromise takes place? ____ ____

11. Can the network trace the telephone numbers of users on dial-up lines, e.g., caller id? ____ ____

12. Does the network restrict help information, system status, and other useful information to authenticated users? ____ ____

	Yes	No

Reporting

1. Is there an audit trail of
   a) failed access attempts (logon failures)? ____ ____
   b) function violations (data or access violations)? ____ ____
2. Are problems tracked? ____ ____
3. Is there a user listing of users and access capabilities? ____ ____
4. Is a log kept of all sensitive or important messages for a certain period of time, such that these messages are reconstructible? ____ ____
5. Are trace and snapshot facilities available to log suspect user activity in real-time? ____ ____
6. Are message handling logs kept so users know when a message was delivered or a transaction processed? ____ ____

Change control

1. Are formal change controls in place for network software and hardware changes? ____ ____
2. Is a history log maintained for application changes? ____ ____
3. Is a log of application versions maintained? ____ ____
4. Is a log maintained of configuration management changes? ____ ____

Userid

1. Are users tied to specific devices? ____ ____
2. Are users only allowed one session per userid? ____ ____

Workstations

1. Are terminals timed out after a predetermined period of inactivity? ____ ____
2. Is there automatic logoff when power-off occurs? ____ ____
3. Are privileges controlled on a workstation or node basis? ____ ____

Network management

1. Has responsibility for network security and administration been assigned? ____ ____
2. Are administration functions monitored? ____ ____
3. Have special software routines been written to provide graceful degradation of service to users? ____ ____
4. Are critical and sensitive network software routines protected via hash totals, file authentication codes, encryption, or other methods so modification of such routines is detected? ____ ____

	Yes	No
5. Is third-party software used?	____	____
6. Can passwords or sensitive data be captured?	____	____

File server site protection

1. Are there controls over physical access? ____ ____
2. Are transactions simultaneously recorded, i.e., are these mirrored drives? ____ ____
3. Is there a UPS attached to the LAN? ____ ____
4. Are all wiring closets locked when not being used by network or support personnel? ____ ____
5. Is virus detection and prevention software used? ____ ____

Following is a mini-dictionary of words from the Internet worm retrieved at Purdue University through the use of reverse-engineering. The words were used in addition to the standard UNIX dictionary on the system.

The list is different in that it contains none of the usual hacker choices such as *hobbit, dwarf, skywalker, gandalf* or *conan*. Nor does it contain common women's names such as *jennifer* or *kathy* or common men's names such as *thomas* or *steven*. No profanity exists either, yet we know from concerted attacks that curse words or phrases are very popular. Note that you will find a very high hit rate when you run a list of curse words against your organization's password file.

I offer this list with no explanation, but I do suggest you put these words in any routines you might have to check passwords!

aaa	arthur	beverly	chester
academia	athena	bicameral	cigar
aerobics	atmosphere	bob	classic
airplane	aztecs	brenda	clusters
albany	azure	brian	coffee
albatross	bacchus	bridget	coke
albert	bailey	broadway	collins
alex	banana	bumbling	commrades
alexander	bananas	burgess	computer
algebra	bandit	campanile	condo
aliases	banks	cantor	cookie
alphabet	barber	cardinal	cooper
ama	baritone	carmen	cornelius
amorphous	bass	carolina	couscous
analog	bassoon	caroline	creation
anchor	batman	cascades	creosote
andromache	beater	castle	cretin
animals	beauty	cat	daemon
answer	beethoven	cayuga	dancer
anthropogenic	beloved	celtics	daniel
anvils	benz	cerulean	danny
anything	beowulf	change	dave
aria	berkeley	charles	december
ariadne	berliner	charming	defoe
arrow	beryl	charon	deluge

Appendix B

desperate	fidelity	guntis	kathleen
develop	finite	hacker	kermit
dieter	fishers	hamlet	kernel
digital	flakes	handily	kirkland
discovery	float	happening	knight
disney	flower	harmony	ladle
dog	flowers	harold	lambda
drought	foolproof	harvey	lamination
duncan	football	hebrides	larkin
eager	foresight	heinlein	larry
easier	format	hello	lazarus
edges	forsythe	help	lebeque
edinburgh	fourier	herbert	lee
edwin	fred	hiawatha	leland
edwina	friend	hibernia	leroy
egghead	frighten	honey	lewis
eiderdown	fun	horse	light
eileen	fungible	horus	lisa
einstein	gabriel	hutchins	louis
elephant	gardner	imbroglio	lynne
elizabeth	garfield	imperial	macintosh
ellen	gauss	include	mack
emerald	george	ingres	maggot
engine	gertrude	inna	magic
engineer	ginger	innocuous	malcolm
enterprise	glacier	irishman	mark
enzyme	gnu	isis	markus
ersatz	golfer	japan	marty
establish	gorgeous	jessica	marvin
estate	gorges	jester	master
euclid	gosling	jixian	maurice
evelyn	gouge	johnny	mellon
extension	graham	joseph	merlin
fairway	gryphon	joshua	mets
felicia	guest	judith	michael
fender	guitar	juggle	michelle
fermat	gumption	julia	mike

minimum	persona	rolex	sossina
minsky	pete	romano	sparrows
moguls	peter	ronald	spit
moose	philip	rosebud	spring
morley	phoenix	rosemary	squires
mozart	pierre	roses	strangle
nancy	pizza	ruben	stratford
napoleon	plover	rules	stuttgart
nepenthe	plymouth	ruth	subway
ness	polynomial	sal	success
network	pondering	saxon	summer
newton	pork	scamper	super
next	poster	scheme	superstage
noxious	praise	scott	support
nutrition	precious	scotty	supported
nyquist	prelude	secret	surfer
oceanography	prince	sensor	suzanne
ocelot	princeton	serenity	swearer
olivetti	protect	sharks	symmetry
olivia	protozoa	sharon	tangerine
oracle	pumpkin	sheffield	tape
orca	puneet	sheldon	target
orwell	puppet	shiva	tarragon
osiris	rabbit	shuttle	taylor
outlaw	rachmaninoff	signature	telephone
oxford	rainbow	simon	temptation
pacific	raindrop	simple	thailand
painless	raleigh	singer	tiger
pakistan	random	single	toggle
pam	rascal	smile	tomato
papers	really	smiles	topography
password	rebecca	smooch	tortoise
patricia	remote	smother	toyota
penguin	rick	snatch	trails
peoria	ripple	snoopy	trivial
percolate	robotics	soap	trombone
persimmon	rochester	socrates	tubas

tuttle	vicky	will	wormwood
umesh	village	william	yacov
unhappy	virginia	williamsburg	yang
unicorn	warren	willie	yellowstone
unknown	water	winston	yosemite
urchin	weenie	wisconsin	zap
utility	whatnot	wizard	zimmerman
vasant	whiting	wombat	
vertigo	whitney	woodwind	

Following is a list of LAN security products grouped by type.

Access control systems

FREEZE!!
Command Software Systems, Inc.
1061 E. Indiantown Road, Suite 500
Jupiter, FL 33477
(407) 575-3200

FREEZE!! is access control software for PCs and workstations.

C:Cure
Leprechaun Software International, Ltd.
2619 Sandy Plains Road
Marietta, GA 30066
(404) 971-8900

C:Cure is a hardware device that allows write-protection of a hard drive.

Data Security Plus
PC Guardian
1133 East Francisco Blvd.
San Rafael, CA 94901
(800) 288-8126

Data Security Plus is program approval, virus protection, directory locking, audit trail, and forced backup software package for single-user or multiuser DOS-based PCs and LANs.

Net/DACS
Pyramid Development Corp.
70 Inwood Road
Rocky Hill, CT 06067
(203) 257-4223

Net/DACS is user identification and authentication software for Novell NetWare.

COMLOCK
IRILOCK
Techmar Computer Products, Inc.
98-11 Queens Blvd.
Rego Park, NY 11374
(800) 922-0015

COMLOCK is a family of access control sofware for disks. IRILOCK protects executable files on floppy or hard disks.

Audit software

SAFE-Guard Professional /OS/2
Uti-maco Safeguard Systems, Inc.
750 Old Main Street
Rocky Hill, CT 06067
(800) 394-4230

SAFE-Guard is identification, authentication, administration, and verification software for DOS and OS/2. The software controls rights, audit, and object reuse.

Auditor Plus
Braintree Technology, Inc.
62 Accord Park Drive
Norwell, MA 02061-1606
(617) 982-0200

Auditor Plus is a VMS security management and auditing system.

LT Auditor 386
Blue Lance Software
1700 West Loop South, Suite 1100
Houston, TX 77027
(713) 680-1187

LT Auditor 386 is network management software for monitoring, recording, and reporting network activity.

LANGARD
Command Software Systems, Inc.
1061 E. Indiantown Road, Suite 500
Jupiter, FL 33477
(407) 575-3200

LANGARD is a LAN security and auditing program.

Auditor
Leprechaun Software International, Ltd.
2619 Sandy Plains Road
Marietta, GA 30066
(404) 971-8900

Auditor is software that collects workstation information and changes on hardware configuration, files, and applications.

The Network Security Monitor (NSM)
Network-1, Inc.
P.O. Box 8370
Long Island City, NY 11101-9714
(800) NET-WRK1

NSM is full-featured network security monitoring and auditing software that collects critical information on network security status for all nodes on your network.

Backup software

ARCserve
Cheyenne Software, Inc.
55 Bryant Avenue
Roslyn, NY 11576
(516) 484-5110

ARCserve is a NetWare automated backup and restore software package.

Autoback
Leprechaun Software International, Ltd.
2619 Sandy Plains Road
Marietta, GA 30066
(404) 971-8900

Autoback is automatic backup software for LAN Manager, LANtastic, NetWare, and VINES workstations.

Network Archivist NLM
Palindrome Corporation
600 E. Delphi Road
Napierville, IL 60563
(708) 505-3300

Network Archivist NLM is NetWare backup, disaster recovery, and data archiving software.

BACK-Guard
Uti-maco Safeguard Systems, Inc.
750 Old Main Street
Rocky Hill, CT 06067
(800) 394-4230

BACK-Guard is a user-friendly, SAA-compliant, fast-backup program that transfers files onto diskettes or other media.

Client-server software

OCSG/Kerberos Client-server Development Toolkit
Open Computing Security Group
2451 152nd Avenue N.E.
Redmond, WA 98052
(206) 883-8721

The Kerberos Development Toolkit provides libraries and routines to develop secure client-server applications.

Trusted ORACLE7
Oracle Corp.
500 Oracle Parkway
Redwood Shores, CA 94065
(415) 506-7000

Trusted ORACLE7 is high-security database management software package designed to meet TSEC B1 criteria and ITSEC E3 requirements.

COP Communication security systems

Astronautics Corporation of America
P.O. Box 523
Milwaukee, WI 53201
(414) 447-8200

COP (Communication Oriented Processor) is an intelligent communications control system that adapts and directs the flow between selected resources.

FAXserve
Cheyenne Software, Inc.
55 Bryant Avenue
Roslyn, NY 11576
(516) 484-5110

FAXserve is a high performance server-based solution for network facsimile services.

Defender
Digital Pathways, Inc.
201 Ravendale Drive
Mountain View, CA 94043
(415) 964-0707

Defender is a line of secure dial products.

FasTraq
Leemah DataCom Security Corporation
3948 Trust Way
Hayward, CA 94545-3716
(510) 786-0790

FasTraq is a security modem with secure call-in, glare-proof callback, and second line callback.

Disaster recovery software

NETWORKS
CHI/COR Information Management
300 South Wacker Drive
Chicago, IL 60606
(312) 322-0150

NETWORKS addresses LAN recovery planning, including backup and archiving, recovery planning, and hot-site services.

Recovery Architect
Dataguard Recovery Services, Inc.
P.O. Box 37144
Louisville, KY 40233-7144
(502) 426-3434

Recovery Architect is a PC-based disaster recovery planning tool.

Encryption/ decryption

LTPASS for Lotus 1-2-3, Quattro Pro, and Symphony
PXPASS for Paradox
WRPASS for Wordperfect
XLPASS for Excel
AccessData
87 East 600 South
Orem, UT 84058
(800) 658-5199

These products decrypt passwords for the listed software.

Encryption Plus
PC Guardian
1133 East Francisco Blvd.
San Rafael, CA 94901
(800) 288-8126

Encryption Plus is encryption software for any local drive except the C:.

SecurCOM
Quince
121 Dundas Street East, Suite 207
Belleville, ON
K8N 1C3
(613) 967-2843

SecurCOM is a hardware encryption device for any Ethernet or IEEE 802.3 LAN.

IRICRYPT
Techmar Computer Products, Inc.
98-11 Queens Blvd.
Rego Park, NY 11374
(800) 922-0015

IRICRYPT is a DOS-resident utility for encrypting files written to disk.

Fault-tolerant

SystemPro
Compaq Computer Corp.
P.O. Box 692000
Houston, TX 77269-2000
(713) 374-4711

SystemPro offers hardware-based disk mirroring.

NetFRAME
NetFRAME Systems, Inc.
1545 Barber Lane
Milpitas, CA 95035
(800) 852-3726

NetFRAME servers offer error-correcting memory. High-end units have redundant power supplies.

Information security

CA-UNICENTER
Computer Associates International, Inc.
711 Stewart Avenue
Garden City, NY 11530-4787
(516) 227-3300

CA-UNICENTER is a UNIX security product.

WATCHDOG DIRECTOR LAN
Fischer International Systems
4073 Merchantile Avenue
Naples, FL 33942
(800) 237-4510

WATCHDOG DIRECTOR LAN is a central security administration product.

Bindview Network Control System
LAN Support Group, Inc.
2425 Fountainview, Suite 390
Houston, TX 77057
(713) 789-0882

Bindview NCS is reporting and analyzing software for NetWare.

Trusted Access
Program Manager Plus
Lassen Software, Inc.
5923 Clark Road, Suite F
P.O. Box 2319
Paradise, CA 95967-2319
(800) 338-2126

Trusted Access provides logon authentication and continuous, transparent walkaway security. Program Manager Plus is a secure menu system designed to separate end users from the DOS command line and provide basic virus detection.

Empower Remote
Magna Corp.
332 Commercial Street
San Jose, CA 95112
(408) 282-0900

Empower Remote is network security administration software for large Macintosh networks.

Network management

REMOTELY POSSIBLE
Avalan Technology, Inc.
116 Hopping Brook Park
Holliston, MA 01746
(800) 441-2281

REMOTELY POSSIBLE is LAN remote control utility for Novell and NETBIOS networks (Windows and DOS).

LT Event
LT HelpDesk
Blue Lance Software
1700 West Loop South, Suite 1100
Houston, TX 77027
(713) 680-1187

LT Event is a mainframe-like scheduler. LT HelpDesk is a service/work order processing system.

Monitrix
Cheyenne Software, Inc.
55 Bryant Avenue
Roslyn, NY 11576
(516) 484-5110

Monitrix is a NetWare management and monitoring solution.

Expert Sniffer
Network General
4200 Bohannon Drive
Menlo Park, CA 94025
(800) 846-6601

Expert Sniffer is a network troubleshooting tool.

LAN SCHEDULER
Microwork Co.
47 West St. Andrews
Deerfield, IL 60015
(708) 940-8979

LAN SCHEDULER is security, conditional jobs scheduling, and job priority software.

The Network Event Manager (NEM)
The Network Mapping Utility (NMU)
Network-1, Inc.
P.O. Box 8370
Long Island City, NY 11101-9714
(800) NET-WRK1

NEM is a real-time management tool that allows the network or systems manager to specify events on the network to monitor and then execute commands to take action on the event. NMU is a network utility that learns about nodes, protocols, names, and other information on the network.

Disk Manager-N
NetOptimizer
Net·Utils
Ontrack Computer Systems, Inc.
6321 Bury Drive
Eden Prairie, MN 55346
(800) 752-1333

Disk Manager-N is installation software that initializes, partitions, and prepares a hard disk for Novell network file server. NetOptimizer is file server reorganization software for Novell that helps protect and recover data. Net·Utils is hard disk maintenance software for Novell.

Network operating systems

AppleShare
Apple Computer, Inc.
20525 Mariani Ave.
Cupertino, CA
(408) 996-1010

AppleShare is a Macintosh-based peer-to-peer local area network.

LANtastic
Artisoft, Inc.
691 East River Road
Tucson, AZ 85704

LANtastic is a DOS-based peer-to-peer local area network.

VINES
Banyan Systems Incorporated
115 Flanders Road
Westboro, MA 01581
(617) 898-1000

Vines is a device-to-device communications system.

OS/2 LAN Manager
IBM Corp. (personal computers)
P.O. Box 1328
Boca Raton, FL 33428

LAN Manager is an OS/2-based peer-to-peer local area network.

NetWare
Novell, Inc.
122 E. 1700 S.
Provo, UT 84601
(801) 379-5900

NetWare is a device-to-device communication system.

Physical security

Security Force
Globus Systems, Inc.
1447 McAllister Street
San Francisco, CA 94115
(415) 292-6744

Security Force is software that protects hardware against theft by using a buddy system to check on microcomputers on the network.

Electronic Asset Protection
Knogo
350 Wireless Boulevard
Hauppauge, NY 11788
(800) 645-4224

Electronic Asset Protection systems prevent theft of computers and software using invisible detection systems and tags.

Network security

SECNET
Concord-Eracom
7370 Bramalea Road, Units 18-19
Mississauga, Ontario
L5S 1N6
(416) 672-0252

SECNET is a PC-to-host security product.

Net/Assure
Cordant, Inc.
11400 Commerce Park Drive
Reston, VA 22091-1506
(800) 843-1132

Net/Assure provides identification and authentication, audit trails, discretionary access control, and automatic transparent DES encryption.

Safeword
Enigma Logic, Inc.
2151 Salvio Street, Suite 301
Concord, CA 94520
(510) 827-5707

Safeword is security software for Banyan, Novell, Stratus, and UNIX.

Power systems

Ferrups
Fortress
Best Power Technology, Inc.
P.O. Box 280
Necedah, WI 54646
(800) 356-5794

Ferrups and Fortress are UPS for LANs.

Risk management

RiskWatch
Expert Systems Software, Inc.
8201 Corporate Drive, Suite 620
Landover, MD 20785
(301) 731-4666

RiskWatch is risk management software used for formal analysis of applications and networks.

Baysien Decision Support System [BOSS]
Ozier, Peterse & Associates
870 Market Street, Suite 1001
San Francisco, CA 94102
(415) 989-9092

BOSS is risk management software used for formal analysis of applications and networks.

Virus protection

D-FENCE
SWEEP, SWEEP for NetWare, SWEEP for VAX/VMS and Pathworks
VACCINE
Alternative Computer Technologies
P.O. Box 1218
West Chester, OH 45071
(513) 755-1958

D-FENCE is a memory-resident utility that prevents the use of unauthorized floppy disks. SWEEP is virus-scanning and removal software. VACCINE is virus prevention software.

Central Point Anti-Virus for NetWare
Central Point Software, Inc.
15220 N.W. Greenbrier Parkway
Beaverton, OR 97006
(503) 690-2260

Central Point Anti-Virus (CPAV) for NetWare is an NLM offering server protection and real-time scanning.

InocuLAN
Cheyenne Software, Inc.
55 Bryant Avenue
Roslyn, NY 11576
(800) 243-9462

InocuLAN is a server-based network anti-virus program.

F-Prot Professional
Command Software Systems, Inc.
1061 E. Indiantown Road, Suite 500
Jupiter, FL 33477
(407) 575-3200

F-Prot Professional is a standalone virus detection, prevention, and removal program.

Victor Charlie
Computer Security Associates
P.O. Box 2001
Columbia, SC 29202
(803) 796-6591

Victor Charlie secures the areas on PCs where viruses operate.

Disk Defender
Director Technologies, Inc.
906 University Place
Evanston, IL 60201
(312) 491-2334

Disk Defender is an anti-virus system.

Untouchable Network NLM
Fifth Generation Systems, Inc.
10049 N. Reiger Road
Baton Rouge, LA 70809
(800) 873-4384

Untouchable Network NLM provides integrity checking on a NetWare server.

Virus Buster
Leprechaun Software International, Inc.
2619 Sandy Plains Road
Marietta, GA 30066
(404) 971-8900

Virus Buster is virus-detection and prevention software for 3Com, LANtastic, NetWare, OS/2 LAN Manager, Token Ring, and VINES.

Clean-Up
NetShield NLM
ViruScan
VShield
McAfee Associates, Inc.
3350 Scott Boulevard, Bldg. 14
Santa Clara, CA 95054-3107
(408) 988-3832

Clean-Up is virus-removal software, and restores files inoculated by ViruScan. NetShield NLM provides virus-detection products for NetWare. ViruScan is virus-detection software. VShield is virus-prevention software.

PC ScanMaster
NetShield NLM
Network-1, Inc.
P.O. Box 8370
Long Island, NY 11101-9714
(800) NET-WRK1

PC ScanMaster and NetShield NLM are virus-detection products for NetWare. NetPro also has Banyan VINES virus-protection software.

Dr. Solomon's Anti-Virus Toolkit
Ontrack Computer Systems, Inc.
6321 Bury Drive
Eden Prairie, MN 55346
(800) 752-1333

Dr. Solomon's Anti-Virus Toolkit detects and identifies all known viruses and variants for DOS, Windows, and OS/2 environments.

Virus Prevention Plus
PC Guardian
1133 East Francisco Blvd.
San Rafael, CA 94901
(800) 288-8126

Virus Prevention Plus controls the execution of programs, preventing unapproved and possibly infected programs from running.

Vi-Spy
RG Software
6900 East Camelback Road, Suite 630
Scottsdale, AZ 85251
(602) 423-8000

Vi-Spy is a LAN virus detection, removal, protection, and scheduling program.

Drive-In Anti-Virus
Safetynet, Inc.
55 Bleeker Street
Millburn, NJ 07041-1414
(800) 851-0188

Drive-In Anti-Virus is anti-virus and menu services software for LANs.

Integrity Master
Stiller Research
2625 Ridgeway Street
Tallahassee, FL 32310
(800) 622-2793

Integrity Master is LAN virus protection, data integrity, security, and change management program.

Norton AntiVirus
Symantec/Peter Norton Group
2500 Broadway, Suite 200
Santa Monica, CA 90404
(310) 453-4600

Norton AntiVirus is virus software for networks.

AntiVirusPlus
Techmar Computer Products, Inc.
98-11 Queens Blvd.
Rego Park, NY 11374
(800) 922-0015

AntiVirusPlus is virus detection, prevention, and restoration software.

PC Rx
Trend Micro Devices, Inc.
2421 W. 205th Street, Suite D 100
Torrance, CA 90501
(310) 782-8190

PC Rx is virus scanning and removal software for LANs.

VIR-Guard
Uti-maco Safeguard Systems, Inc.
750 Old Main Street
Rocky Hill, CT 06067
(800) 394-4230

VIR-Guard is user-friendly, SAA-compliant, anti-viral software.

ViruSafe/LAN
Xtree Company
4115 Broad Street, Building #1
San Luis Obispo, CA 93401-7993
(805) 541-0604

ViruSafe/LAN is virus-prevention and -detection software.

Organizations

Following are organizations who are directly concerned with LAN security or have special interest groups (SIG) who focus on the subject.

American Institute of Certified Public Accountants (AICPA)
1211 Avenue of the Americas
New York, NY   10036

American Society for Industrial Security (ASIS)
1655 N. Fort Meyer Drive,
Suite 1200
Arlington, VA   22209

Association for Computing Machinery (ACM)
Special Interest Group on Computers and Security (SIGCAS)
11 W. 42 St.
New York, NY   10036

Association for Computing Machinery (ACM)
Special Interest Group on Security, Audit and Control (SIGSAC)
c/o Steve Clemons
Norfolk Southern
8 N. Jefferson St.
Roanoke, VA   24042-0006

Association for Information Management (AIM)
7380 Parkway Drive
La Mesa, CA   92401

Association for Systems Management (ASM)
P.O. Box 38370
Cleveland, OH   44138-0370

Association of Contingency Planners (ACP)
P.O. Box 73-149
Long Beach, CA   90801-0073

Association of the Institute for Certification of Computer Professionals (AICCP)
2200 E. Devon Avenue, Suite 268
Des Plaines, IL   60018

Bank Administration Institute (BAI)
60 Gould Center
Rolling Meadows, IL   60008

Business Resumption Planners Association (BRPA)
P.O. Box 1078
Niles, IL   60648-5078

Business and Industry Council for Emergency Planning and Preparedness (BICEPP)
P.O. Box 9457
Newport Beach, CA   92658

Canadian Information Processing Society (CIPS)
430 King Street West, Suite 205
Toronto, Ontario
M5V 1L5

Canadian Institute of Chartered Accountants (CICA)
150 Bloor Street West
Toronto, Ontario
M5S 2Y2

Canadian Standards Association (CSA)
178 Rexdale Boulevard
Rexdale, Ontario
M9W 1R3

COMMON
401 North Michigan Avenue
Chicago, IL   60611

Computer and Business Equipment Manufacturers Association (CBEMA)
311 First St. NW, Suite 500
Washington, DC 20001

Computer Professionals for Social Responsibility (CPSR)
P.O. Box 717
Palo Alto, CA 94301

Computer Security Institute (CSI)
360 Church St.
Northboro, MA 01532

Data Administration Management Association (DAMA)
152 W. Northwest Highway, Suite 103
Palatine, IL 60067

Data Entry Management Association (DEMA)
101 Merrit, 7 Corporate Park
Norwalk, CT 06851

Data Processing Management Association (DPMA)
505 Busse Highway
Park Ridge, IL 60068-3191

Digital Equipment Computer Users Society (DECUS)
219 Boston Post Road (BP02)
Marlboro, MA 01752

Disaster Recovery Institute
5647 Telegraph Road
St. Louis, MO 630129

EDP Auditors Association (EDPAA)
P.O. Box 88180, 300 Schmale
Carol Stream, IL 60188-0180

GUIDE
401 North Michigan Avenue
Chicago, IL 60611

Information System Security Association (ISSA)
401 North Michigan Avenue
Chicago, IL 60611

IEEE Social Impact Group, Computer Security
1730 Massachusetts Ave.
Washington, DC 20036-1903

Institute for the Certification of Computer Professionals (ICCP)
2200 E. Devon Avenue, Suite 268
Des Plaines, IL 60018

Institute of Internal Auditors (IIA)
249 Maitland Avenue, Box 1119
Altamonte Springs, FL 32701

International Information Systems Security Certification Consortium, Inc. (ISC²)
P.O. Box 98
Spencer, MA 01562-0098

MIS Training Institute
498 Concord Street
Framingham, MA 01701

National Centre for Computer Crime Data (NCCCD)
904 Daniel Court
Santa Cruz, CA 95062

National Computer Security Association (NCSA)
227 West Main Street
Mechanicsburg, PA 17055

Quality Assurance Institute (QAI)
7575 Dr. Phillips Boulevard,
 Suite 350
Orlando, FL   32819

SHARE
401 North Michigan Avenue
Chicago, IL   60611

Bibliography

Computer crimes Bequai, August. 1983. *How to Prevent Computer Crime*. New York: John Wiley & Sons.

BloomBecker, Buck. 1990. *Spectacular Computer Crimes*. Homewood, IL: Dow Jones-Irwin.

Bowcott, Owen and Sally Hamilton. 1990. *Beating The System*. London: Bloomsbury Publishing, Inc.

Comer, Michael J., Patrick M. Ardis, and David H. Price. 1988. *Bad Lies in Business*. Maidenhead: McGraw-Hill Book Company (UK).

Cornwall, Hugo. 1987. *Data Theft*. London: Heinemann Professional Publishing Limited.

Farr, Robert. 1975. *The Electronic Criminals*. New York: McGraw-Hill.

Hafner, Katie and John Markoff. 1991. *Cyberpunk: Outlaws and Hackers on the Computer Frontier*. New York: Simon & Schuster.

Jennings, Karla. 1990. *The Devouring Fungus*. New York: W. W. Norton.

Parker, Donn B. 1975. *Computer Abuse Assessment*. Menlo Park, CA: SRI.

_____. 1976. *Crime by Computer*. New York: Scribner's Sons.

_____. 1983. *Fighting Computer Crime*. New York: Scribner's Sons.

Schwartu, Winn. 1991. *Terminal Compromise*. United States: Inter Pact Press.

Whiteside, Thomas. 1978. *Computer Capers: Tales of Embezzlement and Fraud*. New York: Thomas Y. Crowell Co.

Contingency planning Catania, Salvatore C., Walter J. Dick and Martin E. Silverman. 1980. *Contingency Planning: A Discussion of Strategies*. USA: Coopers & Lybrand.

Federal Information Processing Standards Publication 87. March 1981. *Guidelines for ADP Contingency Planning*. National Bureau of Standards.

Isaac, Irene. November 1985. *Guide on Selecting ADP Backup Process Alternatives*. National Bureau of Standards, NBS Special Publication 500-134.

Janulartis, Victor. February 1985. "Creating a Disaster Recovery Plan." *Infosystems*.

_____. February 1985. "Getting a Grip on Disaster Planning Needs." *Infosystems*.

NBS Special Publication 500-85. July 1981. *Executive Guide to ADP Contingency Planning*. National Bureau of Standards.

Controls

American Institute of Certified Public Accountants. 1977. *The Auditor's Study and Evaluation of Internal Control in EDP Systems*. New York: AICPA.

Beniger, James R. 1986. *The Control Revolution*. Cambridge, MA: Harvard University Press.

Boritz, Jefim E. 1987. *Computer Control & Audit Guide*. Waterloo, ON: University of Waterloo Press.

Brink, Victor Z. and Herbert Witt. 1982. *Modern Internal Auditing: Appraising Operations and Controls*. 4th ed. New York: John Wiley & Sons.

Canadian Institute of Chartered Accountants. 1986. *Computer Control Guidelines*. Toronto: CICA.

_____. 1991. *Managing and Using Microcomputers*. Toronto: CICA.

Davis, G.B. 1968. *Auditing & EDP*. New York: AICPA.

EDP Auditors Foundation. April 1990. *Control Objectives*. Carol Stream, IL: EDPAF.

Govindan, Marshall and John Picard. 1990. *Manifesto on Information Systems Control and Management: A New World Order*. Toronto: McGraw-Hill Ryerson.

Harper, R.M. Fall 1986. "Internal Control of Microcomputers in Local Area Networks." *Journal of Information Systems:* 67-80.

Institute of Internal Auditors. 1977. *Systems Auditability & Control*. Altamonte Springs, FL: IIA.

Moeller, Robert R. 1989. *Computer Audit, Control and Security*. New York: John Wiley & Sons.

Office of the Auditor General of Canada. 1983. *Audit Guide: Auditing EDP: Conducting EDP Applications Audits*. Ottawa: Queen's Printers.

_____. 1983. *Audit Guide: Auditing EDP: Conducting EDP Facilities Audits*. Ottawa: Queen's Printers.

_____. 1983. *Audit Guide: Auditing EDP: Conducting the EDP Financial Controls Audit*. Ottawa: Queen's Printers.

Perry, William. 1983. *Auditing Information Systems: A Step-by-Step Approach*. Carol Stream, IL: EDP Auditors Foundation.

Porter, W. Thomas and William E. Perry. 1981. *EDP Controls and Auditing* 3rd ed. Boston: Kent Publishing Company.

Ruthberg, Zella G. and Robert McKenzie, eds. April 1980. *Audit and Evaluation of Computer Security*. National Bureau of Standards, NBS Special Publication 500-19.

Ruthberg, Zella G., ed. October 1977. *Audit and Evaluation of Computer Security II: System Vulnerabilities and Controls*. National Bureau of Standards, NBS Special Publication 500-57.

Encryption

Bamford, James. 1982. *The Puzzle Palace*. New York: Houghton Mifflin.

Branstad, Dennis. February 1978. *Computer Security and the Data Encryption Standard*. National Bureau of Standards, NBS Special Publication 500-27.

Denning, Dorothy E. R. 1983. *Cryptography and Data Security*. Reading, MA: Addison-Wesley.

Federal Information Processing Standards Publication 46. 15 January 1977. *Data Encryption Standard*. National Bureau of Standards.

Federal Information Processing Standards Publication 74. April 1981. *Guidelines for Implementing and Using the NBS Data Encryption Standard*. National Bureau of Standards.

Federal Information Processing Standards Publication 81. 2 December 1980. *DES Modes of Operation*. National Bureau of Standards.

Federal Information Processing Standards Publication 113. March 1985. *Standard on Computer Data Authentication*. National Bureau of Standards.

Gait, Jason. November 1977. *Validating the Correctness of Hardware Implementations of the NBS Data Encryption Standard*. National Bureau of Standards, NBS Special Publication 500-20.

_____. August 1980. *Maintenance Testing for the Data Encryption Standard*. National Bureau of Standards, NBS Special Publication 500-61.

Gardner, Martin. 1989. *Penrose Tiles to Trapdoor Ciphers*. New York: W. H. Freeman and Company.

Kahn, David. 1983. *Kahn on Codes*. New York: Macmillan Company.

_____. 1967. *The Codebreakers*. New York: Macmillan Company.

Katzen, Harry Jr. 1977. *The Standard Data Encryption Algorithm*. New York: Petrocelli Books.

Lysing, Henry. 1974. *Secret Writing*. New York: Dover Publications.

Seberry, Jennifer and Josef Pieprzyk. 1989. *Cryptography: An Introduction to Computer Security*. Englewood Cliffs: NJ: Prentice-Hall.

Smid, Miles E. October 1979. *A Key Notarization System for Computer Networks*. National Bureau of Standards, NBS Special Publication 500-54.

Rivest, R. L., A. Shamir and L. Adleman. 1978. "A Method for Obtaining Digital Signatures and Public-Key Cryptosystems." *Communications of the ACM 21, No. 2*: 120-126.

Espionage

Carroll, John M. 1966. *The Secrets of Electronic Espionage*. New York: E.P. Dutton.

Cooper, Miles. 1974. *Without Cloak and Dagger —The Truth About the New Espionage*. New York: Simon and Schuster.

Cornwall, Hugo. 1991. *The Industrial Espionage Handbook*. London: Random Century.

Eells, Richard and Peter Nehemkis. 1984. *Corporate Intelligence and Espionage*. New York: Macmillan Publishing Company.

Stoll, Clifford. 1989. *The Cuckoo's Egg*. New York: Doubleday & Company.

Tuck, Jay. 1986. *High-Tech Espionage*. New York: Random House Inc.

Ethics

Blanchard, Kenneth and Norman Vincent Peale. 1989. *The Power of Ethical Management*. New York: Ballantine Books.

Forester, Tom and Perry Morrison. 1991. *Computer Ethics: Cautionary Tales and Ethical Dilemmas in Computing*. 2nd ed. Cambridge, MA: The MIT Press.

Johnson, D. 1985. *Computer Ethics*. Englewood Cliffs, NJ: Prentice-Hall.

_____. 1985. *Ethical Issues in the Use of Computers*. Belmont, CA: Wadsworth.

Lieberstein, Stanley H. 1979. *Who Owns What Is In Your Head?* New York: A. Howard Wyndham Company.

Madden, Carl H. 1972. *Clash of Culture: Management in an Age of Changing Values*. Washington, DC: National Planning Association.

Madsen, Peter and Jay M. Shafritz, editors. 1990. *Essentials of Business Ethics*. New York: Meridian.

Parker, Donn, Susan Swope and Dr. Bruce N. Baker. 1990. *Ethical Conflicts in Information and Computer Science, Technology and Business*. Wellesley, MA: QED Information Sciences, Inc.

Shapiro, Norman Z. and Robert H. Anderson. 1985. *Toward an Ethics and Etiquette for Electronic Mail*. Santa Monica, CA: Rand Corporation.

Hackers Armor, John C. August 30, 1983. "Computer Bandits Should be Outlawed." *Newsday*.

Browne, Malcolm W. November 1983. "Locking Out the Hackers." *Discover*.

Cornwall, Hugo. 1988. *Hacker's Handbook III*. London: Century Hutchinson Limited.

Gibson, William. 1986. *Count Zero*. New York: Berkley.

_____. 1989. *Mona Lisa Overdrive*. New York: Berkley.

_____. 1984. *Neuromancer*. New York: Berkley.

Kidder, Tracy. 1981. *The Soul of a New Machine*. Boston: The Atlantic Monthly Press.

Landreth, Bill. 1989. *Out of the Inner Circle*. Redmond, WA: Tempus Books.

Levy, Steven. 1984. *Hackers*. New York: Doubleday & Company.

Markoff, John. 1993. "Cellular Phreaks and Code Dudes." *Wired*. 1 (1): 60-105.

Raymond, Eric, ed. 1991. *The New Hacker's Dictionary*. Cambridge, MA: MIT Press.

Ryan, Thomas J. 1977. *The Adolescence of P-1*. New York: Collier.

Sterling, Bruce. 1990. *Crystal Express*. New York: Ace Books.

_____. 1988. *Islands in the Net*. New York: Arbor House.

_____. 1992. *The Hacker Crackdown: Law and Disorder on the Electronic Frontier*. New York: Bantam Books.

Sterling, Bruce, ed. 1986. *Mirrorshades: The Cyberpunk Anthology*. New York: Arbor House.

Vinge, Vernor. 1987. *True Names __ and Other Dangers*. New York: Baen Publishing.

Information systems

Becker, H.B. 1983. *Information Integrity —A Structure for its Definition and Management*. New York: McGraw-Hill, Inc.

Burnham, David. 1983. *The Rise of the Computer State*. New York: Random House.

Hanson, Dirk. 1982. *The New Alchemists —Silicon Valley and the Microelectronics Revolution*. Boston: Little, Brown and Company.

Gartner Group. December 1990. *Information Industry Scenario—1995–2000*.

Goldstine, Herman H. 1980. *The Computer: From Pascal to von Neumann*. Princeton, NJ: Princeton University Press.

Melzer, Morton E. 1967. *The Information Center: Management's Hidden Asset*. New York: American Management Association.

Metcalfe, Robyn Shotwell. 1988. *The New Wizard War*. Redmond, WA: Tempus Press.

Postman, Neil. 1992. *Technopoly: The Surrender of Culture to Technology*. New York: Alfred A. Knopf.

Pressman, Roger S. and S. Russell Herron. 1991. *Software Shock: The Danger & The Opportunity*. New York: Dorset House Publishing.

Rosenthal, Lynne S. January 1985. *Guidance on Planning and Implementing Computer System Reliability*. National Bureau of Standards, NBS Special Publication 500-121.

Senn, J. A. 1982. *Information Systems in Management*. Belmont, CA: Wadsworth.

Roszak, T. 1986. *The Cult of Information*. New York: Pantheon.

Weitzen, H. Skip. 1988. *Infopreneurs*. New York: John Wiley and Sons.

Local area networks

Corrigan, Patrick H. and Aisling Guy. 1989. *Building Local Area Networks with Novell's NetWare*. Redwood City, CA: M & T Books.

Datapro Research Corporation. 1985. *All About Local Area Networks and PABX Systems*. Delran, NJ: Datapro.

Day, Michael. 1992. *Enterprise Series: Downsizing to NetWare*. Carmel, IN: New Riders Publishing.

Harper, R.M., A.H. Friedberg and M.J. Cerullo. Fall 1987. "Local Area Networks: The PC Connection." *Journal of Accounting & EDP*:4-11.

King, Adrian J. 1991. *RUNNING LANtastic*. NewYork: Bantam Computer Books.

Kosiur, Dave and Nancy E. H. Jones. 1992. *Macworld Networking Handbook*. San Mateo, CA: IDG Books.

Sawicki, Ed. 1992. *LAN Desktop Guide to Security: NetWare Edition*. Carmel, IN: SAMS.

Stalling, William. 1990. *The Business Guide to Local Area Networks*. Carmel, IN: Howard W. Sams & Company.

Management

Carlzon, Jan. 1987. *Moments of Truth*. Cambridge: MA: Ballinger Publishing Co.

Naisbitt, John. 1982. *Megatrends*. New York: Warner Books.

Ouchi, William G. 1981. *Theory Z*. New York: Avon Books.

Rifkin, Jeremy with Ted Howard. 1980. *Entropy: A New World View*. New York: The Viking Press.

Toffler, Alvin. 1980. *The Third Wave*. New York: William Morrow.

_____. 1990. *Powershift*. New York.

Ziglar, Zig. 1988. *See You at The Top*. Gretna, LA: Pelican Press.

Privacy

Federal Information Processing Standards Publication 41. May 1975. *Computer Security Guidelines for Implementing the Privacy Act of 1974.* National Bureau of Standards.

Fong, Elizabeth. June 1977. *A Database Management Approach to Privacy Act Compliance.* National Bureau of Standards, NBS Special Publication 500-10.

Westin, Alan F. 1972. *Databanks in a Free Society.* New York: Quadrangle Books.

_____. December 1976. *Computers, Health Records, and Citizen Rights.* National Bureau of Standards, NBS Monograph 157.

_____. July 1979. *Computers, Personnel Administration, and Citizen Rights.* National Bureau of Standards, NBS Special Publication 500-50.

Westin, Alan F. and Florence Isbell. January 1977. *A Policy Analysis of Citizen Rights Issues in Health Data Systems.* National Bureau of Standards, NBS Special Publication 469.

Security

Biba, K. J. June 1975. "Integrity Considerations for Secure Computer Systems." *Report MTR-3153.* Bedford, MA: Mitre Corporation.

Buck, Edward R. 1982. *Introduction to Data Security and Controls.* Wellesley, MA: QED Information Sciences Inc.

Campbell, Robert. 1980. *A Guide to Automated Systems Security.* Woodbridge, VA: Advanced Information Management Inc.

Carroll, John. 1987. *Computer Security.* 2nd ed. Woburn, MA: Butterworths.

Clark, D. D. and D. R. Wilson. April 27–29 1987. "A comparison of commercial and military computer security policies." *Proceedings of the 1987 IEEE Symposium on Security and Privacy.*: 184-194.

Clavell, James ed. 1983. *The Art of War: Sun Tzu.* New York: Delacorte Press.

Cooper, J. Arlin. 1989. *Computer and Communications Security.* New York: McGraw-Hill.

Copeland, James Arlin. 1984. *Computer-Security Technology.* Lexington, MA: Lexington Books.

Cronin, Daniel J. 1986. *Microcomputer Data Security.* New York: Prentice-Hall.

Davies, D. W. and W. L. Price. 1984. *Security for Computer Networks*. New York: John Wiley & Sons.

DeMaio, Harry B. 1992. *Information Protection and Other Unnatural Acts*. New York: AMACOM.

Denning, D. E. May 1976. "A Lattice Model of Secure Information Flow." *Communications of the ACM 19*. No. 5.: 236-243.

Department of Defense. December 1985. *Department of Defense Trusted Computer System Evaluation Criteria*. DoD 5200.28-STD.

Federal Information Processing Standards Publication 31. June 1974. *Guidelines for ADP Physical Security and Risk Management*. National Bureau of Standards.

Federal Information Processing Standards Publication 39. February 1974. *Glossary for Computer Systems Security*. National Bureau of Standards.

Federal Information Processing Standards Publication 48. April 1, 1977. *Guidelines on Evaluation of Techniques for Automated Personal Identification*. National Bureau of Standards.

Federal Information Processing Standards Publication 73. June 1980. *Guidelines for Security of Computer Applications*. National Bureau of Standards.

Federal Information Processing Standards Publication 83. September 1980. *Guidelines on User Authentication Techniques for Computer Network Access Control*. National Bureau of Standards.

Federal Information Processing Standards Publication 88. August 1981. *Guideline on Integrity Assurance and Control in Database Applications*. National Bureau of Standards.

Federal Information Processing Standards Publication 102. September 1983. *Guideline for Computer Security Certification and Accreditation*. National Bureau of Standards.

Federal Information Processing Standards Publication 112. 30 May 1985. *Password Usage Standard*. National Bureau of Standards.

Fisher, Royal. 1984. *Information Systems Security*. Englewood Cliffs, NJ: Prentice-Hall.

Gasser, Morrie. 1988. *Building a Secure System*. United States: Van Nostrand Reinhold.

Hoffman, Lance. 1977. *Modern Methods for Computer Security and Privacy*. Englewood Cliffs, NJ: Prentice-Hall.

Institute for Computer Sciences and Technology. *Security of Personal Computer Systems: A Management Guide*. National Bureau of Standards, NBS Special Publication 500-120.

Lamere, J.M. 1985. *La Sécurité Informatique*. Paris: Dunod Informatique.

Lobel, Jerome. 1986. *Foiling the System Breakers*. New York: McGraw-Hill.

Martin, James. 1973. *Security, Accuracy and Privacy in Computer Systems*. Englewood Cliffs, NJ: Prentice-Hall Inc.

National Research Council. 1991. *Computers at Risk: Safe Computing in the Information Age*. Washington, DC: National Academy Press.

NBS Special Publication 451. September 1976. *Database Directions: The Next Steps*. National Bureau of Standards.

Neugent, William, John Gilligan, Lance Hoffman and Zella G. Ruthberg. October 1985. *Technology Assessment: Methods for Measuring the Level of Computer Security*. National Bureau of Standards, NBS Special Publication 500-133.

Orceyre, Michel J. and Robert H. Courtney, Jr., edited by Gloria R. Bolotsky. June 1978. *Considerations in the Selection of Security Measures of Automatic Data Processing Systems*. National Bureau of Standards, NBS Special Publication 500-33.

Parker, Donn B. 1981. *Managers Guide to Computer Security*. Reston, VA: Reston Publishing Inc.

Pfleeger, Charles P. 1989. *Security in Computing*. Englewood Cliffs, NJ: Prentice-Hall Inc.

Ruder, Brian and J. D. Madden, edited by Robert P. Blanc. January 1978. *An Analysis of Computer Security Safeguards for Detecting and Preventing Intentional Computer Misuse*. National Bureau of Standards, NBS Special Publication 500-25.

Ruthberg, Zella G. and William Neugent. April 1984. *Overview of Computer Security Certification and Accreditation.* National Bureau of Standards, NBS Special Publication 500-109.

Steinauer, Dennis D. January 1985. *Security of Personal Computer Systems: A Management Guide.* National Bureau of Standards, NBS Special Publication 500-120.

Turn, Rein, ed. 1984. *Advances in Computer System Security.* Vol. 2. Dedham, MA: Artech House.

Wood, Helen. May 1977. *The Use of Passwords for Controlled Access to Computer Resources.* National Bureau of Standards, NBS Special Publication 500-9.

Risk assessment

Bannister, J.E. and P.A. Bawcutt. 1981. *Practical Risk Management.* London: Witherby.

Demski, J. 1980. *Information Analysis, 2nd ed..* Reading, MA: Addison-Wesley.

Demski, J. and G. Feltham. 1976. *Cost Determination: A Conceptual Approach.* Ames: Iowa State University Press.

Federal Information Processing Standards Publication 31. June 1974. *Guidelines for ADP Physical Security and Risk Management.* National Bureau of Standards.

Federal Information Processing Standards Publication 65. August 1979. *Guidelines for Automatic Data Processing Risk Analysis.* National Bureau of Standards.

International Business Machines. January 1984. *Security Risk Assessment in Electronic Data Processing Systems.* First Edition. White Plains: New York.

Schmucker, Kurt J. 1984. *Fuzzy Sets, Natural Language Computations, and Risk Analysis.* Rockville, MD: Computer Science Press.

Viruses & worms

Brunner, John. 1976. *The Shockwave Rider.* New York: Harper & Row.

Cherryh, C. J. 1988. *Cyteen: The Betrayal.* New York: Popular Library.

_____. 1988. *Cyteen: The Rebirth.* New York: Popular Library.

_____. 1988. *Cyteen: The Vindication.* New York: Popular Library.

Cohen, Fred. 1984. "Computer Viruses: Theory and Experiments." *Proceedings of the 7th National Computer Security Conference.* 240-263.

Deloitte Haskins & Sells/Information Systems Security Association. 1989. *Computer Viruses.* New York: DH&S.

Dembart, Lee. November 1984. "Attack of the Computer Virus." *Discover.*

Denning, Peter J. May–June 1988. "Computer Viruses." *American Scientist,* Vol. 76: 236-238.

Fites, Philip, Peter Johnston and Martin Kratz. 1989. *The Computer Virus Crisis.* Toronto: Nelson Canada.

Gerrold, David. 1972. *When Harlie Was One.* Ballantine Books.

Hoffman, Lance J. 1990. *Rogue Programs: Viruses, Worms and Trojan Horses.* United States: Van Nostrand Reinhold.

Hogan, James P. 1991. *Entoverse.* New York: Ballatine Books.

Howitt, Doran. November 19, 1984. "Of Worms and Booby Traps." *InfoWorld.*

Kane, Pamela. 1989. *V.I.R.U.S. Protection.* New York: Bantam Books.

Lundell, Allan. 1989. *Virus!.* Chicago: Contemporary Books.

McAfee, John and Colin Haynes. 1989. *Computer Viruses, Worms, Data Diddlers, Killer Programs and Other Threats to Your System.* New York: St. Martins Press.

Reid, Brian. February 1987. "Reflections on Some Recent Widespread Computer Breakins." *Communications of the ACM. Vol. 30, No. 2,*: 103-105.

Roszak, T. 1981. *Bugs.* New York: Doubleday.

Shoch, John and Jon A. Hupp. March 1982. The Worm Programs—Early Experience with a Distributed Computation." *Communications of the ACM. Vol. 25, No. 3:* 172-180.

Stang, David J. 1990. *Computer Viruses.* Washington, DC: National Computer Security Association.

Stephenson, Neal. 1992. *Snow Crash.* New York: Bantam Books.

Thomas, Quentin. 1992. *Chains of Light.* New York: Penguin Books.

Glossary

access The ability and means necessary to approach, to store or to retrieve data, to communicate with, and to make use of any resource of a computer system.

access category One of the classes whereto a user, a program, or a process in a system can be assigned because of the resources or groups of resources that each user, program, or process is authorized to use.

access control mechanisms Hardware or software features, operating procedures, management procedures, and various combinations of these designed to detect and prevent unauthorized access and permit authorized access to a system.

access guidelines Guidelines for the modification of specific access rights. A general framework drawn up by the owner or custodian to instruct the data set security administrator on the degree of latitude that exists for the modification of rights of access to a file without the specific authority of the owner or custodian.

access list A catalog of users, programs, or processes and the specifications of access categories whereto each is assigned.

access period A segment of time, generally expressed on a daily or weekly basis, when access rights prevail.

access type An access right to a particular device, program, or file. For example, Read, Write, Execute, Append, Allocate, Modify, Delete, Create.

accessibility The ease with which information can be obtained.

accidental Outcome from the lack of care or any situation where the result is negatively different from that intended. For example, poor program design, poor planning.

accountability The quality or state that enables violations or attempted violations of system security to be traced to individuals who can then be held responsible.

accurate Having no errors. Correct. Exact. Faithful. Precise. Proper. Right. True. Veracious. Veridical.

algorithm A step-by-step procedure, usually mathematical, for doing a specific function, e.g., a PIN verification algorithm or an encryption algorithm.

analog A system based on a continuous ratio, such as voltage or current values.

analog transmission A communications scheme using a continuous signal, varied by amplification. Broadband networks use analog transmissions.

analytical attack An attempt to break a code or cipher key by discovering flaws in its encryption algorithm.

application The user's communication with the installation; a software program or program package allowing a user to perform a specific job, such as word processing or electronic mail.

application program/software A program written for or by a user that applies to his or her work.

application system A collection of programs and documentation used for an application.

architecture The general design of hardware or software, including how everything fits together.

ARCnet (Attached Resource Computer Network) A local area network scheme developed by Datapoint.

assembler A language translator that converts a program written in assembly language into an equivalent program in machine language. The opposite of a disassembler.

assembly language A low-level programming language in which individual machine-language instructions are written in a symbolic form that is easier to understand than machine language itself.

assets Any object that has value, be it real or virtual, excluding fixtures, furniture, and real estate.

asynchronous A method of data communication where transmissions are not synchronized with a signal. Local area networks transmit asynchronously.

attacks The method used to commit security violations, such as masquerading and modification.

audit trail A chronological record of system activities sufficient to enable the reconstruction, review, and examination of the sequence of environments and activities surrounding or leading to each event in the path of a transaction from its inception to output of results.

auditability The physical or mental power to perform an examination or verification of financial records or accounts.

authenticate (1) To confirm that the object is what it purports being. To verify the identity of a person (or other agent external to the protection system) making a request. (2) The act of identifying or verifying the eligibility of a station, originator, or individual to access specific categories of information.

authorize To grant necessary and sufficient permissions for the intended purpose.

automated security monitoring The use of automated procedures to ensure that the security controls implemented within a system are not circumvented.

ANSI Acronym for American National Standards Institute that sets standards for many technical fields.

ASCII Acronym for American Standard Code for Information Interchange; pronounced "ASK-ee."

AWG (American Wire Gauge) The adopted standard wire sizes, such as No. 12 wire, No. 14. The larger the gauge number of the wire, the smaller the wire; therefore, a No. 14 wire is smaller than a No. 12 wire.

backbone Connection points in a network carrying messages between distributed LANs.

backup (n) A copy of a disk or of a file on a disk. (v) To make a spare copy of a disk or of a file on a disk.

backup procedures The provisions made for the recovery of data files and program libraries, and for the restart or replacement of equipment after the occurrence of a system failure or disaster.

background A task or program that runs while the user is doing something else. The most common example is a print spooler program. Used in contrast to foreground.

background processing The ability to complete tasks in the background.

bandwidth The range of frequencies available for signaling; the difference expressed in Hertz between the lowest and highest frequencies of a band.

BASIC (Beginner's All-purpose Symbolic instruction Code) A high-level programming language that is easy to use. Used mainly for microcomputers.

batch The processing of a group of related transactions or other items at planned intervals.

baud Unit of signaling speed. The speed in baud is the number of discreet conditions or events per second.

bit Contraction for binary digit. The smallest unit of information that a computer can hold. The value of a bit (1 or 0) represents a simple two-way choice, such as yes or no, on or off, positive or negative, something or nothing.

boot To start up by loading the operating system into the computer. Booting up is often accomplished by first loading a small program which then reads a larger program into memory. The program is said to "pull itself up by its own bootstraps"—hence the term "bootstrapping" or "booting."

bps (bits per second) Unit of data transmission rate.

breach A break in the system security that results in admittance of a person or program to an object.

bridge   A device used to connect LANs by forwarding packets addressed to other similar networks across connections at the Media Access Control Level. Routers, which operate at the Protocol Level, are also called bridges.

broadband   A transmission system in which signals are encoded and modulated into different frequencies and then transmitted simultaneously with other signals.

broadcast   A LAN data transmission scheme in which data packets are heard by all stations on the network.

brute-force attack   A computerized trial-and-error attempt to decode a cipher or password by trying every possible combination. Also known as exhaustive attack.

buffer   A temporary holding area of the computer's memory where information can be stored by one program or device and then read at a different rate by another; for example, a print buffer.

bug   An error in a program that prevents its functioning as intended. The expression reportedly comes from the early days of computing when an itinerant moth shorted a connection and caused a breakdown in a room-sized computer.

Bulletin Board System (BBS)   An electronic system that supports communication via modem among computers. Typically, a bulletin board system supports public and private electronic mail, uploading and downloading of public-domain files, and access to online databases. Large, commercial bulletin board systems, such as CompuServe and GEnie, can support many users simultaneously; smaller, local boards permit only one caller at a time.

bus   A common connection. Networks that broadcast signals to all stations, such as Ethernet and ARCnet, are considered bus networks.

byte   A unit of information having eight bits.

CAAT (Computer-Assisted Audit Technique)   Any audit technique that uses the computer as an audit tool.

callback   A procedure established for identifying a terminal dialing into a computer system by disconnecting the calling terminal and reestablishing the connection by the computer system's dialing the telephone number of the calling number.

catalog   A list of files stored on a disk. Sometimes called a directory.

central processing unit (CPU)   The "brain" of the computer; the microprocessor performing the actual computations in machine language.

centralized system   For security systems, one where passwords are created and accounted for centrally. The passwords are distributed to the users.

certification The technical evaluation, made as part of and in support of the accreditation process, establishing the extent that a particular computer system or network design and implementation meet a prespecified set of security requirements.

channel An information transfer path within a system. Can also refer to the mechanism by which the path is effected.

character Letter, numerical, punctuation, or any other symbol contained in a message.

chip Slang for a silicon wafer imprinted with integrated circuits.

classified Subject to prescribed asset-protection controls, including controls associated with classifications.

classify The assignment of a level of sensitivity and priority and hence, security control, to data.

clear text Information in its readable state (before encryption or after decryption).

client In a client/server database system, the computer (usually a workstation) that makes service requests.

client/server A network system design in which a processor or computer designated as a server (file server, database server, etcetera) provides services to other client processors or computers.

collision A garbled transmission resulting from simultaneous transmissions by two or more workstations on the same network cable.

communication link An electrical and logical connection between two devices. On a local area network, a communication link is the point-to-point path between sender and recipient.

communication program A program that enables the computer to transmit data to and receive data from distant computers through the telephone system.

compartmentalization The breaking down of sensitive data into small, isolated blocks for reducing the risk to the data.

compiler A language translator that converts a program written in a high-level programming language (source code) into an equivalent program in a lower-level language, such as machine language (object code), for later execution.

completeness Having all or necessary parts. Whole.

compromise The loss, misuse, or unauthorized disclosure of a data asset.

condition An operating situation when a threat arises. The condition is necessary and desirable for operations.

conditional value   Value that ensues if a particular event occurs.

confidential   Loss, misuse, or unauthorized disclosure of data with this protection classification could, at most, have a major negative impact. Such an incident would be harmful to the organization.

confidentiality   A parameter showing the privacy of the information (used particularly in costing functions involving information that has a security classification or is considered proprietary or sensitive).

configuration   (1) The total combination of hardware components—central processing unit, video display device, keyboard, and peripheral devices—forming a computer system. (2) The software settings allowing various hardware components of a computer system to communicate with each other.

control program   A program designed to schedule and supervise the performance of data processing work by a computing system.

controlled sharing   Reducing the scope or domain of authorization to an arbitrarily small set or sphere of activity.

convertibility   The ease that an asset can be misappropriated.

cost   Sacrifice or forgoing made for goods or services. It can take the form of an outlay cost or an opportunity cost.

cost/time contamination   A parameter indicating the affect of the contamination of the information.

cost/time interruption   A parameter indicating the affect of an interruption of the information.

crash   A malfunction caused by hardware failure or error in the program.

critical   Data with this preservation classification is essential to the organization's continued existence. The loss of such data would cause a serious disruption of the organization's operation.

criticality   A parameter indicating dependence of the organization on the information.

crosstalk   The unwanted transmission of a signal on a channel that interfaces with another adjacent channel. Signal interference created by emissions passing from one cable element to another.

cryptoanalysis   The steps and operations performed, in converting messages (cipher) into plain text (clear) without initial knowledge of the key employed in the encryption algorithm.

cryptographic system   The documents, devices, equipment, and associated techniques used as a unit to provide a single means of encryption (enciphering or encoding).

cryptography Transformation of plain text into coded form (encryption) or from coded form into plain text (decryption).

cryptology The field that includes both cryptoanalysis and cryptography.

custodian An employee or agent of the organization who has been assigned administration or control responsibility for an EDP asset (from owner). Custodian is an employee or agent having authorized possession (physical or logical) of data (from owner).

custody The authorized possession of an EDP asset.

customer related Information that identifies or relates specifically to a customer of the organization.

damage Impairment of the worth or usefulness of the information.

data Processable information with the associated documentation. The input that a program and its instructions perform on and that determines the results of processing.

database (1) A collection of information organized in a form that can be readily manipulated and sorted by a computer user. (2) Short for database management system.

database management system A software system for organizing, storing, retrieving, analyzing, and modifying information in a database.

database server The "back-end" processor that manages the database and fulfills database requests in a client/server database system.

data contamination A deliberate or accidental process or act that results in a change in the integrity of the original data.

data diddling Unauthorized alteration of data as it is entered or stored in a computer.

data integrity Verified correspondence between the computer representation of information and the real-world events that the information represents. The condition of being whole, complete, accurate and timely.

data leakage The theft of data or software.

data protection Measures to safeguard data from undesired occurrences that intentionally or unintentionally lead to modification, destruction, or disclosure of data.

data security The result achieved through implementing measures to protect data against unauthorized events leading to unintentional or intentional modification, destruction, or disclosure of data.

data security administrator The individual charged with administering the security requirements of the owner, steward, or custodian.

data security auditor   An independent reviewer who formally tests compliance with business control and asset protection requirements.

data storage   The preservation of data in various data media for direct use by the system.

data-dependent protection   Protection of data at a level commensurate with the sensitivity level of the individual data elements, instead of with the sensitivity of the entire file, including the data elements.

debug   (colloquial term) To find and correct an error or the cause of a problem or malfunction in a computer program. Usually synonymous with troubleshoot.

debugger   A utility program that allows a programmer to see what is happening in the microprocessor and in memory while another program is running.

decipher   To convert, by use of the appropriate key, cipher text (encoded, encrypted) into its equivalent plain text (clear).

decrypt   Refer to *decipher*.

dedicated file server   A file server that cannot be used as a user's workstation.

deficiency   A weakness in organization, administration, programs, or machines that results in the appearance of threats .

degauss   Application of a variable, alternating current field for demagnetizing magnetic recording media, usually tapes.

delay   The act of delaying or being delayed, to cause to be detained or late. See *cost/time interruption*.

deliberate   Actions intended to harm. The results of such deliberate actions might well be different from those expected by perpetrators or victims. For example, arson and vandalism.

destruction   To render an asset ineffective or useless; a recognizable loss. For example, if a file must be recovered from backup storage or reconstituted.

digital   A system based on discrete states, typically the binary conditions of *on* or *off*.

digital transmission   A communications system that passes information encoded as pulses. Baseband networks use digital transmissions, as do microcomputers.

directory   A pictorial, alphabetical, or chronological list of the contents of a disk. A directory is sometimes called a catalog. Used by the operating system to keep track of the contents of the disk.

disclosure The act or an instance of revelation or exposure. A disclosure can be obvious, such as the removal of a tape from a library, or it can be concealed, such as the retrieval of a discarded report by an outsider or disgruntled employee.

discretionary controls Security controls applied at the user's option; that is, they are not required. Access control lists (ACLs) are typical of such optional security features. Discretionary controls are the opposite of mandatory controls.

disk A data storage device in which data is recorded on a number of concentric circular tracks on magnetic medium.

distributed system For security systems, one where passwords are created by the users. The passwords can be accounted for centrally.

documentation A complete and accurate description and authorization of a transaction and each operation a transaction passes through. The written (can be automated) description of a system or program and how it operates.

domain Set of objects that currently can be directly accessed by a principal (subject).

download To transfer a file from a large computer or BBS to a personal computer. *Upload* is the opposite operation.

eavesdropping Unauthorized interception of data transmissions.

embarrassment A parameter indicating the sensitivity of an organization to public knowledge of the impacting of the information because of an event.

employee related The information identifies or relates specifically to an employee of the organization.

emulation The imitation of a computer system, performed by a combination of hardware and software, that allows programs to run between incompatible systems.

encipher To convert plain text (clear) into unintelligible form by a cipher system.

encrypt See *encipher*.

Ethernet A local area network protocol developed by Xerox.

expected lifetime A parameter indicating the length of time the information is operative or has value to its owners.

exposure A quantitative rating (in dollars per year) expressing the organization's vulnerability to a given risk.

EDP assets Computers, computing installations, terminals, supporting facilities, data processing services, and data processing input/output, software and data.

fail safe   The automatic termination and protection of programs or other processing operations when a hardware or software failure is detected in a system.

fail soft   The selective termination of affected nonessential processing when a hardware or software failure is detected in a system.

field   A particular type or category of information in a database management program, e.g., a variable.

file   A single, named collection of related information stored on magnetic medium.

file server   A computer that provides network stations with controlled access to shareable resources.

fraud   A deliberate deception perpetrated for unlawful or unfair gain.

gateway   A device that provides routing and protocol conversion among physically dissimilar networks and computers, e.g., LAN to Host, LAN to LAN, X.25 and SNA gateways.

grant   Authorize.

hacker   A computer enthusiast; also, one who seeks to gain unauthorized access to computer systems.

handshaking   A dialogue between a user and a computer, a computer and another computer, or a program and another program for identifying a user and authenticating his identity through a sequence of questions and answers based on information either previously stored in the computer or supplied to the computer by the initiator of the dialogue.

hardware   In computer terminology, the machinery that forms a computer system.

Hertz (Hz)   A measure of frequency or bandwidth. The same as cycles per second.

hierarchical database   A database organized in a treelike structure.

host computer   The computer that receives information from and sends data to terminals over telecommunication lines. The computer that is in control in a data communication network. The host computer can be a mainframe computer, minicomputer, or microcomputer.

hub   (1) A device used on certain network topologies that modifies transmission signals, allowing the network to be lengthened or expanded with additional workstations. The hub is the central device in a star topology. (2) A computer that receives messages from other computers, stores them, and routes them to other computer destinations.

identification   The process that enables, generally using unique machine-readable names, recognition of users or resources as identical with those previously described to a system.

IEEE (Institute of Electrical and Electronic Engineers)   One of several groups whose members are drawn from industry and who attempt to establish industry standards. The IEEE 802 committee has published numerous definitive documents on local area network standards.

information   Input, output, software, data, and all related documentation.

information pool   Data designated as accessible by authorized individuals.

initialize   (1) To set to an initial state or value in preparation for some computation. (2) To prepare a blank disk to receive information by organizing its surface into tracks and sectors; same as format.

integrity   Freedom from errors.

interface   A device or program that allows two systems or devices to communicate with each other. An interface provides a common boundary between the two systems, devices or programs.

input/output (I/O)   The process by which information is transferred between the computer's memory and its keyboard or peripheral devices.

installation   The organizational unit (staff, machines, and programs) that executes automatic data processing.

intentional   See *deliberate*.

Internal Use Only   Loss, misuse, or unauthorized disclosure of data with this protection classification could have at most a minimal negative impact. Such an incident would cause some harm to an organization.

interruption of business   On-going costs versus costs that could cease. See *cost/time interruption*.

isolation   The containment of users and resources in a system, so users and processes are separate from one another and from the protection controls of the operating system.

I/O device (input/output device)   A device that transfers information into or out of a computer.

job   A combined run of one or more application programs automatically processed in sequence in the computer. The job is normally the unit that the authorization and checking procedures of the requesting user are concerned.

key   In cryptography, a sequence of symbols that controls the operations of encryption and decryption.

key generation   The origination of a key or of a set of distinct keys.

local area network (LAN) A communications system using directly connected computers, printers, and hard disks allowing shared access to all resources on the network.

logic bomb Malicious action, initiated by software, that inhibits the normal system functions; a logic bomb takes effect only when specified conditions occur.

logical access Access to the information content of a record or field.

logical file Data that a file contains.

logon The process of accessing a file server or computer after physical connection has been established.

mainframe A large central computer intended to meet the computing needs of a large organization. The largest mainframes can handle thousands of dumb terminals and use gigabytes of secondary storage.

mandatory controls Security controls imposed by the system on all users. Mandatory controls are the opposite of discretionary controls.

master key A key used to encrypt another key. The master key is not used to protect data.

microcomputer A general term referring to a small computer having a microprocessor.

modification An asset altered partly so the form or quality of it has been changed somewhat. A file can appear intact and may be perfectly usable, but it can contain erroneous information.

multilevel device A device used in a manner that permits it to simultaneously process data of two or more security lev els without risk of compromise. To accomplish this, sensitivity labels are normally stored on the same physical medium and in the same form (i.e., machine-readable or human-readable) as the data being processed.

need-to-know The necessity for access to, knowledge of, or possession of sensitive information to fulfill official duties. Responsibility for determining whether a person's duties require that he have or have access to certain information, and whether he is authorized to receive it, rests upon the owner of the information involved and not upon the prospective recipient.

NetBIOS (Network Basic Input/Output System) A PC networking software component introduced by IBM in 1984. It has become a standard interface allowing different makes of network hardware and software to exchange information.

network A collection of interconnected, individually controlled computer printers and hard disks, with the hardware and software used to connect them.

network station Any PC or other device connected to a network by means of a network interface board and some communication medium. A network station can be a workstation, bridge, or server.

node A point of interconnection to a network. Normally, a point at which a number of terminals are located.

object A passive entity that contains or receives data. Access to an object potentially implies access to the informat ion it contains.

operating system Software that controls the internal operations (housekeeping chores) of a computer system. Operating systems are specific to the type of computer used.

originator The primary individual responsible for causing the file to be created on the system as directed by the owner. For procedure-generated files, the person who authorized the running of the job is responsible. Another frequently used term for originator is *custodian*.

owner An employee or agent of the client assigned responsibility for making and communicating certain judgments and decisions regarding business control and selective protection of assets, and for monitoring compliance with specified controls.

package A generic term referring to any group of detailed computer programs necessary to achieve a general objective, for example, an accounts receivable package would include all programs necessary to record transactions in customers' accounts, produce customers' statements, et cetera.

packet A group of bits transmitted as a whole on a network.

pandemic Many newer viruses are prevalent over a wide geographic area. The Columbus Day virus was thought to have originated in Europe, yet it found its way to North America.

password Privileged information given to, or created by the user, entered into a system for authentication purposes. A protected word or secret character string used to authenticate the claimed identity of an individual, a resource or access type.

password system auditor The individual responsible for reconciling all maintenance done on the system with authorized requests, ensuring procedures are complied with, and verifying that maintenance activities are properly authorized.

password system manager The individual responsible for maintaining the authentication list and investigating and documenting user requests. The PSM also should investigate password-related violations and enforce user compliance with password system procedures. The PSM or designate is responsible for the secure distribution of passwords.

password system user The individual or group that has been duly authorized to retain a password and access a resource through the password system.

penetration A successful unauthorized access to a system.

peripheral Any device used for input/output operations with the computer's central processing unit (CPU). Peripheral devices are typically connected to the microcomputer with special cabling and include such devices as modems and printers.

permission A particular form of allowed access, e.g., permission to Read as contrasted with permission to Write.

physical security Physical protection of assets achieved through implementing security measures.

piggybacking Gaining illicit access to a computer facility by following an authorized employee through a controlled door; also known as tailgating.

plain text Intelligible text or signals that have meaning and can be read or acted upon without the application of any decryption.

polling A means of controlling devices on a line.

prescript A rule that must be followed before access to an object is permitted, by that introducing an opportunity for human judgment about the need for access, so that abuse of the access is discouraged.

principal The entity in a computer system to which authorizations are granted; thus, the unit of accountability in a computer system.

print server A device and/or program that manages printers. Print service is often provided by the file server but can also be provided from a separate LAN PC.

prior probability The probability representing the likelihood of occurrence of an event; that is a control will function as specified before experimental evidence about the event has been observed.

privacy The right of an individual to control or influence what information related to them can be collected and stored and by whom and to whom that information may be disclosed.

privileges A means of protecting the use of certain system functions that can affect system resources and integrity. System managers grant privileges according to the user's needs and deny them to restrict the user's access to the system. See *need-to-know*.

processing A systematic sequence of operations performed on data.

propagation When a principal, having been authorized access to some object in turn authorizes access to another principal.

protocol A set of characters at the beginning and end of a message that enables two computers to communicate with each other.

queue A method for managing separate requests to process data, usually, to be printed.

quiescent period A period during which there is no activity on the workstation or PC.

read A fundamental operation that results only in the flow of information from an object to a subject.

read access Permission to read data.

realization costs The agent of an intentional threat incurs realization costs in perpetrating the event. One such cost to the agent is his own exposure, a value calculated from the probability of getting caught and the cost if caught. Before an agent attempts to perpetrate the event, the agent is assumed to determine an event value that is very subjective, but might include the value to the agent of any information obtained, or simply the desirability (i.e., value) of perpetrating the event. The expected cost to the agent resulting from attempts to perpetrate an event.

record Collection of related information treated as one unit within a file.

recovery cost Parameter associated with restoring an organization to operate as before an event.

reference monitor Mechanism that enforces the security rules, by mediating the creation of subjects, granting subjects access to objects according to the requirements of the authorization database, and recording events as necessary in the audit trail.

replicability The ease which the information can be duplicated.

resource In a system, any function, device, or data collection that can be allocated to users or programs.

resource sharing The concurrent use of a resource by more than one user, job, or program.

revoke To take away previously authorized access from some principal.

risk The potential that a given threat has of occurring within a specific period. The potential for realization of unwanted, negative consequences of an event.

risk analysis An analysis of system assets and vulnerabilities to establish an expected loss from certain events based on estimated probabilities of the occurrence of those events.

risk averse Individual's utility for monetary amounts increases at decreasing rate. Thus, a risk averter is generally willing to pay less than the expected monetary value of fair gamble.

risk congruence Sharing of the same attitudes to risk-taking among superior and subordinates.

risk financing Financing of any shortfall in expected future assets and earnings resulting from the impact of uncertainty.

risk management An element of managerial science concerned with the identification, measurement, control, and minimization of uncertain events. An effective risk management program encompasses the following four phases: (1) risk assessment, as derived from an evaluation of threats and vulnerabilities; (2) management decision; (3) control implementation; and (4) effectiveness review.

risk neutral Utility is directly proportional to monetary amounts. The utility function is linear; it always bears a constant relationship to monetary amounts.

risk seeking Opposite of *risk averse*. The individual's utility for monetary amounts increases at an increasing rate. A risk seeker is generally willing to pay more than the expected monetary value of fair gambles.

scavenging Randomly searching for valuable data in a computer's memory or in discarded or incompletely erased magnetic media.

security Protection of all those resources that the client uses to complete its mission.

security equivalence A security feature that allows the supervisor to quickly and easily assign one user or group the same rights as another user or group.

security filter A set of software routines and techniques used in systems to prevent automatic forwarding of specified data over unprotected links or to unauthorized persons.

security kernel The central part of a computer system (software and hardware) that implements the basic security proce dures for controlling access to system resources.

security level The combination of a hierarchical classification and a set of nonhierarchical categories that represents the sensitivity of information.

security policy The set of laws, rules, and practices that regulate how an organization manages, protects, and distributes sensitive information.

security policy model An informal presentation of a formal security policy model.

sensitive Loss, misuse, or unauthorized disclosure of data with this protection classification would have a serious negative impact. Such an incident would be very harmful to the organization. A data classification category.

sensitive program   An application program whose misuse through unauthorized activity could lead to serious misappropriation or loss of assets.

sensitivity   The characteristic of a resource that implies its value or importance, and can include its vulnerability.

server   Network device that provides services to client stations. Servers include file servers, disk servers, and print servers.

shielding   Protective covering that eliminates electromagnetic and radio frequency interference.

sneakers   Computer professional who seeks to test security by attempting to gain unauthorized access to computer systems.

software   Programs and routines to be loaded temporarily into a computer system, for example, compilers, utilities, operating system and application programs.

spatial coherence   Consistency and completeness of information. Concerned with the validity of the interpretation model used for selection and processing.

spatial pertinence   Degree which an item of information is relevant to its intended organizational function. Information must be selected and processed according to a local organization's needs.

steward   An employee or agent of the client entrusted by the owner with management of EDP assets.

subject   An activity entity, generally a person, process, or device that causes information to flow among objects or changes the system state. Technically, a process/domain pair.

subject security level   A subject's security level is equal to the security level of the objects whereto it has both Read and Write access. A subject's security level must always be dominated by the clearance of the user the subject is associated with.

substantive testing   The collection of sufficient competent evidential matter to render an opinion. Two components of substantive testing are analytical review procedures and direct tests.

supervisor   The network supervisor is the person responsible for the operation of the network. The network supervisor maintains the network, reconfiguring and updating it as the need arises.

supporting facilities   Facilities supporting computing installations such as data entry, communication, and power supply areas.

system defensiveness   Part of system integrity. Nonexistence of inappropriate behavior. Components include security, reliability, availability, recoverability, and auditability.

system integrity   Behavior of hardware/software system that does the right thing; further, it does these things right and does them when they are needed.

telecommunication   Electronic transfer of information via telephone lines from computer to computer. See *electronic mail; BBS; modem.*

temporal coherence   Degree which diverse information elements, such as closing dates and sales figures, reflect the same time period.

temporal pertinence   Timeliness of information.

threat   One or more events that can lead to either intentional or unintentional modification, destruction, or disclosure of data. An eventuality which, should it occur, would lead to an undesirable effect on the environment.

threat realization cost   The cost to a perpetrator of performing an attack. This could be financial, punitive, embarrassment, etc.

topology   The physical layout of the network cabling.

transaction   A set of operations that completes a unified task.

transient   An abrupt change in voltage, of short duration.

transportability   The ease which information can be transported.

trapdoor   A set of special instructions, originally created for testing and troubleshooting, that bypasses security procedures and allows direct access to a computer's operating system or to other software.

Trojan Horse   A program, purporting to do useful work, that conceals instructions to breach security whenever the software is invoked.

user   Used imprecisely to refer to the individual who is accountable for some identifiable set of activities in a computer system.

user group   A computer club in which computer users exchange tips and information, publish a newsletter, support a local BBS, and listen to sales pitches from vendors at meetings. A meeting of like-minded individuals who practice information sharing, e.g., GUIDE, SHARE, DECUS, ISSA, and EDPAA. See Appendix D for a list of user groups.

utilities   Useful programs that allow you to rename, copy, format, delete, and otherwise manipulate files and volumes.

utility   The quality or state of being useful. Something designed for practical use.

vaporware   Software announced by vendors but not available.

virus   A program, usually a Trojan Horse, that copies itself into new databases and computers whenever the infected, parent program is invoked.

volume   A storage device, such as a disk pack, mass storage system cartridge, or magnetic tape. For our purposes, diskettes, cassettes, mag cards and such are treated as volumes.

vulnerability   The cost that an organization would incur if an event happened.

wideband   A communications channel that has greater bandwidth than voice-grade lines.

wiretapping   Monitoring or recording data as it moves across a communications link; also known as traffic analysis.

working key   Key used to encrypt data. The working key is not used to protect other keys.

workstation   Desktop computer that performs local processing and accesses LAN services.

worm   Program that deletes data from a computer's memory.

write   Fundamental operation that results only in the flow of data from a subject to an object.

write access   Permission to write an object.

xenophobe   One who fears, mistrusts, and dislikes foreigners or what is foreign or strange. A good access control mechanism must balance xenophobia and paranoia.

zeitgeist   The moral and intellectual atmosphere characteristic of an epoch or age, roughly the spirit of the times. The present zeitgeist regarding computer hackers is they are clever individuals who should be rewarded.

Index

A

access control, 49, 76
  client-server applications, 197
  data/asset control statements, 84
  database systems, 193, 197
  electronic mail, 189
  host system, 249-250
  physical security, 95
  products and suppliers, 261-262
  remote, 250
  software security, 98-99
accidents, 40, 41
accounting management, network management, 184
administrative/organizational security, 74-88
  asset valuation, 82
  audits, 88
  classification of data/assets, 82, **83-87**
  passwords, 77, **78-82**
  responsibility for security, 87-88
  security policy, 74, **75-77**
Adolescence of P-1, The, 113
agents, threat agents, 41
American Airlines, 4
American Hospital Supply, 4
analog communications, 5, **6**
anomie, "normlessness" of current ethical era, 71
Apple, 146, 223
AppleShare, 124, 146, 147-151
AppleTalk architecture, 20
application software (*see* software security)
applications systems, disaster recovery, 92
ARCnet, 24-**25**, 118, 123
Ardis, Patrick M., personnel security author, 93
Art of War, 13
artificial intelligence, 109
Artisoft (*see* LANtastic)
assets (*see* data/assets)
asymmetrical encryption, 96-**97**
audits, 76, 88
  software products and suppliers, 262-263
authentication
  biometrics, 105-107
  communications/electronics security, 95, 97
  electronic mail, 189
  electronic signatures, 97
  passwords, 80, 99-105
  software security, 99

B

backup procedures, 76
  ease of backup, 137
  frequency of backup, 136-137
  hardware security, 135-138
  offsite storage of backups, 138
  password systems, 81-82
  reasons for backup, 135-**136**
  recovery speed, 137
  speed of backup, 137
  software products and suppliers, 263
Bacon, Francis, 213
bacteria, 113
Bagdikian, Ben H., quotation, 209
Banyan (*see* VINES)
baseband transmission rates, 32-33
batch processing servers, 128
Baxter, 4
Bell Labs, 138
  viral-game development, 112
Beniger, James R., future-trends author, 213
biometrics, 105-107
  fingerprinting, 106
  hand geometry, 106
  keystroke dynamics, 106
  retinal patterns, 106
  signature analysis, 106
  voice verification, 106
black-box testing of software, 110
Blanchard, Ken, ethics author, 74
bridges, 201-203, **202**
Brink, Victor Z., 45
broadband technology, 16
broadband transmission rates, 32-33
brouters, 205
Brunner, John, science-fiction author, 11, 113
bulletin board systems (BBS), shareware, 145-146
bus configuration topology, **21**
Business Communications Co., Inc., fiberoptics research, 120

Business Research Group, LAN growth study (1991), 17

C

cabling for LANs, 18, 118-122
  coaxial cable, 120, **120**
  fiberoptics, 120-**121**, 122
  IBM standards, 123
  private telephone exchanges, 122
  shielded twisted-pair, 119, **119**
  standards, 122-123
  Token Ring 802.5 standard, 123
  unshielded twisted-pair (UTP), 118-**119**
callback options, communications/electronics security, 129
Canadian Alliance Against Software Theft (CAAST), 115
carelessness as threat, 41
Carlzon, Jan, 73
carrier detection protocols, 27
CASE software development tools, 108
CD-ROM, 229
cellular telephones, 214-215
chain letters, 113
change analysis and control, 49-50, 251
Chaos Computer Club, Germany, 11
checklist, LAN security, 248-251
Cherryh, fiction author, hackers as folk heros, 11
CISE software development tools, 108
client-server applications, 193-198, **196**
  access control, 197
  benefits, 195-197
  host-based vs. client-server apps, 193, **195**
  logon accounts, 197
  privilege granting, 197
  products and suppliers, 264
  structured query language (SQL), 195
  uses, 193-195
  views, 197
Clinton, Bill, fiberoptic-network support, 121
coaxial cable, 120, 120
coherence of data, 108
collision avoidance/detection protocols, 27-**28**, 203
Comer, Michael J., personnel security author, 93

communications interconnection devices: bridge, router, 18
communications servers, dial-out/dial-in services, 128-130
communications/electronics security, 95-97, 199-208
  authentication, 95, 97
  bridges, 201-203, **202**
  brouters, 205
  callback options, 129
  communications servers, 128-130
  components of networks, 200
  connectivity, 200
  dial-in services, 129-130
  dial-out services, 128-129
  disaster recovery, 92
  encryption/decryption security, 95-96, 130
  gateways, 205, **205**
  guidelines to communication security, 200
  interception of transmission, 95-96
  interconnection devices, 200, **200**
  interconnectivity, 205, **205**
    LAN-to-host computer, **206**-207
    LAN-to-LAN, 205
    LAN-to-WAN, 206
  interference reduction/elimination, 95
  internetworking, 200
  LAN-to-host computer interconnectivity, **206**-207
  LAN-to-LAN interconnectivity, 205
  LAN-to-wan interconnectivity, 206
  modems, 207-**208**
  passthrough options, 129
  password security, 130
  products and suppliers, 264
  repeaters, 201, **201**
  routers, 203-**204**
  shielding workstations, 95
  telecommuting, 213, 220-222
  vaulting, electronic vaulting, 97
  vaulting, televaulting, 97
  wireless LAN, 213, 214-217
Computers and Privacy..., U.S. GAO survey on personal data (1990), 16
Computerworld, 114
concurrency control, database systems, 192
conduct (*see* ethics)

confidential data/assets, 84, 85
configuration management, network management, 184
connectors and connections, 123
Conrad, Cynthia, bank-access theft case, 74, 77
content analysis, 39
contention protocols, 27
contention-free protocols, 29
contingency plans, 49
  password system failure, 81
Control Revolution, The, 213
control systems for LANs, 7, 9-10, 43-55, 66, 70
  access control, 49
  action taking, 50-51
  areas of control, 46
  change analysis, 49-50
  communications/electronics security, 199-208
  contingency plans, 49
  corporate culture vs. control, 53
  corrective controls, 46
  detective controls, 45-46
  difference analysis, 50
  disaster recovery, 47
  feasibility studies, 49
  feedback and control, 44
  formal vs. informal controls, 47, **47**
  Gartner Group report, user-control (1990), 7
  hardware security (*see* hardware security)
  human element, effects of control on people, 54-55
  issues of control: access vs. security, 46-47
  licensing of software, 47, 49
  loop, control loop, **44**
  management's role, 50, **51**-52
  measuring results of control systems, 49-50
  objectives of control, 44, 48-49
  password control, 79, 80, 82
  performance gap determination, 50
  physical security, 49
  preventive controls, 45
  problems with control, 55
  process of developing control systems, 48-51
    access control, 49
    change analysis, 49-50
    contingency planning, 49
    difference analysis, 50
    feasiblity studies, 49
    licensing of software, 49
    management's action, 50
    measuring results, 49-50
    objective development, 48-49
    performance gap determination, 50
    physical security, 49
    reappraisal of existing systems, 51
    requirements in writing, 48
    risk management, 49
    standards for architecture, 49
    taking action, 50-51
    training programs, 49
  reappraisal of existing systems, 51
  relationship of control to customers, 53
  risk management, 49, 54
  scenario of control function, 45
  software (*see* software security)
  standards, 47, 49
  threat/control matrix, **63**
  training programs, 49
  types of control, 45-46
controller, network controller, 18
cooperative processing, 213, 217-220
  ensemble processing, 220
  groupware, 218-220
  hypercomputers, 220
  varathane, electronic, 218
  workflow software, 217-218
Core War viral-game, 112
corrective controls, 46
Cost of Downtime, The, 134
cost-benefit analysis, 57-66
crackers, 11
Critical data/assets preservation classification, 86, 87
custodianship of data, 75-76
Cyberpunk, 11
cyberpunks, 11

D

da Vinci, Leonardo, 213
damage prevention, physical security, 95
data (*see* data/assets)
data encryption algorithm (DES), 97
data/assets
  aggregate classifications for protection, 86

application of classification to data/assets, 83
classification of data/assets, 76, 82, **83-87**
coherence of data, 108
competitive data/assets, 85
Confidential classification, 84, 85
control statements, 84
criteria for classification, 84-85
criteria for protection, 86
Critical preservation classification, 86, 87
customer-related data/assets, 85
deriving a protection classification, 85-88
deriving protection classifications, 85
Do Not Copy control statement, 84
employee-related data/assets, 85
Encrypt for Storage control statement, 84
Encrypt for Transmission control statement, 84
financial data/assets, 85
For XXX Use Only control statement, 84
identifying assets, 61
impact assessment, 87
integrity of data/assets, 85
Internal Use Only classification, 84, 85
ownership vs. custodianship of assets, 75-76
pertinence of data, 108
preservation classifications, 86, 87
protection classifications, 84
Public classification, 84, 86
quality of data/assets, 107-108
reputation of business/organization, 85
security-related data/assets, 85
Sensitive classification, 84, 85
service-related data/assets, 86
spatial coherence, 108
spatial pertinence, 108
subjective criteria for classification, 85
temporal coherence, 108
temporal pertinence, 108
Useful preservation classification, 86, 87
Valuable preservation classification, 86, 87

valuation of assets, 61, 82
database systems, 191-193
  access control, 193, 197
  client-server applications, 193-198
  concurrency control, 192
  file locks, 193
  logon accounts, 197
  password security, 198
  privilege granting, 197
  security management, 192, **193**
  structured query language (SQL), 193
  threats, **194**
  transaction control, 192
  views, 197
Datapoint, 25
Deming, W.Edwards, quality control, 107
denial of service, 40
detective controls, 45-46
device restraints, 131
diddlers, data diddlers, 12
difference analysis, control systems for LANs, 50
Digital, 24, 25
disaster recovery, 47, 76, 88-93, 213, 243-246
  accidents, 40
  administration of disaster recovery plan, 93
  applications systems, 92
  avoiding disasters, 93
  communications subplans, 92
  criteria/relative importance of asset protection/recovery, 91-92
  emergency notification plan, 92
  exposures assessment, 90
  hardware, 92
  identification of critical functions, 89
  impact assessment, 90
  maintaining recovery plans, 91
  natural disasters, 40, 88
  offsite inventory, 92
  planning, 89-90
  preparing for disaster, self-assessment quiz, 93
  qualification of disaster, 92
  recorded disasters, 1987–1993, **245**
  revising recovery plans, 91
  sample recovery plan, 92-93
  self-assessment quiz, 93
  sequence for disaster recovery, 93

disaster recovery (*cont.*)
  software, 92, 265
  strategy for recovery, 92
  Ten Commandments of disaster plans/business resumption, 91-92
  terrorist attack, 88
  testing recovery plans, 90-91
  time frame for recovery, 92
  water damage, 41
  workstations, 92
disclosure, 38-39
disk arrays, 135
disk drive initialization routines, 131
disk servers (*see also* file servers), 124
diskettes and storage security, 133
distributed processing, 241, **241**
Do Not Copy data/asset control statement, 84
downtime, cost of downtime, 134
Driver, William, quotation, 1
duplexing hard drives, 134-135
Durkheim, Emile, ethics discussion, 71

E

effectiveness reviews, risk management, 66
electronic mail, 185-191
  access control, 189
  authentication, 189
  benefits of e-mail, 185, 187
  control objectives for electronic mail, 189-**190**
  forwarding mail problems, 190-191
  growth of electronic mail, 1991-1995, **186**
  integrity-protection for data, 189
  "junk mail" problems, 189-190
  labeling services, 189
  non-repudiation services, 189
  privacy and confidentiality issues, 187, 189
  security-management services, 189
  store-and-forward systems, 187-188
  threats to electronic mail, 187-**188**
electronic signatures, 97
electronic varathane, 218
emergencies (*see* disaster recovery)
emergency notification plan, 92
employee security (*see* personnel security)
Encrypt for Storage data/asset control statement, 84
Encrypt for Transmission data/asset control statement, 84
encryption/decryption, 95-96
  asymmetrical encryption, 96-**97**
  communications/electronics security, 130
  data encryption algorithm (DES), 97
  data/asset classifications, 84
  public-key encryption, 96-**97**
  software for encryption/decryption, 265-266
  symmetrical encryption, 96, **96**
ensemble processing, 220
entropy vs. need for continuous software testing, 110-111
Entropy: A New World View, 220
environmental security (*see* physical security)
Epson America Inc., e-mail privacy case, 187
errors
  human error, 40
  programming errors, 41
espionage, 12
Ethernet, 24-25, 118, 123, 203
ethics, 70-74
  anomie or "normlessness" of current era, 71
  codes of ethical behavior, 72-73
  committment to company vs. ethical behavior, 72
  espionage, 12
  legality vs. ethicality, 74
  management's ethics pervade workplace, 72
  reporting unethical behavior, 73
  standards of conduct, 72-73
  technostress, 71
  zeitgeist of current era, 71
expert systems, 109
exposure of LAN, 42

F

Farquhar, David, 98
fault management, network management, 184
fault-tolerance
  hardware, 134

products and suppliers, 266
  software, 107
fax servers, 128
feasibility studies, 49
feedback for control systems, 44
fiber distributed data interface (FDDI), 29, 32
Fiber Optics Technology..., 120
fiberoptic cables, 120-**121**, 122
  hypercomputers, 220
  Internet development, 121-122
fiction, hackers, crackers and cyberpunks as folk heros, 11
file locks, database systems, 193
file servers, 18, 123-126
  action of file service in data exchange, 20-21
  AppleShare, 124
  central-server systems, 124-125
  dedicated vs. non-dedicated servers, 125
  disk servers vs. file servers, 124
  distributed systems, 124-125
  hubs, 126
  purpose of file servers, 125
  site protection, 252
file transfer, 191, **191**
fingerprinting, 106
firing policies, personnel security, 94
flu shot anti-viral programs, 114
For XXX Use Only data/asset control statement, 84
Ford Motor Company, quality control, 107
Foreign Corrupt Practices Act, 9
forging, 40
frames, token passing protocols, 29
Friedenberg, Edgar, quotation, 67
future developments in LAN security, 209-246
  cooperative processing, 213, 217-220
  disaster/disaster recovery, 213, 243-246
  hypercomputers, 220
  image processing, 213, 222-237
  paradigm shift in technological/societal development, 212-213
  personal communication networks (PCN), 214
  rightsizing, 213, 237-243

  technology developments, technological ages of mankind, 212
  telecommuting, 213, 220-222
  wireless LAN technology, 213, 214-217

G

Gartner Group, report on user-control (1990), 7
gateways, 205, **205**
General Motors, quality control, 107
Gibson, William, fiction author, hackers as folk heros, 11
Goldhaber, Nat, Apple-IBM joint venture chairman, 223
Gore, Albert, fiberoptic-network support, 121
groupware, 144-**145**, 218-220
growth of LANs in U.S., 17

H

hackers, 11
Hammer, Michael, paper on access vs. control, 53
hand-geometry biometrics, 106
hard drives (*see* hardware security)
hardware security, 18, 98, 117-142
  backup procedures, 135-138
  batch processing servers, 128
  cabling, 118-122
    coaxial cable, 120, **120**
    configurations common to LANs, 122
    fiberoptics, 120-**121**, 122
    IBM standards, 123
    private telephone exchanges, 122
    shielded twisted-pair, 119, **119**
    standards, 122-123
    Token Ring 802.5 standard, 123
    unshielded twisted-pair (UTP), 118-**119**
  communications servers, 128-130
  connectors and connections, 123
  device restraints, 131
  disaster recovery, 92
  disk arrays, 135
  disk drive initialization routines, 131
  diskettes and storage, 133
  diskless workstations, 98, 133
  downtime, cost of downtime, 134
  duplexing of hard drives, 134-135
  fault-tolerant systems, 134

hardware security (*cont.*)
  fax servers, 128
  file servers, 123-126
    AppleShare, 124
    central-server systems, 124-125
    dedicated vs. non-dedicated servers, 125
    disk vs. file servers, 124
    distributed systems, 124-125
    hubs, 126
    purpose of file server, 125
  key locks, 131
  leaking transmission signals, 133-134
  mirroring of hard drives, 134-135
  noise, 140, **140**
  peripheral sharing, 126-130, **127**
  power supplies
    interruptions to power supply, 140-142, **140**
    noise, 140, **140**
    spikes, **139**-140
    standby, 141, **141**
    static discharge, 138-139
    surges, **139**-140
    UPS, 141-**142**
  print servers, 126-128
  redundant array of independent disks (RAID), 135
  removable hard disks, 133
  spikes, **139**-140
  static discharge, 138-139
  surges, **139**-140
  uninterruptible power supply (UPS), 141-**142**
  workstation security, 130-134
Harvard Business Review, 53
Hewlett-Packard, 24, 25
hiring policies, personnel security, 94
Hoffman, Lance, passwords author, 102
honesty (*see* ethics)
Household Finance Corp. (HFC), bank-access theft case, 74, 77
Howard, Ted, future-trends author, 220
Hubner, Hans, 11
hubs, 126
human error, 40
Huxley, Aldous, quotation, 35
hypercomputers, 220

I

IBM, 4, 24, 25, 113, 123, 146, 223
image processing, 213, 222-237
  benefits, 223
  CD-ROM, 229
  components of image processing systems, 223-224, 226-228, **227**
  cost-benefit analysis, 237
  departmental systems, 233
  enterprise systems, 233-234
  monitors, 223, 226
  multimedia processing, 233
  networks, 223
  operating systems, 228
  optical character recognition (OCR), 226, 229
  optical disk storage systems, 223, 225, 226, 229
  paper vs. image processing, 225
  printers, 223, 228, 229-230
  scanners, 223, 224, 226, 228-229
  servers, 223, 224
  software, image management, 228, 230-231
  standalone systems, 233
  trends in image processing, 234-236
  uses and applications, 222-223, 231-234, 234-236
  workstations, 228
  WORM disks, 229
impact assessment
  data/asset loss/corruption, 87
  disaster recovery, 90
inexperienced users as threat, 40
Information Age, 4
information as power (*see also* data/assets), 4-14
  controlling information, 7, 9-10
  "demystification" of technology/professions, 7-8
  network influence on corporate organization, **6**, 7
  security products and suppliers, 266-267
InfoWorld, 114
initialization routines, 131
IntelliQuest, 135
interconnectivity, 205, **205**
interface, network interface, 18, 23-26
  ARCnet, 24-**25**

Ethernet vs. Token Ring, **26**
Ethernet, 24-**25**
percent of installation, **26**
popularity of Big Three, **25**
standards, 24
Token Ring, 24-**25**
interference, RF, reducing/eliminating interference, 95
internal-use-only data/assets, 84, 85
International Data Corp., LAN growth study (1992), 17
International Standards Organization (ISO), 19-20
Internet, 121-122
  1990 breach by R. Tappan, 11-12
inventory, disaster recovery, 92
isolation transformers, 140

J

Janus Associates, 104
job descriptions, personnel security, 94

K

Kaleida, Apple-IBM joint venture, 223
Kates, Jim, password-fraud example, 104
key locks, 131
keystroke-dynamics biometrics, 106
Konami Inc., 114

L

LAN development and organization, 8-9, 15-33
  analog communications, 5, **6**
  AppleShare networks, 147-151
  AppleTalk architecture, 20
  baseband transmission rates, 32-33
  basic structure of LAN, 16
  batch processing servers, 128
  bridges, 201-203, **202**
  broadband technology, 16
  broadband transmission rates, 32-33
  brouters, 205
  cabling (*see* cabling for LANs)
  client-server applications, 193-198
  communications interconnection devices, 18, 201-205
  communications servers, 128-130
  components of networks, 18, 200
  connectors and connections, 123, 200
  controller, network controller, 18
  cooperative processing, 213, 217-220
  data exchange processes, 20-21
  database systems, 191-193
  downtime, cost of downtime, 134
  electronic mail, 185-191
  ensemble processing, 220
  fax servers, 128
  file servers, 18, 20-21, 123-126
  file transfer, 191, **191**
  gateways, 205, **205**
  growth of LANs in U.S., 17
  hardware for LANs, 18
  hubs, 126
  image processing, 213, 222-237
  influence of networking on corporate organization, **6**, 7
  interconnection devices, 200, **200**
  interconnectivity, 205, **205**
    LAN-to-host computer, **206**-207
    LAN-to-LAN, 205
    LAN-to-WAN 206
  interface, network interface, 18, 20, 23-26
    ARCnet, 24-**25**
    Ethernet vs. Token Ring, **26**
    Ethernet, 24-**25**
    LocalTalk for Macintosh networks, 25
    percent of installation, **26**
    popularity of Big Three interfaces, **25**
    standards for interface, 24
    Token Ring, 24-**25**
  internetworking, 200
  LAN-to-host computer interconnectivity, **206**-207
  LAN-to-LAN interconnectivity, 205
  LAN-to-WAN interconnectivity, 206
  LANtastic networks, 151-160
  layers in LAN, OSI model, 19-20
  local area wireless networks (LAWN), 216
  LocalTalk, 25
  Macintosh computer networks, 25
  mainframe environment circa 1980, 4, **5**
  metropolitan area networks (MAN), 18, 200
  microcomputer development, 4-5
  modems, 207-**208**
    analog communications, 5, **6**
  NetWare networks, 160-170

LAN development and organization (*cont.*)
  network management, 183-185
  network operating systems (NOS), 146-181
  networking development, 6-7
  operating systems, 20
  OS/2 LAN Server, 170-174
  packet switching networks, data exchange process, 20-21
  print servers, 126-128
  private branch exchange (PBX), 18
  productivity gains associated with LANs, 16
  protocols, 20, 26, 27-32
    carrier detection, 27
    collision detection, 27-**28**
    contention, 27
    contention-free, 29
    fiber distributed data interface (FDDI), 29, 32
    future developments, 32
    token passing, 29, **30**, **31**
  repeaters, 201, **201**
  rightsizing, 213, 237-243
  routers, 203-**204**
  selection criteria for LAN design, 33
  speed of data transmission, broad- vs. baseband, 32-33
  speed of data transmission, kilo-, mega- and gigabits, 32-33
  standards for networks, ISO and OSI, 18, 19-20
  telecommuting, 213, 220-222
  telephone-line LANs, 18
  topology, 20, 21-23
    bus configuration, 21, **21**
    ring configuration, 21-**22**
    star configuration, 22-**23**
    tree configuration, 23-**24**
  VINES networks, 174-181
  wide area network (WAN), 18, 200
  wireless LAN technology, 213
  workstations, 130-134
LAN security (*see also* threats), 9, 1-14, 69-115
  acceptance of risk, 76
  access control, 76
    host system, 249-250
    remote access, 250
  administrative/organizational security, 74-88
  AppleShare networks, 147-151
  application software, 185-198, **186**
  asset valuation, 82
  audits, 76, 88, 115
  authentication systems (*see* authentication)
  awareness of security measures, 76
  backup procedures, 76
    hardware security, 135-138
  batch processing servers, 128
  biometrics, 105-107
  cabling, 118-122
  change control, 251
  checklist, 248-251
  classification of data/assets, 76, 82, **83-87**
  client-server applications, 193-198
  communications servers, 128-130
  communications/electronics security, 95-97
  connectors and connections, 123
  control systems (*see* control systems for LANs)
  cooperative processing, 213, 217-220
  cost-benefit analysis, 57-66
  crackers, 11
  cyberpunks, 11
  database systems, 191-193
  diddlers, data diddlers, 12
  disaster recovery, 76, 88-93
  disk arrays, 135
  downtime, cost of downtime, 134
  duplexing hard drives, 134-135
  electronic mail, 185-191
  employees as threats, 13
  ensemble processing, 220
  espionage, 12
  ethics and security, 70-74
  fault-tolerant hardware, 134
  fax servers, 128
  file servers, 123-126
  file transfer, 191, **191**
  future developments (*see* future developments in LAN security)
  hackers, 11
  hardware security, 98, 117-142
  hypercomputers, 220
  image processing, 213, 222-237

impact assessment, data/asset loss/corruption, 87
importance of data security in corporate structure, 10
internetworking and connectivity, 200
LANtastic networks, 151-160
leaks, leaking transmission signals, 133-134
liability in case of abuse/loss, 9
local area wireless networks (LAWN), 216
management's role in security, 13
mirroring hard drives, 134-135
need for security, 10-13
NetWare networks, 160-170
network management, 183-185, 251
network operating systems (NOS), 146-181
noise, 140, **140**
number of users vs. increase threat to security, 16
open systems vs. security, 13
OS/2 LAN Server, 170-174
ownership vs. custodianship of data, 75-76
passwords (*see* passwords)
peripheral sharing, 126-130, **127**
personnel security, 93-94
physical security, 94-95
policy, security policy, 74, **75-77**
power supply interruption, 140-142, **140**, **141**
print servers, 126-128
privacy concerns, 16
quality control, software security, 107-111
reporting security violations, 76, 250-251
responsibility for security, 76, 87-88
rightsizing, 213, 237-243
risk management, 10, 57-66
scenarios of possible security breach, 41-42
security policy, 74, **75-77**
self-assessment quiz on security, 14
software security, 98-115, 143-198
spikes in power supply, **139**-140
static discharge, 138-139
surges in power supply, **139**-140
telecommuting, 213, 220-222
threats, 10-13
training programs, 94
user ID, 251
valuation of data/assets, 17, 82
VINES networks, 174-181,
viruses (*see* viruses)
wireless LAN technology, 213
workstation security, 130-134, 251
LANtastic, 146, 151-160
Lawrence Livermore Laboratories, ethics course, 71
layers in LAN, OSI model, 19-20
Le Suicide, 71
Leading Edge, 114
liability in case of data abuse/loss, 9
licensing of software, 47, 49, 115
local area wireless networks (LAWN), 216
LocalTalk, 25, 118
logon accounts, database systems, 197
loss-cost analysis, risk management, 62-63

M

mainframe environment circa 1980, 4, **5**
management's role in security, 13, 63-65, **64**
  control systems for LANs, 50, **51**-52
    controlling, 52
    directing, 52
    organization, 52
    planning, 51-52
    staffing, 52
  controlling, 52
  directing, 52
  ethics, standards of conduct, 70-74
  organization, 52
  planning, 51-52
  risk management, 63-65, **64**
    acceptance of risk, 64
    avoidance of risk, 64-65
    transference of risk, 65
  staffing, 52
Market Intelligence, wireless-LAN growth study, 215
masquerading, 39
Massachussetts Institute of Technology (MIT), 11
McIlroy, M. Douglas, viral-game developer, 112
McLuhan, Marshall, quotation, 67

measuring results of control systems, 49-50
Megatrends, 4, 212
message stream modification, 38
metropolitan area networks (MAN), 18, 200
Michaelangelo virus, 114
microcomputers, 4-5
mirroring hard drives, 134-135
Mitnick, Kevin, 11
mobile communications, 214-215
modems, 5, **6**, 207-**208**
Modern Methods for Computer Security and Privacy, 102
Morris, Robert T., 11-12
multimedia processing, 233

N

Naisbitt, John, future-trends author, 4, 212, 213
name management, network management, 184
natural disasters, 40, 88
NCR, 216
Nestle, electronic mail system, 185
NetWare, 24, 135, 146, 160-170
network management, 183-185, 251
  accounting management, 184
  Common Management Information Protocol (CMIP), 183
  configuration management, 184
  control functions, 184-185
  fault management, 184
  ISO network management architecture, 183, **183**
  monitoring function, 184-185
  name management, 184
  operating systems, products and suppliers, 268-269
  performance management, 184-185
  products and suppliers, 267-268
  security management, 185, 270
  Simple Network Management Protocol (SNMP), 183
network operating systems (NOS), 146-181
  access control, trophy, 146-147
  AppleShare, 146, 147-151
  IBM vs. Mac platforms, 146
  LANtastic, 146, 151-160

name or directory services, 146
NetWare, 146, 160-170
operation of NOS, 146
OS/2 LAN Server, 146, 170-174
summary of LAN NOS, **182**
VINES, 146, 174-181
networks (*see* LAN development and organization; LAN security; network management; network operating systems)
Neuromancer, 11
New Atlantis, 213
Nicholson, Emma, 17
noise, 140, **140**
nondisclosure agreements, personnel security, 94
Nostradamus, 213
Novell (*see* NetWare), 146

O

office security (*see* physical security)
offsite inventory, disaster recovery, 92
open systems, security problems of open systems, 13
Open Systems Interconnection (OSI), 19-20
operating systems, 20, 181, 183
  image processing systems, 228
  network (NOS) (*see* network operating systems)
  network, products and suppliers, 268-269
OS/2, 25
optical character recognition (OCR), 226, 229
optical disk storage, image processing, 223, 225, 226, 229
organizational security (see administrative/organizational security)
organizations and associations, 276-278
OS/2, 25
OS/2 LAN Server, 146, 170-174
Ouchi, William G., quality-control techniques, 109
ownership of data, 75-76

P

packet switching, network data exchange, 20-21

paradigm shift, technological/societal development, 212-213
passcodes (*see* passwords)
passthrough options, communications/electronics security, 129
Password Management Guidelines, 101
Password Usage Standard, 99
passwords, 77, **78-82**, 99-105, 249
  acknowledgment of password reception, 80
  applications for passwords, 78
  applications software, 198
  authentication of passwords, 80
  authentication period, 99
  backup passwords, 81-82
  changing passwords, 80
  combinations, possible combinations of given characters, **101**-102
  communications/electronics security, 130
  composition of passwords, 99
  compromised passwords, 80, 82
  contingency procedures, 81
  control of passwords, 79, 80, 82
  creation of passwords, 79
  database systems, 198
  deviations from passwords-standards, 78
  dictionary of passwords, 254-257
  distribution of passwords, 79, 102
  entry of passwords without observation, 102-103
  expiration of passwords, 81, 82
  generation of passwords, 79
  guidelines for use of passwords, 103-105, **104**
  length of password, 101-102
  lifetime of passwords, 102
  logoff automatic on password failure, 81
  logon attempt limits, 80
  multiple-account passwords, 80
  need-to-know access rights, 80
  one owner/one account systems, 81
  ownership of passwords, 103
  poor password choices, 101
  purpose of passwords, 78
  report generator password systems, 81
  reporting on password use, 81
  scope of password systems, 78
  source of passwords, 103
  suppression of passwords, 80
  transformations used in passwords, 100, **100**
  transmission of passwords, 103
  use of passwords, 79
  user responsibility for password security, 82
PC LAN Integration and Management User Trends, 17
Peale, Norman Vincent, ethics author, 74
performance gaps, 50
performance management, network management, 184-185
peripheral security (*see* hardware security)
Perry, Bill, quality-control techniques, 111
personal communication networks (PCN), 214
personnel security, 93-94
  awareness of security measures, 76
  candidate screening and checkout procedures, 94
  firing policies, 94
  hiring policies, 94
  job descriptions, 94
  nondisclosure agreements, 94
  orientation courses to security, 94
  passwords, user responsibility, 82
  reference-checking, 94
  responsibility of employees to security, 76
  training programs, 94
pertinence of data, 108
physical security, 49, 94-95
  access control, 95
  damage prevention, 95
  media protection, 95
  power supply interruptions, 95
  products and suppliers, 269
  supplies protection, 95
planning, 51
Popcorn, Faith, future-trends author, 213
Power of Ethical Management, The, 74
power supplies
  brownout, 141, **141**

power supplies (*cont.*)
  interruptions to power supply, 40, 95, 140-142, **140**, **141**
  isolation transformers vs. noise, 140
  noise, 140, **140**
  products and suppliers, 270
  spikes, **139**-140
  standby power supply, 141, **141**
  static discharge, 138-139
  surges, **139**-140
  transients, 140, **140**
  undervoltage, 140, **140**
  uninterruptible power supply (UPS), 141-**142**
predictive analysis, risk management, 62
preventive controls, 45
Price, David H., personnel security author, 93
print servers, 126-128
printers, image processing systems, 229-230
privacy, 16
  electronic mail, 187, 189
private branch exchange (PBX), 18
privileges, database systems, 197
productivity gains associated with LANs, 16
products and suppliers
  access control systems, 261-262
  communications security systems, 264
  encryption/decryption, 265-266
  fault-tolerant systems, 266
  information security, 266-267
  network management, 267-268
  network operating systems, 268-269
  network security, 270
  physical security, 269
  power systems, 270
  risk management, 270
  software, audit, 262-263
  software, backup, 263
  software, client-server, 264
  software, disaster recovery, 265
  software, encryption/decryption, 265-266
  virus protection, 271-273
programming errors, 41
protocols, 20, 26, 27-32
  carrier detection, 27
  collision detection, 27-**28**
  collision-avoidance, 203
  Common Management Information Protocol (CMIP), 183
  contention, 27
  contention-free, 29
  fiber distributed data interface (FDDI), 29, 32
  future developments, 29, 32
  Simple Network Management Protocol (SNMP), 183
  token passing, 29, **30**, **31**
public data/assets, 84, 86
public-domain software (*see* shareware)
public-key encryption, 96-**97**

Q

qualitative analysis of risk, 60-61, 66
quality control, software security, 107-111
  CASE tools, 108
  CISE software development tools, 108
  entropy and need for continuous testing, 110-111
  expert systems and artificial intelligence, 109
  productivity measurements, 108
  reliability of software, 109
  spatial and temporal coherence of data, 108
  spatial and temporal pertinence of data, 108
  testing software, 110-111
quantitative analysis of risk, 60-61, 66

R

rabbits, 113
reappraisal of existing control systems, 51
recovery (*see* disaster recovery)
redundant array of independent disks (RAID) technology, 135
references, personnel security, 94
remote access control, 250
reneging, 39-40
repeaters, 201, **201**
reporting security violations, 76, 250-251

repudiation, 40
retinal-pattern biometrics, 106
Rifkin, Jeremy, future-trends author, 213, 220
rightsizing, 213, 237-243
ring configuration topology, 21-**22**
risk management, 10, 49, 57-66, **60**
  acceptance of risk, 64, 76
  analyzing risk, 60-63, 66
    asset identification, 61
    asset valuation, 61
    loss-cost analysis, 62-63
    predictive analysis, 62
    quantitative vs. qualitative analysis, 60-61, 66
    safeguard identification, 63
    steps , 61-63
    threat identification, 61-62
    threat/vulnerability mergers, 62
    vulnerability identification, 62
  asset identification, 61
  asset valuation, 61
  avoidance of risk, 64-65
  control implementation, 66
  control systems for LANs, 54
  cost-benefit analysis, 58-59
  effectiveness reviews, 66
  loss-cost analysis, 62-63
  management's role in risk management, 63-65
  predictive analysis, 62
  products and suppliers, 270
  qualitative vs. quantitative risk analysis, 60-61, 66
  risk, definition of risk, 59-60
  safeguard identification, 63
  threat identification, 61-62
  threat/control matrix, **63**
  threat/vulnerability mergers, 62
  transference of risk, 65
  vulnerability identification, 62
routers, 203-**204**
Ryan, Thomas J., science-fiction author, 113

S

safeguards identification, 63
Scandinavian Airlines system, 73
scanners (*see* image processing)
scientific prefixes, 32-**33**

screening procedures, personnel security, 94
security management, network management, 185
security policy, 74, **75-77**
  acceptance of risk, 76
  access control, 76
  audits, 76
  awareness of security measures, 76
  backup procedures, 76
  classification of data/assets, 76
  custodianship of data, 75-76
  disaster recovery, 76
  ownership of data, 75-76
  reporting violations, 76
  responsibilities of employees to security, 76
  scope of policy, 75
self-assessement quiz on disaster-preparedness, 93
self-assessment quiz on security, 14
sensitive data/assets, 84, 85
shareware, 145-146
shielded twisted-pair, 119, **119**
shielding, 95
Shockwave Rider, 113
Shors, Alana, e-mail privacy case, 187
signature-analysis biometrics, 106
signatures, electronic, 97
Simple Network Management Protocol (SNMP), 183
site security (*see* physical security)
software products and suppliers
  audit software, 262-263
  backup software, 263
  client-server, 264
  disaster recovery software, 92, 265
  encryption/decryption, 265-266
Software Protection Association (SPA), 115
software security, 98-115, 143-198
  access control, 98-99
  AppleShare networks, 147-151
  application software, 185-198, **186**
  audits, 115
  authentication, 99
  biometrics, 105-107
  black-box testing, 110
  Canadian Alliance Against Software Theft (CAAST), 115

software security (*cont.*)
    CASE software development tools, 108
    CISE software development tools, 108
    client-server applications, 193-198
    cooperative processing, 217-220
    database systems, 191-193
    electronic mail, 185-191
    ensemble processing, 220
    entropy and need for continuous testing, 110-111
    expert systems and artificial intelligence, 109
    fault-tolerant software, 107
    file transfer, 191, **191**
    groupware, 144-**145**, 218-220
    integrity of software, 107-111
    LANtastic networks, 151-160
    licensing of software, 115
    multiuser software, 144
    NetWare networks, 160-170
    network management software, 183-185
    network operating systems (NOS) (*see* network operating systems)
    operating systems, 181, 183
    OS/2 LAN Server, 170-174
    passwords, 198
    public-domain shareware, 145-146
    quality control for software, 107-111
    reliability of software, 109
    shareware, 145-146
    single-user software, 144
    Software Protection Association (SPA), 115
    testing software for defects, 107, 110-111
    varathane, electronic, 218
    VINES networks, 174-181
    viruses (*see* viruses)
    white-box testing, 110
    workflow software, 217-218
speed of data transmission
    broad- vs. baseband, 32-**33**
    kilo-, mega- and gigabits, 32-33
spikes, **139**-140
spoofing, 40
staffing, 52
standards for LANs, 18, 47, 49
    cabling standards, 122-123
    International Standards Organization (ISO), 19-20
    Open Systems Interconnection (OSI), 19-20
star configuration topology, 22-**23**
static discharge, 138-139
Sterling, fiction author, hackers as folk heros, 11
Stoned virus, 114
structured query language (SQL), 193, 195
Sun, 24, 25
suppliers and manufacturers, 260-273
surges, **139**-140
Sutton, Willie, 17
symmetrical encryption, 96, **96**

T

3Com, 24
3M Corp., 135
"technostress", 71
telecommuting, 213, 220-222
telephone lines for LANs, 18
televaulting, 97
Teller, Edward, quotation, 209
terrorist attacks, 88
testing software for defects, 107, 110-111
Third Wave, The, 4, 220
threat agents, 41
threat/control matrix, **63**
threats, 10-13, 17, 37-42, **39**, **244**
    academically inclined intruders, 11-12
    accidents, 40, 41
    agents, threat agents, 41
    carelessness, 41
    content analysis, 39
    control/threat matrix, **63**
    crackers, 11
    cyberpunks, 11
    database systems, **194**
    denial of service, 40
    diddlers, data diddlers, 12
    disaster recovery, 90
    disclosure, 38-39
    electronic mail, 187-**188**
    employees, disgruntled employees, 13
    errors, human error, 40
    errors, programming errors, 41
    espionage, 12

exposures, 42
fiction, hackers, crackers and cyberpunks as folk heros, 11
forging, 40
hackers, 11
identifying threats, 61-62
inexperienced users, 40
masquerading, 39
message stream modification, 38
natural disasters, 40
number of users vs. increase in threat, 16
power-supply interruptions, 40
reneging, 39-40
repudiation, 40
scenarios of possible security breach, 41-42
spoofing, 40
traffic analysis, 39
viruses (*see* viruses)
vulnerabilities, 42
vulnerability/threat mergers, 62
water damage, 41
wiretapping, 40
Toffler, Alvin, future-trends author, 4, 7-8, 213, 220
token passing protocols, 29, **30**, **31**
Token Ring, 24-**25**, 118
  cabling standard, 123
tokens, token passing protocols, 29
topology for LANs, 20, 21-23
  bus configuration, 21, **21**
  ring configuration, 21-**22**
  star configuration, 22-**23**
  tree configuration, 23-**24**
traffic analysis, 39
training programs, 49, 94
transaction control, database systems, 192
transients, 140, **140**
tree configuration topology, 23-**24**
tribbles, 113
True Names, 11
Tzu, Sun, Chinese general on security, 13

U

uninterruptible power supply (UPS), 141-**142**
UNIX, 135

unshielded twisted-pair (UTP) cabling, 118-**119**
Useful data/assets preservation classification, 86, 87
user ID, 251

V

Valuable data/assets preservation classification, 86, 87
varathane, electronic, 218
vaulting, electronic vaulting/televaulting, 97
views, database systems, 197
VINES, 146, 174-181
Vinge, fiction author, hackers as folk heros, 11
viruses, 13, 112-115
  bacteria, 113
  chain letters, 113
  curing viral infection, 114-115
  effects of viruses, 112
  flu shot programs, 114
  history of viruses and computers, 112
  Michaelangelo virus, 114
  preventing viral infection, 113-**114**
  products and suppliers, 271-273
  rabbits, 113
  Stoned virus, 114
  symptoms of viral infection, 113
  threat, 112
  tribbles, 113
  worms, 112-113
voice verification biometrics, 106
vulnerabilities, 42
  identifying vulnerabilities, 62
  threat/vulnerability mergers, 62

W

water damage, 41
WaveLAN, 216
white-box testing of software, 110
wide area networks (WAN), 18, 200
Wilkinson, John, quotation, 35
wireless LANs, 213, 214-217
  growth of wireless LAN, 215-217, **215**, **216**
  local area wireless networks (LAWN), 216
  mobile communications, 214-215
Wireless Office: LAN, PBX..., 215

wiretapping, 40
Witt, Herbert, 45
workflow software, 217-218
workstation security, 130-134, 251
  device restraints, 131
  disaster recovery, 92
  disk initialization routines, 131
  diskettes and storage, 133
  diskless workstations, 98, 133
  image processing, 228
  key locks, 131
  removable disks, 133
  security measures, 98
worms, viruses, 112-113
write once read many (WORM) disks, 229

X
Xerox, 25

Z
Ziglar, Zig, 246

Other Bestsellers of Related Interest

LAN PERFORMANCE OPTIMIZATION
Martin A. W. Nemzow

Resolve your most stubborn network performance problems with this practical resource for LAN managers and consultants. This book-disk package will help you locate and eliminate bottlenecks in local area networks quickly. The diagnostic tools provided are equally effective with Banyan Vines, Novell Netware, UB Access One, Unix, Sun, NFS, IBM LAN Server, Microsoft LAN Manager, Ethernet, Token Ring, and FDDI network operating systems.
- 230 pages • 90 illustrations. • 5.25" disk.

Book No. 024629-7 *$29.95 paperback only*

WRITING DR DOS® BATCH FILES
Ronny Richardson

Boost the performance and increase the efficiency of the DR DOS operating system with this first and only book/disk package on batch file programming for DR DOS. After a complete batch file programming tutorial, you'll discover how to create your own batch files using DR DOS commands and the batch file utilities included on the FREE 3.5" companion disk. A screen compiler, a batch file utility kit, and a quick-reference summary of the DR DOS command language round out this thoroughly practical, easy-to-follow guide.
- 464 pages • 79 illustrations • 3.5" disk

Book No. 052364-9 *$32.95 paperback only*

NETWORKING WITH LANtastic®
Michael S. Montgomery

With this instructive book you'll have an easy-to-read alternative to the program documentation—a comprehensive guide to setting up and running an efficient, high-performance LANtastic network. The author describes proven techniques for sharing files, printing, and using peripherals. Focusing on ways to configure LANtastic to meet specific needs and how to ensure maximum productivity, he shows you how to plan and design networks, install LANtastic software, use program functions and menus, and more.
- 632 pages • 199 illustrations

Book No. 042907-3 *$22.95 paperback*
Book No. 042906-5 *$34.95 hardcover*

BUILDER LITE: Developing Dynamic Batch Files
Ronny Richardson

With this software and Richardson's accompanying user's manual, even beginners will be able to build and test sophisticated batch files in as little as 10 minutes. Richardson's step-by-step tutorial demonstrates how to write batch files that manipulate displays, create menus, make calculations, customize system files, and perform looping operations. This isn't a demo package, either. Builder Lite was developed by Doug Amaral of hyperkinetix, inc., especially for this book.
- 368 pages • 61 illustrations • 3.5" disk

Book No. 052363-0 $32.95 paperback
Book No. 052362-2 $44.95 hardcover

DR. BATCH FILE'S ULTIMATE COLLECTION
Ronny Richardson

Boost productivity, enhance DOS performance, and save hundreds of unnecessary keystrokes with this practical library of programs—no programming skills required. Assembled here and on the FREE 3.5" companion disk are over 120 of the most useful batch files available for creating and using keyboard macros, saving and reusing command lines, tracking down viruses in COMMAND.COM, and much more.
- 440 pages • 146 illustrations • 3.5" disk

Book No. 052359-2 $29.95 paperback
Book No. 052358-4 $39.95 hardcover

NORTON DESKTOP® FOR WINDOWS® 2.0: An Illustrated Tutorial
Richard Evans

"Evans tells the reader virtually everything necessary to use the Norton Utilities... Recommended."
Computer Shopper on a previous edition

This example-packed guide gives you step-by-step, illustrated instructions for using each Norton Desktop library—including valuable troubleshooting advice and solutions to common problems. Evans, whose previous books on the Norton Utilities have sold more than 50,000 copies, not only shows you how to optimize the Norton Desktop Utilities, he also demonstrates the use of Norton Disk Doctor and Norton Backup.
- 240 pages • 109 illustrations

Book No. 019883-7 $19.95
Book No. 019882-9 $29.95

Prices Subject to Change Without Notice.

Look for These and Other TAB Books at Your Local Bookstore

To Order Call Toll Free 1-800-822-8158
(24-hour telephone service available.)

or write to TAB Books, Blue Ridge Summit, PA 17294-0840.

Title	Product No.	Quantity	Price

☐ Check or money order made payable to TAB Books

Charge my ☐ VISA ☐ MasterCard ☐ American Express

Acct. No. _____ Exp. _____

Signature: _____

Name: _____

Address: _____

City: _____

State: _____ Zip: _____

Subtotal $ _____

Postage and Handling
($3.00 in U.S., $5.00 outside U.S.) $ _____

Add applicable state and local sales tax $ _____

TOTAL $ _____

TAB Books catalog free with purchase; otherwise send $1.00 in check or money order and receive $1.00 credit on your next purchase.

Orders outside U.S. must pay with international money in U.S. dollars drawn on a U.S. bank.

TAB Guarantee: If for any reason you are not satisfied with the book(s) you order, simply return it (them) within 15 days and receive a full refund.

About the Author

In his 19 years in information systems, Peter Davis worked in data processing in large scale installations in the financial industry and government sectors, where he was involved in the development and implementation of applications and specification of requirements. Most recently, he worked as director of information systems audit for the Office of the Provincial Auditor in Ontario, Canada. In addition, Peter was a principal in an international public accounting firm's information systems audit practice. He has acted as the Canadian representative for a U.S. company specializing in the manufacture and integration of communications products. Peter is now principal of Peter Davis & Associates, a training and consulting firm specializing in the security, audit, and control of information systems.

He is an internationally known speaker on security and audit, frequently speaking at local user meetings and international conferences sponsored by professional organizations and industry groups. In addition, he has had numerous articles published on security and audit.

Peter is a member of the international committee formed to develop Generally Accepted System Security Principles (GSSP). He is also an Advisory Council member for the Computer Security Institute.

Peter Davis received his Bachelor of Commerce degree from Carleton University. He also is a Certified Management Accountant (CMA), Certified Information Systems Auditor (CISA), Certified Systems Professional (CSP), Certified Data Processor (CDP), Information Systems Professional (ISP), and Certified Information Systems Security Professional (CISSP).

He currently lives in Toronto, Ontario, with his wife and daughter.